JAMES THOMSON

Essays for the Tercentenary

LIVERPOOL ENGLISH TEXTS AND STUDIES

General editors: JONATHAN BATE and BERNARD BEATTY

✣

Literature and Nationalism
edited by VINCENT NEWEY and ANN THOMPSON
Volume 23. 1991. 296pp. ISBN 0-85323-057-9

Reading Rochester
edited by EDWARD BURNS
Volume 24. 1995. 240pp. ISBN 0-85323-038-2 (cased), 0-85323-309-8 (paper)

Thomas Gray: Contemporary Essays
edited by W. B. HUTCHINGS and WILLIAM RUDDICK
Volume 25. 1993. 287pp. ISBN 0-85323-268-7

Nearly Too Much: The Poetry of J. H. Prynne
by N. H. REEVE and RICHARD KERRIDGE
Volume 26. 1995. 224pp. ISBN 0-85323-840-5 (cased), 0-85323-850-2 (paper)

A Quest for Home: Reading Robert Southey
by CHRISTOPHER J. P. SMITH
Volume 27. 1996. 256pp. ISBN 0-85323-511-2 (cased), 0-85323-521-X (paper)

Outcasts from Eden: Ideas of Landscape in British Poetry since 1945
by EDWARD PICOT
Volume 28. 1997. 344pp. ISBN 0-85323 531-7 (cased), 0-85323-541-4 (paper)

The Plays of Lord Byron
edited by ROBERT F. GLECKNER and BERNARD BEATTY
Volume 29. 1997. 400pp. ISBN 0-85323-881-2 (cased), 0-85323-891-X (paper)

Sea-Mark: The Metaphorical Voyage, Spenser to Milton
by PHILIP EDWARDS
Volume 30. 1997. 240pp. ISBN 0-85323-512-0 (cased), 0-85323-522-8 (paper)

Passionate Intellect: The Poetry of Charles Tomlinson
by MICHAEL KIRKHAM
Volume 31. 1999. 320pp. ISBN 0-85323-534-0 (cased), 0-85323-553-8 (paper)

'The New Poet': Novelty and Tradition in Spenser's Complaints
by RICHARD DANSON BROWN
Volume 32. 1999. 320p. ISBN 0-85323-803-3 (cased), 0-85323-813-8 (paper)

Translating Life: Studies in Transpositional Aesthetics
edited by SHIRLEY CHEW and ALISTAIR STEAD
Volume 33. 1999. 421p. ISBN 0-85323-674-7 (cased), 0-85323-684-4 (paper)

James Thomson:
Essays for the Tercentenary

*

Edited by
RICHARD TERRY
University of Sunderland

LIVERPOOL UNIVERSITY PRESS

First published 2000 by
LIVERPOOL UNIVERSITY PRESS
Liverpool L69 7ZU

©2000 Liverpool University Press

The right of Richard Terry
to be identified as the editor of this work
has been asserted by him in accordance with
the Copyright, Design and Patents Act, 1988

British Library Cataloguing-in-Publication Data
A British Library CIP Record is available

ISBN 0-85323-954-1 (hardback)
0-85323-964-9 (paperback)
Typeset in Stempel Garamond
by BBR, Sheffield
Printed by Bell & Bain, Glasgow

Contents

Illustrations

Introduction: Thomson's 'fame'

RICHARD TERRY

Thomson's life, unlike that of some of his literary contemporaries, did not generate a great number of anecdotes, and the most famous one in which his name figures relates to a posthumous incident concerning not so much the author himself as his most celebrated literary work, *The Seasons*. Hazlitt tells of how, rambling in North Devon with Coleridge, the two of them stopped off at a country inn. Finding a battered copy of *The Seasons* lying in the parlour, Coleridge, so Hazlitt recounts, picked it up with a flourish and then pronounced: '*That* is true fame'.[1] Coleridge's meaning is not entirely certain, since fame at this time was something of an amphibian concept, but he is probably paying homage both to the breadth and to the longevity of Thomson's post-mortal reputation. Although Coleridge's exclamation springs directly from a palpable piece of evidence for the book's endurance and wide dissemination, it also caps a sequence of early critical responses to Thomson in which the poet's fame is prophesied, remarked upon or celebrated.

The prediction of Thomson's fame goes back even to the appearance of 'Winter' in 1726, an event which led Aaron Hill, later the poet's friend, to inform him of his premonition that 'Time ... shall lend her soundless depth, to float your fame'.[2] When Sir Gilbert Elliot of Minto, an early patron of Thomson's, received a copy of the first edition of *The Seasons*, he also felt sufficient confidence to assert that 'There's a book that will make him famous all over the world, and his name immortal'.[3] After his death, and in large part due to the wide or 'universal' appeal of *The Seasons*, Thomson acquired the reputation of a poet almost uniquely gifted with poetic fame. In 1785, John Pinkerton, for example, regrets that *The Seasons* should be the most incorrect 'of any works which have obtained considerable applause', and forecasts that this shortcoming will ultimately see to it

1

that 'the fame of *The Seasons* will not be of long existence'.[4] Yet three years later, William Cowper, in a letter to a Mrs King, states, again notwithstanding certain frailties of poetic style, that Thomson 'was however a true poet and his lasting fame has proved it'.[5] Moreover, only five years later, Percival Stockdale can look back at Thomson's posterity and declare that 'Perhaps no poems have been read more generally, or with more pleasure, than the Seasons of Thomson'.[6]

There is no evidence that Thomson courted the poetic fame with which he was posthumously to be blessed. The supposition of an innate authorial desire for fame was, even by the late seventeenth century, a tired conceit; and, in the following century, the topos is in large part supplanted by poets' publicly disavowing the desire for, or pouring scorn on the feasibility of, a lasting fame. Thomson, himself, seems to have been of this party: in *Liberty*, for instance, he calls upon the direct inspiration of the Goddess Liberty as he aspires to an objective 'nobler than Poetic fame'.[7] Similarly, in *The Castle of Indolence*, the occupants of the wizard's vale entertain themselves by gazing into a 'Mirror of Vanity' in which one of the groups held up as epitomizing the 'Vanity of Life' are authors feverish for post-mortal renown:

> Why, Authors, all this Scrawl and Scribbling sore?
> To lose the present, gain the future Age,
> Praisèd to be when you can hear no more,
> And much enrich'd with Fame when useless worldly Store.[8]

This rebuke to fame, it should be said, figures as part of a more general cynicism, spread by the wizard's spell, towards energetic pursuits of all kinds; but the suggestion that the quest for fame must ultimately terminate in self-defeat, its possession always deferred past the point at which it can be enjoyed by its recipient, had already become a commonplace. Ironically, this recognition is returned back on Thomson by Lord Lyttelton in the Prologue he supplied for the posthumous 1749 production of *Coriolanus*. Where one might have expected some rhapsodizing of the poet's immortal name, instead Lyttelton chooses to admonish the growing cult of Thomson's fame, cautioning that the poet 'superior now to Praise or Blame,/ Hears not the feeble Voice of

Human Fame'.[9] The very same point had been made in Edward Young's seminal poem *Love of Fame: the Universal Passion* (1725–28), which mocked poets 'who thirst for glory, strive/ To grasp, what no man can possess alive!'; and the irony intrinsic to posthumous applause ('of being celebrated by generations to come with praises which we shall not hear') was only a year after Lyttelton's Prologue to be vexed over at length in Johnson's *Rambler* 49 (4 September 1750).[10]

So much for Thomson's fame in the fifty years or so after his death: in our own century, his posterity has not been so uninterruptedly gratifying. The tendency, evident in his own time, for him to be identified with one work alone has become even more pronounced. In 1951, for example, Douglas Grant entitled his biography of the poet *James Thomson: Poet of 'The Seasons'*, capitalizing on, but also entrenching, this restrictive association. The near erasure of Thomson as a playwright is evident perhaps in nothing so much as the difficulty of obtaining the standard scholarly edition of his dramatic works, John Greene's *Plays of James Thomson*; and, while *Liberty* and *The Castle of Indolence* have received intermittent attention, the tendency has always been to approach them as historical or biographical documents, of interest less for themselves than for the ideas they contain. Moreover, even *The Seasons* failed to avoid being tarnished by the disparagement of mid-eighteenth-century verse meted out by T. S. Eliot and F. R. Leavis. Leavis, for example, in his *Revaluation* (1936) classes Thomson's poetry amongst that of Gray, Dyer, Akenside and Shenstone as not 'bearing a serious relation to the life of its time', and as merely trading in the 'literary and conventional'.[11]

Yet on the whole the last fifty years have been buoyant ones for the reputation of *The Seasons*, if not for the rest of Thomson's *oeuvre*. Contrary to Leavis's remark above, *The Seasons* has come to be seen as a poem remarkable for its intersection with numerous shaping issues and phenomena of its own time. Its appreciation in these terms is sealed as early as Alan Dugald McKillop's *The Background of Thomson's Seasons* (1942), which sets the poem in a range of intellectual contexts, and Marjorie Hope Nicolson's seminal study of literary and scientific relations

'*Newton Demands the Muse*': Newton's '*Opticks*' and the *Eighteenth Century Poets* (1946) in which Thomson commands more coverage than any other author. In a similar way, *The Seasons* has proved an automatic resort for critics wanting to analyse the language of nature description, the aesthetic category of the sublime, the genre of georgic, the influence of *Paradise Lost* on Augustan verse, eighteenth-century theodicy, the idea of 'pre-Romanticism' and even, very recently, contemporary agricultural practices.[12] This sense of the poem's being multifaceted, and therefore reflecting a multiplicity of different lights, is further apparent in one of the landmark treatments of it, Ralph Cohen's *The Art of Discrimination: Thomson's 'The Seasons' and the Language of Criticism* (1964), a voluminous explication not of the poem but of the history of its interpretation. The poem, and its reception, is used to bear witness to an unfolding literary critical tradition.

The impression given by most criticism of *The Seasons* before the 1970s is that of a poem that yields itself to a multiplicity of perspectives but that lacks an overall coherence or 'unifying vision'. This question of the poem's unity, the coherence of its viewpoint regarding the materials it contains, has indeed become the main point at issue in recent criticism. Ralph Cohen, for example, in his *The Unfolding of 'The Seasons'* (1970) sees the artistry of the work as a matter of how the poem 'holds together' and harmonizes the diversity and changeability of its scenes. As the issue is posed by him, it is both an aesthetic and a philosophical one: how does the poem cohere as a literary artifact? and in what ways does it envision harmony in a world made up of human vicissitude and natural diffuseness?

Cohen's optimism that *The Seasons* does contain a unifying vision has been the point of departure for John Barrell's sustained engagement with the poem.[13] In his *English Literature in History, 1730–1780: An Equal, Wide Survey* (1983) Barrell reads the poem as intent on a strategy of harmonization, conveying to the reader the grounds on which society can be seen as concordant and providentially disposed. This strategy is mediated by the prospect-view, where Thomson depicts the rural landscape as seen from the houses of the landed 'great'.

Barrell's argument rests on a coincidence of the aesthetic and political: the point from which the rural prospect can can best be seen in its essential pictorial unity is the dwelling place of the leisured aristocrat, and correspondingly the point from which existing social relations can best be seen for their underlying coherence is the same place. The unity vouchsafed by the poem comes to be seen as a very partial one, its apprehension reserved exclusively for those occupying a very select station in society.

How to read The *Seasons*, especially so as to see it *whole* or, conversely, to see the partiality of its claims to wholeness, remains central to Thomson criticism. Tim Fulford, for example, has recently produced another strong reading of the poem in terms of the ideology of its landscape descriptions; and John Barrell and Harriet Guest and, more recently, Richard Terry have explored the work through the particular vexed ordonnance of the eighteenth-century long poem.[14] But it would be wrong to imply that explication of Thomson's best-known work is the only front on which Thomson scholarship has being going forward. James Sambrook's *James Thomson 1700–1748: A Life* (1991) is a fitting capstone to his earlier distinguished editorial work on the poet; since Christine Gerrard's seminal work *The Patriot Opposition to Walpole: Politics, Poetry, and National Myth 1725–1742* (1994), it has become possible if not imperative to read Thomson's later writings against his involvement with the anti-Walpole grouping of Whig patriots; work on Thomson as an Anglo-Scottish poet has been stimulated by Mary Jane W. Scott's *James Thomson, Anglo-Scot* (1988); and notwithstanding the difficulty of getting hold of John Greene's indispensable edition of Thomson's plays, we are perhaps seeing the first flickerings of a rekindled interest in Thomson as a dramatist.[15]

Thomson has always been both the beneficiary and the victim of his works' seeming to epitomize issues and phenomena (like the poetic response to Newtonian science, the sublime and so on) of wider significance the *oeuvre* itself. While being a significant poet in his own right, there is a sense in which his work has sometimes been relegated to background for the works of others or for the overarching literary and cultural trends of his time. It is a paradox that his works remain much written about, without there being many critical books devoted exclusively to him. If an editor is permitted an exhortation for future scholarly work, it is that Thomson's plays win the renewed attention they deserve and that his own writings, rather than so much the issues with which they connect, come to occupy the centre ground of Thomsonian criticism and scholarship. That Thomson is a major poet of his time is not in doubt, but there is still scope for the nature of his individual achievement to be redefined.

The present volume of essays substantiates, contributes to, and defines the modern-day terms of Thomson's fame. The poet was born on 7 September 1700 at Ednam in the Scottish borders and died in Richmond on 27 August 1748, after a short illness; the proximity of significant anniversaries of his birth and death was the immediate occasion for commissioning a collection of essays. Although it was hoped that the essays would address a broad range of Thomson's writings and the issues arising from them, my intention was also that the contributors would have liberty to approach whichever of Thomson's texts, and in whichever ways, seemed important to them in the present climate. The upshot is a volume that inevitably shows both clusterings and omissions, but which speaks forthrightly about the current stock of Thomson's fame and about the complexion of his modern-day reception. What emerges is that Thomson remains for our own time a poet who happened also to write plays: the poet, that is, 'of "The Seasons"'. Only one essayist elected to write on Thomson as a dramatist; the poet's personal conviction that *Liberty* was his 'noblest work' is belied here by its having earned much less generous treatment than *The Seasons*; and *The Castle of Indolence*, a poem which at certain times, and especially to the Victorians, has taken on the guise of Thomson's most flawless achievement, has been squeezed to the margins of the received authorial canon.

But in so far as the volume testifies to a continuing fixation of critical concern on *The Seasons*, it also witnesses to a pronounced critical interest in Thomson's fame, or the afterlife enjoyed by his work and reputation. Five contributors, half of the book's entire company, have explored aspects of the poet's posthumous

reception: how his texts became available after his death to politically charged re-readings; how he was at different times co-
opted into and discharged from membership of an exclusively
Scottish literary tradition; and how in the Romantic era the
byword of Thomson's literary 'fame' led to his being sucked into
a literary dispute concerning the nature of popular poetry. In the
last twenty years, the ways in which Thomson's verse has been
read, perhaps especially in our understanding of the ideology of
landscape description, have changed out of all recognition. Yet
the present volume in certain respects goes back to school to
Thomson's own century. The Thomsonian canon represented
here is much the same as that which recommended itself to Dr
Johnson and his contemporaries; and the volume exhibits the
same realization that Thomson's importance is in part a matter of
his literary artistry, but also, to an unusual degree, of a self-won
afterlife through popular dissemination and the endurance of his
poetic reputation.

The following essays fall naturally into two groups, the first
five exploring individual works of Thomson's; and the concluding five addressing aspects of his posthumous reception. We
begin with Brean Hammond's essay, the sole one in the collection to address Thomson specifically as a dramatist. The essay
tries to rescue Thomson's plays from the slur, routinely cast on
early eighteenth-century tragedies, of being affected and bloated
with high sentiment. On the contrary, Hammond finds Thomson's first play *Sophonisba* to be 'an exceptionally promising
theatrical début' which succeeds, at least in part, in creating new
sources of domestic interest in tragedy. Thomson's dramatic
form is intellectually dialogic, constantly setting ideas against
each other. In *Sophonisba*, much as in the play which most influenced it, Addison's *Cato*, the key conflict is between the call of
public duty and the needs of the private self. This is the dilemma
that at the end of the play confronts the Numidian Masinissa,
who has to choose between his love for Sophonisba and his allegiance to the Roman state. Typically, as Hammond reveals, the
way out of the dilemma urged by Thomson, in the voice of
Scipio, is a Shaftesburian 'social love', a 'nameless sympathy ...
That binds, supports, and sweetens human life'.

The next essay, by Bill Hutchings, is a sophisticated challenge to what have become our acquired habits of response to Thomsonian, and wider eighteenth-century, nature description. He argues that recent ideological criticism of *The Seasons* has sometimes taken as its basis the supposition that 'because a description of a prospect cannot simply replicate that prospect ... its semantic function ... [has to] ... lie elsewhere—in the confirmation or subversion of modes of ownership, control and authority'. Hutchings puts the case for reading eighteenth-century description more on its own terms, or against the backdrop of reflections on its operation by the likes of Pope, Johnson, Hutcheson and Lessing. The limitations incident to verse description, as against those that apply to description in the non-verbal media, were something that eighteenth-century writers recognized and indeed took to heart; but Hutchings also shows the ways in which, within the understood constraints, a skilful poet like Thomson could organize descriptive passages so as to realize a 'completely experiential reality, a piece of *virtual life*'.

Robert Inglesfield's essay explores the influence exercised over Thomson by the writings of Anthony Ashley Cooper, the third earl of Shaftesbury. He sets Thomson's 'discipleship' (as one earlier critic put it) in the context of the controversy that raged around Shaftesbury's writings in the late 1720s and 1730s, and he tracks how Shaftesburian notions flicker and modulate through the successive revampings of *The Seasons*. From the outset, Thomson seems to have envisaged a poem that would be an 'expression of Shaftesburian "enthusiasm" for "Nature" and the refined moral and quasi-religious feelings that accompany it'. But he was also drawn to Shaftesbury's habitual invocations of qualities of benevolence and human sympathy as well as to his deism, though there is a watering down of deistic material in the later editions of the poem, especially in the 1744 text, possibly as a result of pressure from George Lyttelton. At the same time as the additions and revisions to *The Seasons* allow us to witness the motions of Thomson's intellectual allegiance to Shaftesbury, so they also witness to the development of his political affiliations. This is an issue taken up by Glynis Ridley, whose essay, building on the seminal work of Christine Gerrard, attempts the first sustained reading of the poem in terms of Patriot politics. The task that Ridley sets herself is to pin down what images or themes of opposition to the Walpolean administration belong exclusively to the Patriot grouping as opposed to being shared cross-factionally. With this in mind, she analyses the poem's depiction of the contemporary trade wars with Spain and executes a painstaking political exegesis of Thomson's celebration of the 'British worthies'. Her essay finishes with a discussion of the political, and in particular anti-Walpolean, associations that group themselves around such neutral-seeming concepts as those of 'virtue' and 'friendship'.

Robin Dix's essay begins with a near-obligatory acknowledgement that *Liberty* is neither a popular work nor one that can easily be claimed as an artistic success. One source of this failure Dix diagnoses as a disharmony between the two main strands of the poem. Thomson's work was intended as a serenade to the principle of 'liberty' (associated with mixed or power-sharing government), charting its course from ancient Greece to Thomson's own time, but the poem also wants to record the progress of the arts, and to illustrate the premise that these can only flourish under conditions of political liberty. Dix's essay analyses the numerous fraught inconsistencies that have to be introduced into the poem for this thesis to be upheld; but he also proposes that the problems that Thomson encounters in *Liberty* are ones that he found the means of resolving in his later poem *The Castle of Indolence*. Here Thomson is able more successfully to sustain the progress theme by jettisoning the causal link between politics and culture and turning from a historical to an allegorical narrative. In doing so, he achieves a new 'suggestiveness' and 'flexibility' of signification, transmuting the laboured contradictions of *Liberty* into 'creative tensions'.

The second group of essays begins with my own contribution, which takes as its point of departure William Collins' well-known commemorative poem 'Ode occasioned by the death of Mr Thomson', and explores what Collins may have meant by his cryptic designation of Thomson as a 'Druid'. The essay mulls over some explicit and implied references to Druids in

Thomson's own writing and considers a growing trend for the native literary history to be mapped as a tradition descending from the Druidical bards, seen as the earliest practitioners of poetry to have inhabited the British Isles. Gerard Carruthers meanwhile sets his discussion against the background of Thomson's 'fall from favour' as a *bona fide* member of the Scottish poetic tradition and of the charge made against him by some modern critics of being 'a man kicking over the traces of his own Scottish culture'. Carruthers's essay attempts to define afresh the nature of the 'Scottish–British' tradition, and seeks to rehabilitate those aspects of Thomson's achievement that an 'essentialistic' view of that tradition has demonized as 'English affectation'. So he suggests, for example, that Thomson's steepage in Milton was 'in large measure in keeping with the Scottish Presbyterian background from which ... [he] ... emerged'; and his 'close-focusing attention to natural detail ... emanates from a reversal of the rather morbid attention to the external world found in Calvinist pietism'. His conclusion overturns the received wisdom that Thomson turns his back on the Scottish tradition; rather he emanates from a Scottish culture 'both manifestly plural and problematic'. Carruthers rounds out his thesis by demonstrating the extent of Thomson's influence on two quintessential exponents of Scots vernacular poetry, Robert Fergusson and Robert Burns.

Tim Fulford's essay explores an idiom or iconography of patriotism that runs through the eighteenth century. This has to do with the British oak, which provided the physical material for the ships of the British navy, but which also symbolized a national indomitability in the face of overseas conflict. Fulford narrates how the image of the oak planted its roots in popular perceptions about British military history and national character, and how it came to be at the centre of debates concerning the very nature of patriotism, and the identity of those who most boasted its possession. In *The Seasons*, Thomson associates patriotism with the Whig aristocrats like Lyttelton whose propagation of oaks on their country estates was seen to epitomize their staunch and selfless patriotism. In 'Rule Britannia', the oak is referred to in the context of ringing prejudices about British resilience and naval power. But Fulford's essay is a lesson in how a political symbol both so public and so fluid as the 'oak' can never be monopolized by a single factional group, and his essay charts how in the late decades of the century it is invested with new meanings, and turned to the service of new causes, in the face of political controversies such as the trial of Queen Caroline in 1820.

John Barrell and Harriet Guest explore how Thomson's words are taken up in the controversies ensuing from the French Revolution of 1789. They begin with the Earl of Buchan's accident-prone attempt to erect a monument to Thomson in his native village of Ednam, and explore why it was that his attempts to solicit subscriptions should prove so notably unsuccessful. The answer they come up with has to do with the interest Buchan had, evident in his biography of the poet, in enlisting the authority of Thomson, and particularly that of *Liberty*, to justify the French Revolution and a measure of parliamentary reform in Britain. Buchan's enlistment of the poem in this way, and the frosty reaction greeting his project on Thomson's behalf, show, as Barrell and Guest demonstrate at greater length, how in the aftermath of 1789, *Liberty* became briefly 'readable' as a vindication of a range of positions supportive of the French Revolution and yet how this situation proved short-lived as polite opinion swung against the events in France. But if Thomson becomes less available to be read politically during the 1790s, then he becomes increasingly adopted as a poet of sentimental domesticity and as a point of reference for a new set of contentions to do with the politics of gender and private life.

The collection concludes with John Strachan's essay on Thomson's 'popularity' during the Romantic era. To many commentators, it was axiomatic not just that *The Seasons* was enormously popular, in terms of the wide readership attracted by its universal themes, but that moreover it stood as a paragon of the kind of literary work whose greatness is a factor of its popularity. For poets like Wordsworth and Coleridge who were acutely conscious of the limited public appeal of their own sort of writing, Thomson's precedent stood as something of a rebuke; and Wordsworth, in particular, tried to debunk the legend of

Thomson's popularity, or at least to suggest its foundation on false premises. Yet not only was *The Seasons* a popular poem in its own right, and one furthermore at the heart of debate about the aesthetic value of popularity *per se*, it also exercised a profound influence on some of the most prolific poetry (as measured in the commercial terms of sizes of print run and values of copyright) of the Romantic era, as that written by Robert Burns and Robert Bloomfield, a poetry that in terms of popular appeal entirely eclipsed that of the Lakers. When we look at a poet like Bloomfield, whose *The Farmer's Boy* was a publishing sensation of its day, we can see, in John Strachan's words, that the Romantic period is 'perhaps more Thomsonian than Wordsworth's and Coleridge's self-representations and critical judgments would imply'.

NOTES

1. The incident is recorded in Douglas Grant, *James Thomson: Poet of 'The Seasons'* (London, 1951), p. 98.
2. 'To Mr James Thomson; on his asking my Advice, to what Patron he should address his Poem, called Winter', in *The Works of the late Aaron Hill, Esq.*, 4 vols (1753), III, 77.
3. Cited from David Erskine, 11th Earl of Buchan, *Essays on the Lives and Writings of Fletcher of Saltoun and the Poet Thomson* (1792), p. 185.
4. Robert Heron [John Pinkerton], *Letters of Literature* (1785), pp. 64–65.
5. Cowper to Mrs King, 19 June 1788, in *The Letters and Prose Writings of William Cowper*, ed. James King and Charles Ryskamp, 4 vols (Oxford, 1979–84), III, 181.
6. The comment was originally penned by Stockdale in 1793. See his *Lectures on the Truly Eminent English Poets*, 2 vols (1807), II, 107.
7. *Liberty, A Poem*, I.396, in *Liberty, The Castle of Indolence and other Poems*, ed. James Sambrook (Oxford, 1986).
8. *The Castle of Indolence, An Allegorical Poem*, Canto I, Stanza LII, in Sambrook, *Liberty ... and other Poems*.
9. *The Plays of James Thomson 1700–1748: A Critical Edition*, ed. John C. Greene, 2 vols (New York, 1987), II, 499.

10. For Young, see *Poetical Works*, with intro. by Rev. John Mitford, 2 vols (London, 1906), II, 93.

11. F. R. Leavis, *Revaluation* (London, 1936), p. 90; see also T. S. Eliot, 'Poetry in the Eighteenth Century' (orig. published 1930), in *The New Pelican Guide to English Literature 4. From Dryden to Johnson*, ed. Boris Ford (London, 1957, 1982), pp. 228–34.

12. For natural description, see John Arthos, *The Language of Natural Description in Eighteenth-Century English Poetry* (Ann Arbor, 1949). For recent work on Thomson and the sublime, see David R. Anderson, 'Thomson, Natural Evil, and the Eighteenth-Century Sublime', in *Studies on Voltaire and the Eighteenth Century*, 245 (1986), 489–99; and Robert Inglesfield, 'James Thomson, Aaron Hill and the Poetic "Sublime"', *British Journal for Eighteenth-Century Studies*, 13 (1990), 215–21. For *The Seasons* as a georgic poem, see John Chalker, *The English Georgic: A Study in the Development of a Form* (London, 1969). For Milton's influence on Thomson, see Dustin Griffin, *Regaining Paradise: Milton and the Eighteenth Century* (Cambridge, 1986). For theodicy in *The Seasons*, see David R. Anderson, 'Emotive Theodicy in *The Seasons*', *Studies in Eighteenth Century Culture*, 12 (1983), 59–76; Anderson, 'Thomson, Natural Evil and the Eighteenth-Century Sublime'; and Richard Terry, '"Through Nature shedding influence malign": Thomson's *The Seasons* as a Theodicy', *Durham University Journal*, New Series 61 (1995), 257–68. For Thomson as a precursor of Wordsworth, see Mary Jacobus, *Tradition and Experiment in Wordsworth's 'Lyrical Ballads' (1798)* (Oxford, 1976). For Thomson and contemporary agricultural practice, see John Goodridge, *Rural Life in Eighteenth-Century English Poetry* (Cambridge, 1995).

13. As well as Barrell's work discussed here, see his *The Idea of Landscape and the Sense of Place, 1730–1840: An Approach to the Poetry of John Clare* (Cambridge, 1972), pp. 12–42; and *Poetry, Language and Politics* (Manchester, 1988), pp. 100–36.

14. Tim Fulford, *Landscape, Liberty and Authority: Poetry, Criticism and Politics from Thomson to Wordsworth* (Cambridge, 1996); John Barrell and Harriet Guest, 'On the Use of Contradiction: Economics and Morality in the Eighteenth-Century Long Poem', in *The New Eighteenth Century: Theory, Politics, English Literature*, ed. Felicity Nussbaum and Laura Brown (New York, 1987), pp. 121–43; Richard Terry, 'Transitions and Digressions in the Eighteenth-Century Long Poem', *Studies in English Literature*, 32 (1992), 495–510.

15. For a recent essay that discusses Thomson as a dramatist, see Julie Ellison, 'Cato's Tears', *ELH*, 63 (1996), 571–601.

'O *Sophonisba! Sophonisba* o!': Thomson the Tragedian

BREAN S. HAMMOND

I

Grizzle. Oh! Huncamunca, Huncamunca, oh!
(Henry Fielding, *The Tragedy of Tragedies; or, the Life and Death of Tom Thumb the Great* (1731), II.5)

Even eighteenth-century scholars tend to know very little more about Thomson as a playwright than that Fielding parodies a line from his play *Sophonisba* (1730) in the rewritten, annotated version of *Tom Thumb*. In fact *Sophonisba* is one of the principal targets in *The Tragedy of Tragedies*, identified by name in Scriblerus Secundus' preface to assist Fielding's argument against notional detractors that it is quite legitimate for his play not to resemble the printed sources from which it presumably derives. Thomson's *Sophonisba*, Scriblerus points out, does not resemble earlier versions of that story by Mairet and Lee, the heroine being entirely devoid of passion: a Queen Elizabeth to their Mary, Queen of Scots. Thereafter, Scriblerus in his role as a learned commentator combining the talents of a Bentley and a Dennis, notes several parallels between his text and Thomson's, the most celebrated of which is given in my epigraph. The courtier Grizzle bleats his love for the Princess Huncamunca, his forlorn sigh fleshed out, so to speak, by some biological, or perhaps metallurgical, evidence:

> *Griz.* Oh! Huncamunca, Huncamunca, oh,
> Thy pouting Breasts, like Kettle-Drums of Brass,
> Beat everlasting loud Alarms of Joy;
> As bright as Brass they are, and oh, as hard;
> Oh, *Huncamunca, Huncamunca*! oh!

15

The footnote to this exquisite passage reads:

> This beautiful Line, which ought, says Mr W—, to be
> written in Gold, is imitated in the new *Sophonisba*;
> Oh! *Sophonisba, Sophonisba*, oh!
> Oh! *Narva, Narva*, oh!
> The Author of a Song call'd Duke upon Duke, hath
> improv'd it.
> *Alas*! O Nick, O Nick, *alas*!
> Where, by the help of a little false Spelling, you have two
> Meanings in the repeated Words.[1]

Grizzle returns to his mammalian fetish, implying that Huncamunca does twice the job of Atlas in supporting her own breasts:
'The milky way is not so white, that's flat,/ And sure thy breasts
are full as large as that.' And a broader structural parallel between
Huncamunca and Thomson's Sophonisba runs through the
scene. In I.3, the King gives the Princess's hand to Thumb: 'Oh!
happy, happy, happy, happy Thumb'—the footnote to which
joyous exclamation alludes to Sophonisba's second husband:
'Massinissa is one fourth less happy than Tom Thumb:/ Oh!
happy, happy, happy.' In II.5, Grizzle persuades his Princess
that her vows to Thumb are null and void because Thumb is
not a complete man. Thomson's plot turns on the fact that
Sophonisba, married to Syphax, can abrogate her vows to him
and take Masinissa for a husband because Syphax is in Roman
captivity (and therefore not a real man).[2]

Into Grizzle's lovelorn anaphora ('Oh! Huncamunca, Huncamunca oh!'), Fielding concentrates his impatience with the entire
development of contemporary tragic drama. *Sophonisba* simply
happens to be the play freshest in his memory because it was
premièred at Drury Lane in February 1730 very shortly before
the earlier version of *Tom Thumb* was performed at the Little
Haymarket. Scriblerus' notes refer to numerous plays mostly
written in the previous century, but he must also have had in
mind very many even less memorable tragedies performed in
recent seasons, mainly at Lincoln's Inn Fields, that derive their
plots from Greek and Roman history: Philip Frowde, *The Fall of
Saguntum*; David Lewis, *Philip of Macedon*; John Sturmy,

Sesostris: or, Royalty in Disguise; Samuel Madden, *Themistocles: or, The Lover of his Country*; Osborn Sidney Wandesford, *Fatal Love: or, The Degenerate Brother*; and Benjamin Martyn, *Timoleon*, to name a few. Madden's *Themistocles, the Lover of his Country. A Tragedy* (London, 1729), represents the standard product. The published version is furnished with a treacly dedication to Frederick, Prince of Wales:

> May you ever tread in [your Royal Parents'] Steps, and, like them, make the Peace, Unanimity, Honour and Welfare of these Kingdoms, and the Preservation of our civil and religious Rights and Liberties, Your perpetual Care.[3]

and insists in its Prologue that the events set in the post-Salamis phase of the Graeco–Persian wars—the conduct of the hero Themistocles—are an inspiration for present-day British Patriots. Since those events concern an ostracized Greek who is now fighting for the Persian enemy and the attempts made by his countryman Aristides to win him back to the fold by delivering him a parchment announcing the repeal of his banishment, contemporary audiences may have spotted a resemblance to Bolingbroke's career.

Fielding, however, was tired of the formula. Such exotically displaced, politicized quasi-allegory, full of high-sounding sentiment and unpronounceable names (Themistocles, Aristides, Nepistolema), was not breaking any new ground for tragedy in a period of unprecedented theatrical activity, experimentation and innovation.[4] Impossibly remote, incapable of creating the kind of audience identification upon which the future of tragic theatre must depend, these plays are memorably written off in the first scene of a farce by Henry Carey, in which characters' names take up the entire iambic pentameter:

SCENE *An Antichamber in the Palace.*
Enter Rigdum-Funnidos, *and* Aldiborontiphoscophornio.
    Rigdum-Funnidos.
ALDIBORONTIPHOSCOPHORNIO!
Where left you *Chrononhotonthologos*?[5]

Unsurprisingly, Fielding becomes an indefatigable proponent of the new domestic tragedy pioneered by George Lillo in the same season as *The Tragedy of Tragedies*; and his rejection of a play like *Sophonisba* is related to his sponsorship of one like *The London Merchant: or, the History of George Barnwell*. Fielding several times echoed the populist sentiment of Lillo's own mission statement in the play's dedication to Sir John Eyles MP, Alderman and Sub-Governor of the South Sea Company:

> Tragedy is so far from losing its Dignity, by being accommodated to the Circumstances of the Generality of Mankind, that it is more truly august in Proportion to the Extent of its Influence, and the Numbers that are properly affected by it. As it is more truly great to be the Instrument of Good to many, who stand in need of our Assistance, than to a very small Part of that Number.[6]

The question to be asked, in terms of an assessment of Thomson's achievement as a dramatist, is whether Fielding was astute in making *Sophonisba* into an exemplary case of the death of tragedy. Are Thomson's plays properly consigned to the world of Huncamuncas, Dollalollas, Nepistolemas and Aldiborontiphoscophornios that float around in that Bermuda triangle of English tragic theatre, the early eighteenth century?[7]

Far from it. *Sophonisba* is on the contrary an exceptionally promising theatrical début, in which I believe Thomson to have been looking for a direction; a way forward that, while it does not quite make Lillo's breakthrough, does nevertheless try, in line with intentions most frequently stated by Aaron Hill, to create new sources of domestic interest in classical tragedy. Although Hill's journal *The Prompter* did not get under way until November 1734, his correspondence of the early 1730s is peppered with references to the need to take theatre more seriously, both in terms of an improved tragic repertoire capable of combating the debased contemporary taste for farce, pantomime and opera, and of proper training courses for actors. Advice rains down upon leading actors from Hill's letters, such as to make him almost a prototypical Stanislawski. Actors are advised to duplicate in themselves the emotions they wish to communicate to audiences and they are then given lessons in the pointing and

delivery of lines such that the emotions are indeed communicated. This essentially theatrical interest in pointing spills over
into Hill's concern when in early 1735 he first saw the printed
text of Thomson's poem *Liberty* and was moved to send back a
marked-up copy correcting the bad paragraphing and punctua-
tion that he had the tact to attribute to the printer. His praise for
Thomson on this occasion suggestively picks up the same terms
as Scipio's for Sophonisba at the end of the play:

> while you are writing of *old Rome*'s liberty, you seem to
> have sucked in, with the *Roman* air, the soul of an *old
> Roman*.[8]

Hill's own writing is conceived at this time as a vehicle for his
ideas on theatre. *Athelwold* (1731), a rewriting of an earlier play,
concentrates to an unprecedented degree on a form of realism to
be gained from historical authenticity. From Richard Rowlands's
A Restitution of Decayed Intelligence in Antiquities (1605), popularly referred to as Verstegan's *Antiquities*, Hill found coloured
woodcuts of the Anglo-Saxon arrival in England and of the
preaching of the Christian faith to Ethelbert King of Kent that
influenced his ideas for costumes designed to standards of what
Hill believed to be accuracy.[9] And much earlier in his career,
anticipating Lillo by a decade, Hill had experimented with bour-
geois tragedy in his play *Fatal Extravagance* (1721). Similarly in
the mid-1730s, his theatrical adaptation of Voltaire's *Zaire* as
Zara was intended as a laboratory for his new aesthetic of the
expressive. Hill continued to take a close personal interest in
Thomson's playwriting career, as his suggestions for a rewriting
of the final two acts of *Agamemnon* (1738) establish. What these
amount to is an underlining in heavy ink of the play's 'Patriot'
political message:

> ... since [Agamemnon] had neglected to execute the *duties*
> of a *king*, he had no longer a *right* to the *power*—That he
> might now learn too late, by the inferiority, which he saw
> himself reduced to, that, from the moment, wherein he
> resigned to a subject the authority to dispose of all offices,
> and assume the cares of a crown, he invested *that Subject*
> with *Monarchy*:—and that, with the same tame Dependance

of *will*, now more useful, and seasonable, than ever, he might content himself with the effect of his folly.[10]

Having been a member of the 'Hillarian circle' for some four years before the première of *Sophonisba*, Thomson was surely infected by his enthusiasm and swayed by his influence; and the author of *The Seasons* made his move into the theatre prompted by the motives and ambitions of a serious dramatist.[11]

II

Scriblerus Secundus is accurate in noting that Thomson neglects the earlier English-language version of the Sophonisba story by Nathaniel Lee. This unhistorically passionate tale of kings and generals in love is accurately described by Derek Hughes:

> Throughout the play, Lee reveals an irreconcileable and intolerable conflict between the demands of public life and the needs of the private self: the tragic counterpart to the conflict between instinct and social existence in contemporary sex comedy ... the march of imperial destiny is relentless and oppressive, and there is no visible guiding principle in history. Though Lee habitually used the new scenic resources to portray omens and other spectacular expressions of divine will, the omens declare catastrophe, not justice, and become increasingly ambiguous, showing that communication between earth and heaven is tenuous and uncertain.[12]

Thomson does not relish this emotional *Sturm und Drang*, and is looking for a cleaner, more intellectually dialogic form. This partly implies the streamlined French version of Corneille, but more important as intertexts are Shakespeare's Roman plays and, above all, Addison's *Cato*.[13] *Cato* was, and was recognized to be, an appropriation of Roman history for the developing ideology of Whiggism; but it can also be seen to be an expression of the cultural-discursive arm of the Whig project—the discourse of 'politeness'. Last-ditch opponent of Caesar's faction in the

Roman civil war, final glimmering light of republican liberty at the dawn of imperial tyranny, Cato is also an exemplary Stoic whose sense of civic duty is so acute that he can weep for the future of an abstraction—'Rome'—when he does not weep over the corpse of his son. Elevation of the public over the private is thus allied to an iron self-control, a reining-in of the emotions, that the play presents as the essence of civilization itself. Cato has two sons, Marcus and Portius, the former of whom is not able to regulate his conduct successfully and whose body therefore becomes a leaky vessel, constantly extruding the passions that overspill their container. The 'reason-versus-passions' contest played out between the two brothers is harnessed to a racial analysis of civilization and barbarism in the parallel face-off between the two African characters Syphax and Juba—the former urging the latter to rebel and support Cato's Roman enemies, the latter in love with Cato's daughter and aspiring to shed his African skin for the Roman identity that he associates with desirable values. In Act II scene 1, Syphax undermines Juba by deploying the ancient Mars and Venus template: Juba's love has rendered him effeminate, has disabled him for active service. Syphax urges Juba to abduct his love, Marcia, and when Juba protests that this would be dishonourable, he speciously contends that the entire history of Rome is founded upon just such a rape—the rape of the Sabine women. Rejecting his diabolical temptations, Juba puts his countryman's advances down to 'our Numidian wiles' and underlines this sense of racial inferiority and guilt with the comment:

> Our Punick Faith
> Is infamous, and branded to a Proverb.
> *Syphax*, we'll join our Cares, to purge away
> Our Country's Crimes, and clear her Reputation.[14]

Although on one level Juba is endorsed as the play's true Roman, the natural successor to Cato since Cato has advised his son Portius to retire from active service, Cato makes clear on his deathbed that he sanctions Juba's marriage to his daughter only because 'Caesar's arms have thrown down all distinction'. Racial miscegenation of this kind is, that is to say, one more 'dire effect' flowing from civil discord.

This play casts a very long shadow over *Sophonisba*, but one is tempted to say that while Addison's play strikes political *attitudes*, Thomson's strives to express genuine political *ideas*. Although, as Derek Hughes's remarks above cited suggest, the conflict between the demands of public life and the needs of the private self was a standard theme in Restoration tragedy—the 'love-versus-honour' predicaments in which all protagonists find themselves—Thomson's play presents this hoary conflict in a much sharper, more up-to-the-moment version. In situations where allegiance to a friend, relation, husband or lover comes into conflict with allegiance to the state, which should the moral individual choose? For writers living at the interface between an older ideology of civic republicanism and an emerging discourse of sensibility that politicizes feeling, this is clearly a crucial question; and it is articulated as such by Bolingbroke in the introduction to his *On the Idea of a Patriot King* where he is excoriating Walpole's record in office:

> I think, and every wise and honest man in generations yet unborn will think, if the history of this administration descends to blacken our annals, that the greatest iniquity of the minister ... is the constant endeavour he has employed to corrupt the morals of men. I say thus generally, the morals; because he, who abandons or betrays his country, will abandon or betray his friend.[15]

This is the central dilemma of Thomson's *Sophonisba*. How should we regard ideologically-driven 'patriots' who are capable of sidelining human emotions and exploiting their personal relationships in the interests of their cause? In a decade in which the term 'patriot' tripped easily off tongues, Thomson's play has an almost Shavian depth of cut. To persevere with the modern analogies, his Sophonisba has some of the terrible beauty of a Maud Gonne.

The historical background to the play is the later stage of the second Punic War between Rome and Carthage. It opens on the point of battle between Syphax, King of the Numidians, and the Roman general Scipio (203 BC) which sees the Romans victorious, Syphax a captive and the Numidian Masinissa reinstated to the crown from which Syphax recently expelled him. Livy 23–30 is the principal ancient source, but if Thomson had wished to, he could have read the bare bones of the story in a recent English-language source, Laurence Echard's *The Roman History, from the Building of the City, to the perfect Settlement of the Empire by Augustus Caesar*, where the story is told thus:

> During these Endeavours, *Syphax* finding his Kingdom would probably return to *Masanissa*, the true Inheritor [because he was now in league with the Roman general Scipio], had gather'd together a numerous Army of unexperienc'd Strangers, and with them march'd against Scipio, but was soon defeated, and himself taken Prisoner. *Masanissa*, the better to regain his Kingdom, marched with all speed to Cirta, the chief City, and by shewing them the King in Bonds, procur'd the Gates to be opened, every one striving to gain the Favour of him, who, as they perceiv'd, would be their King. Among the rest, Queen *Sophonisba*, *Syphax*'s Wife, a Woman of incomparable Beauty, who very earnestly and humbly besought him, *That she might not be deliver'd up into the Hands of the* Romans, her powerful Charms so recommended her Suit, that young *Masanissa* forthwith granted it; and the more effectually to perform his Promise, marry'd her himself that Day. This Action was much disapprov'd of by Scipio at his Arrival soon after, letting him to understand, *That the* Romans *had a Title to her Head, as being their Captive, one of their greatest Enemies, and the principal Cause of all* Syphax's *Treachery*. Upon this therefore, *Masanissa*, in desperate Passion, sent her a Bowl of Poyson; at the receiving of which she only said, *That if her Husband had no better Token to send to his new Wife, she must accept of that;* adding, *That her Death had been more honourable, if her Marriage had been farther from it;* and so boldly drank it off.[16]

So how does Thomson embed this story in dramatic discourse? Sophonisba's two suitors Syphax and Masinissa are clearly modelled on the reason/passion binarism as represented by Marcus and Portius in *Cato*. Given the familiarity of that play, these acting lines would be recognized easily by the audience. Masinissa's character is heightened at the outset by a story told by Sophonisba's lady-in-waiting (Phoenissa) of his martial derring-do. He has endured privations reminiscent of those endured by Shakespeare's Antony, and on appearance he is shown to be noble and merciful, while the imprisoned Syphax is vengeful and unworthy even in captivity. He is inwardly poisoned, embittered, in the grip of an irrational hatred. Whereas Syphax curses the Gods in a language of impassioned excess, Masinissa accepts their decrees. His sense of fairness even stretches to admitting that Sophonisba rejected him 'from a worthy cause,/ From publick spirit did her fault proceed'.[17] In the soliloquy that concludes Act I, Masinissa makes the kind of speech that prompts one recent critic to remark that North Africa, in Addison and Thomson, is 'a classical version of *The Spectator*':

> What dreadful havoc in the human breast
> The passions make, when unconfin'd, and mad,
> They burst, unguided by the mental eye,
> The light of reason; which in various ways
> Points them to good, or turns them back from ill.[18]

These unexceptionably polite sentiments ought to enable us to get our bearings, recognizing Masinissa as a normative character and distinguishing the play's hero from its villain just as easily as we can in *Cato*; but that the protagonist's gender operates to unsettle and complicate the geometry of the whole experience. For this is the story of a '*female* Patriot'. In *this* play, the character who places love for her native land above all personal considerations is a *woman*, a fact that renders her less straightforwardly admirable than Cato, and a far more ambivalent, unsettling onstage presence for the audience.

Sophonisba in Thomson's version was betrothed to Masinissa prior to her marriage to Syphax. Ostensibly, this tees her up for the female fickleness motif, but it is made clear, early and often, that such a calumny does not apply to her. Sophonisba is no Cleopatra. At the outset she intimates to her maid Phoenissa that, despite her husband's crazed devotion to her, the defence of

Carthage was the only reason why she 'Engag'd my loveless marriage-vows with his' (2). She is contemptuous of Masinissa's infatuation with the Roman Scipio, which she sees as a form of slavery. And she is not a conventional female. Her sense of her lineage does not permit her to:

> give her life,
> And heart high-beating in her country's cause,
> Meant not for common aims and houshold cares,
> To give them up to vain presuming man;
> Much less to one who stoops the neck to *Rome*,
> An enemy to *Carthage*, *Masinissa*.

Since Syphax and Masinissa are psychosomatic antitypes, offering her very different qualities, Sophonisba's shuttle-cocking between the two might be acceptable to male audience-members on the grounds of a woman's right to choose. Awkwardly, however, she continues to insist that their personal gifts and attractions have absolutely no part to play in her choices. So at virtually the same moment in which Pope could write that 'Most women have no characters at all', Thomson gives us a woman so full of character that she challenges all that the early eighteenth century thinks is secure knowledge about women. When in Act IV Syphax upbraids his wife with desertion, insulting her with the familiar misogynist perversion of woman's creation:

> Woman!
> The source of all disaster, all perdition!
> Man in himself is social, would be happy,
> Too happy; but the gods, to keep him down,
> Curs'd him with woman! fond, enchanting, smooth,
> And harmless-seeming woman;

Sophonisba responds by asserting female capability:

> Yet know that all, we were not all, at least,
> Form'd for your trifles, for your wanton hours,
> Our passions too can sometimes soar above
> The houshold talk assign'd us, can expand

> Beyond the narrow sphere of families,
> And take in states into the panting heart,
> As well as yours.

Defying Syphax's scorn for 'a female patriot', she goes on to assert that she married him to advance the interests of Carthage then, and is acting entirely consistently by deserting him in favour of Masinissa for the same reason now.

Her absolute way of rejecting the claims of the heart cannot fail to provoke the audience's extreme discomfort, because this is outside the limits of female behaviour as conventionally defined:

> All love, but that of *Carthage*, I despise.
> I formerly to *Masinissa* thee
> Preferr'd not, nor to thee now *Masinissa*,
> But *Carthage* to you both. And if preferring
> Thousands to one, a whole collected people,
> All nature's tenderness, whate'er is sacred,
> The liberty, the welfare of a state,
> To one man's frantic happiness, be shame;
> Here, *Syphax*, I invoke it on my head!   (48)

Sophonisba's firmness of purpose throws Masinissa's vacillating effeminacy into stark relief. Just as Antony is accused of being feminized by his love for Cleopatra and Juba is similarly slurred by Syphax in *Cato*, Masinissa's infatuation is treated as a case of Venus on the ascendant over Mars. Act II stages a very powerful confrontation between the pair in which Sophonisba demands not to be delivered to Roman chains. Her eloquent, passionate pleading makes a conquest of Masinissa's heart. Although he denies this to Narva, the exclamation 'oh! *Narva, Narva* oh!' betrays his real condition. Acceding to Sophonisba's request, Masinissa finds that his narrow military horizons are being expanded and that the certainties of his vocation are giving way to an altogether more philosophical, contemplative cast of mind that does not conduce towards unseaming people from the nave to the chops, in Shakespearean parlance. 'Nor is there ought in war worth what I feel;/ In pomp and hollow state, like this sweet sense/ Of infelt bliss'. After his exclamation to Narva that caused Fielding so much mirth: 'Oh! *Sophonisba*! *Sophonisba*! oh!' (29), love and war are set at odds and Masinissa's occupation's gone: 'I'm sick of war, of the destroying trade,/ Smooth'd o'er, and gilded with the name of glory' (30). The new Masinissa can sound notes of Johnsonian depth:

> There is a time for love, or life were vile!
> A sickly circle of revolving days,
> Led on by hope, with senseless hurry fill'd,
> And clos'd by disappointment. Round and round,
> Still hope for ever wheels the daily cheat;
> Impudent hope! Unjoyous madness all!
> Till love comes stealing in, with his kind hours,
> His healing lips, his cordial sweets, his cares.

As the Roman soldier Narva warns, Masinissa seems at this point to be losing altogether his commitment to civic *virtù* along with his grasp of the *realpolitik* of the situation. Sophonisba is Roman property, which Rome is unlikely to cede. She is a potent destabilizing force in Roman North Africa, intolerable to an imperial power like Rome. Narva it is who re-factors Rome into the equation.

Whereas in Addison's *Cato* the confrontation between Romans and Numidians is straightforwardly between civilization and barbarism, Thomson changes the terms very signficantly. Rome and the Romans are made to signify in more complex, dialogical fashion in his play than in Addison's. At the beginning of Act II, Narva refers to the 'Punic guile' of the Numidians, a phrase culled directly from *Cato*; and he retails an anecdote about Scipio's greatness of soul, designed to remind Masinissa of the Roman virtue that initially converted him to Romanness and rekindle in him the spirit of emulation. (On the battlefield, Scipio waived his right to a captive virgin and restored her to her family.) This is perhaps not entirely consistent with what Narva has already told us about the Romans, that they subordinate personal relationships to affairs of state: 'They, when their country calls,/ Who know no pain, no tenderness, no joy,/ But bid their children bleed before their eyes;/ That they'll regard the light fantastick pangs/ Of a fond heart?'(31). When Masinissa and Sophonisba come together in Act III to replay the Rome versus Carthage/Numidia

contest that has figured so prominently in *Cato*, the audience has
a multivocal appreciation of what is at stake and the task of refer-
eeing is a good deal more difficult:

> *Romans* are the scourge
> Of the red world, destroyers of mankind,
> The ruffians, ravagers of earth; and all
> Beneath the smooth dissimulating mask
> Of justice, and compassion; as if slave
> Was but another name for civiliz'd.
> All vengeance on the *Romans*!—While fair *Carthage*
> Unblemish'd rises on the base of commerce;
> And asks of heaven nought but the general winds,
> And common tides, to carry plenty, joy,
> Civility, and grandeur, round the world.   (36)

To counterpoint civilization and barbarism is one thing; conquest
versus *trade* is altogether a different contest, and one that would
become acutely topical in the run-up to the War of Jenkins'
Ear. Masinissa is reduced to a state of childish petulance by
Sophonisba's unexpected recasting of the terms of the old
debate, but in the grip of the amatory urge he promises to marry
her that very night, while she declares in a cool aside that 'This is
alone for *Carthage*.' Punic guile? Where does 'policy' stop and
malfeasance begin? Sophonisba seems to be entirely vindicated
when, at the end of Act IV, the Roman emissary Laelius tells
Masinissa that Rome will not permit his marriage. How, she
enquires, does Masinissa relish Roman attitudes when they are
actually applied to *him* and interfere with *his* personal liberty?

> How feels their tyranny, when 'tis brought home?
> When, lawless grown, it touches what is dear?
> Pomp for a while may dazzle thoughtless man,
> False glory blind him; but there is a time,
> When ev'n the slave in heart will spurn his chains,
> Nor know submission more.   (55)

So that by the final act, the play appears to have thought itself
into a standstill and it is truly difficult to see what kind of resolution Thomson can bring about.

Scipio the Roman general is the play's *deus ex machina* but he
is far from a facile instrument. Harping upon Masinissa's effeminate condition, Scipio implies that love has ruined his (Roman)
constancy of disposition and solid rationality. Will he abandon
martial glory

> All for a sigh? all for a soft embrace?
> For a gay transient fancy, *Masinissa*?
> For shame, my friend! for honour's sake, for glory!
> Sit not with folded arms, despairing, weak,
> And careless all, till certain ruin comes:
> Like a sick virgin sighing to the gale,
> Unconquerable love!   (60)

But perhaps Scipio knows *Antony and Cleopatra* and Dryden's
All for Love, because he is aware that the answer to the above
could be 'yes'! Dryden's Antony is a precedent for considering
the world well lost. This calls for heavier philosophical artillery.
Scipio then draws a crucial distinction between romantic love and
a socialized form of love that acts as a societal glue. (In addition
to seventeenth-century drama, it seems, Scipio has been reading
those benevolist philosophers like Hutcheson, Butler and later,
Hume, whose thinking is expressed trenchantly by Pope in the
line 'Self love and social are the same'.) Scipio speaks of

> a holy tenderness indeed,
> A nameless sympathy, a fountain-love;
> Branch'd infinite from parents to their children,
> From child to child, from kindred on to kindred,
> In various streams, from citizen to citizen,
> From friend to friend, from man to man in general;
> That binds, supports, and sweetens human life.
> But is thy passion such?   (62)

This philosophical idea performs massive ideological labour. It
reconciles love of one's native land to love of individuals within
the political entity. It reconciles conceptions of the public good
to acts of mercy that can occasionally be permitted to dilute the
rigour of political absolutism. There is still, however, no room
for Sophonisba inside this resolution. She is, Scipio argues,

entirely unworthy of Masinissa's affection—to rational inspection, a betrayer of men. Scipio's final lesson is the *Spectator*-like sponsorship of self-control: 'Real glory/ Springs from the silent conquest of ourselves'; and with impeccable suavity and politesse, he suggests that Masinissa knows what he has to do. Masinissa sends poison to Sophonisba. But Thomson continues to be disturbed by the clarity of this resolution, and it is undermined in two ways. Scipio is made at once to relent his severity; and Sophonisba's death is a *liebestod* very similar in emotional effect to Cleopatra's, her death envisioned as an escape from slavery. Masinissa comes too late to save her, there is a *Lear*ish moment when she seems to stir into life; and Laelius's attempt to imperialize even her death is felt by the audience to be entirely inadequate and to miss the point of her self-sacrifice: 'She had a *Roman* soul; for everyone/ Who loves, like her, his country is a *Roman*' (75).

III

Sophonisba the play and Sophonisba the character are, I have been arguing, distinguished contributions to the 'Patriot' literature of the decade, as might easily appear if the play is compared with, for example, Eliza Haywood's tragedy *Frederick, Duke of Brunswick-Lunenburgh*, premièred at the Theatre-Royal in Lincoln's Inn Fields in the season before Thomson's (1729). This sycophantic piece, dedicated of course to Frederick, Prince of Wales, is a celebration of Brunswick ancestry that offers two roles for women: Adelaid, in love with Frederick, a deranged harpy maddened by jealousy; and Anna, Frederick's faithful, virtuous and upright wife. Frederick himself is a model of nobility and personal virtue, whose desire to hold imperial sway is represented to be an extension of this personal virtue. He is so good that not to want to be ruled by him is an *ipso facto* sign of villainy; and how could Adelaid conceivably have taken seriously the youthful protestations of love made to her by Frederick? Thomson's play transcends this entirely, providing a rich provocation to political discussion. Mary Jane Scott, although she does not think highly of Thomson as a dramatist, can find in *Sophonisba* support for her biographical hypothesis that the Rome/Carthage contest in the play figures the Anglo-Scot's divided attitude to the Union:

> ... the heroine's self-sacrifice in the face of Rome's superior power parallels Scotland's sacrifice of her national identity in the recent Union with the dominant English nation.[19]

This is an attractive reading in many ways, though Scott does not perceive that within it, Scipio's speech would surely have to perform the function of a legitimation of Britishness. The point is, however, that Thomson's play is rich because it embodies political views dialogically and conflictually in a way that is precisely appropriate to the theatre. And this in turn is perhaps because Thomson was aware of a broad revaluation of some of the cultural semiotics attaching to the salient events in Roman history.

As we have seen, Addison's *Cato* attached to the Roman republic the values of political liberty, sabotaged by the onset of Caesarist imperialism. By 1738, however, Aaron Hill was arguing for a complete U-turn in this culturally dominant reading of the last days of the Roman republic. In a curious treatise entitled *Enquiry into the Merit of Assassination: with a View to the Character of Caesar ... and his Designs on the Roman Republic*, Hill argued that 'Caesar was the noblest PATRIOT of Antiquity; and died a Martyr to that Public Liberty, which, by an unaccountable Malignity of Fortune, he has been so long accus'd of violating'.[20] After the expulsion of the kings, Hill argues, Rome was a democracy but the Senate violently enslaved the people into an aristocratic and then an oligarchic dependency. Hence the Senate became an usurping, tyrannical violator of civil liberty. Caesar quite properly overthrew this usurpation as a means of freeing his country from tyranny and he had the people's mandate for taking arms against the Pompeian and 'aristocratical' factions in the Senate headed by Cicero and Cato. This reading is clearly as far away from Addison's as one can get, and although it is expediently adjusted to the prevailing rhetoric of the anti-Walpole opposition in the late 1730s, neither the theory nor the play written to illustrate it, *The Roman Revenge*, found favour in the eyes of Bolingbroke and Pope. This was too much to swallow, even for them, and the play was never performed. Without wishing to stretch Hill's influence on Thomson too far, one can argue from *Sophonisba* that some of the old certainties about Whig republicanism are under active renegotiation, and this flux makes the play more effective as theatre than is the more obviously propagandist *Cato*. Thomson was not always capable of writing such effective political theatre. His achievement in *Sophonisba* was rivalled in only one play in the opinion of this commentator, the much later *Tancred and Sigismunda* (1745), which must be the topic for another discussion.

NOTES

1.   Henry Fielding, *The Tragedy of Tragedies; or The Life and Death of Tom Thumb the Great with the Annotations of H.Scriblerus Secundus* (1731), ed. L. J. Morrissey (Edinburgh, 1970), p. 70.

2.   The reader will notice inconsistency in the spelling of the name 'Massinissa'. This is because in the first edition, Thomson spells it 'Masinissa', which I will retain when referring to his play.

3.   Samuel Madden, *Themistocles, the Lover of his Country. A Tragedy* (London, 1729), A3f.

4.   Robert D. Hume, *Henry Fielding and the London Theatre 1728–1737* (Oxford, 1988) provides the best account of Fielding's theatrical experiments.

5.   Henry Carey, *Chrononhotonthologos* (1734) quoted from *Burlesque Plays of the Eighteenth Century*, ed. Simon Trussler (London, Oxford, New York, 1969), p. 217.

6.   George Lillo, *The London Merchant: or, the History of George Barnwell* (London, 1731) quoted from *The Dramatic Works of George Lillo*, ed. James L. Steffensen (Oxford, 1993), p. 151.

7.   Mary Jane W. Scott expresses a typically low opinion of Thomson's achievement in this play and generally in *James Thomson, Anglo-Scot* (Athens and London, 1988), ch. 8, though she does argue strongly that the plays are vehicles for his divided sensibility as an Anglo-Scot who celebrated post-Union Britain while retaining sympathy for the native liberties of

Scotland. Hence he is torn between Roman civilization and Carthaginian energy.

8. Hill to Thomson, 17 January 1735, in Aaron Hill, *Works*, 4 vols (London, 1754), I, 282.

9. Richard Rowlands, *A Restitution of Decayed Intelligence in Antiquities* (Antwerp, 1605), opp. pp. 117, 144. On the political significance of 'Patriot Gothic', see Christine Gerrard, *The Patriot Opposition to Walpole: Politics, Poetry and National Myth, 1725–1742* (Oxford, 1994), ch. 5.

10. Hill, *Works*, II, 49.

11. On Hill and Thomson, see James Sambrook, *James Thomson 1700–1748: a Life* (Oxford, 1991), pp. 38–44 and *passim*.

12. Derek Hughes, *English Drama 1660–1700* (Oxford, 1996), p. 101.

13. See Bonnie Nelson, 'The Stage History of James Thomson's *Sophonisba*: The Rise and Fall of a Patriot Queen', *Journal of the American Society for Theatre Research*, 23.1 (May 1982), 103–07.

14. Joseph Addison, *Cato* (2nd ed., 1713), p. 29.

15. Henry St John, Lord Bolingbroke, *On the Idea of a Patriot King* (1749) quoted from *The Works of Lord Bolingbroke*, 4 vols (Philadelphia, 1841, repr. Farnborough, Hants, 1969), II, 373.

16. Laurence Echard, *The Roman History, from the Building of the City, to the perfect Settlement of the Empire by Augustus Caesar*, 2 vols (8th ed., London, 1719), II, 213–15.

17. Quotations from *Sophonisba* are from the first edition of 1731.

18. Julie Ellison, 'Cato's Tears', *English Literary History*, 63.3 (1996), 571–601 (p. 579). Ellison's article is the most sophisticated treatment of the relationship between race, gender and political ideology in *Cato* and *Sophonisba* currently available. She does not, however, take Scipio's final speech in *Sophonisba* into account, and that presents a challenge to her overall reading.

19. Scott, *James Thomson*, p. 208. Scott considers that Thomson's allowing his dramas to serve 'mostly as vehicles for his social and political views' (p. 209) is the reason why he is not an effective dramatist. My reading suggests that such views are embodied dialogically and conflictually in a way that is precisely appropriate to the theatre. Scott comes close to suggesting that actually to *have* ideas is the downfall of a dramatist.

20. Aaron Hill, *Enquiry into the Merit of Assassination: with a View to the Character of Caesar ... and his Designs on the Roman Republic* (London, 1738), A2–A2f.

'Can Pure Description Hold the Place of Sense?': Thomson's Landscape Poetry

W. B. HUTCHINGS

I. The Limits of Description

It all depends what one means by 'pure description'. The phrase, of course, is Pope's, a self-deprecating nod in the direction of the early pastoral poetry he wrote before he learnt to moralize his song:

> Soft were my Numbers, who could take offence
> While pure Description held the place of Sense?[1]

Warburton, in his notes on these lines from the *Epistle to Arbuthnot*, drew attention to the equivocal meaning of the adjective 'pure', as signifying 'either *chaste* or *empty*'. Is the poet's stooping to truth a fall from the chastity of innocence to the sensuality of experience? Or is his growth into maturity marked by a change from the vacuity of ignorance to the plenitude of experience? Warburton himself resolves the ambiguity by indulging in a sensory parallel appropriate for the gourmet Pope:

> [Pope] has given in this line what he esteemed the true Character of *descriptive poetry*, as it is called. A composition, in his opinion, as absurd as a feast made up of sauces. The use of a picturesque imagination is to brighten and adorn good sense; so that to employ it only in *description*, is like childrens [sic] delighting in a prism for the sake of its gaudy colours; which when frugally managed, and artfully disposed, might be made to represent and illustrate the noblest objects in nature.[2]

Description, then, is the concern of those who, knowing no better, are content to feast on the tinsel and glitter of immature imagination. The adult imagination feasts on solider fare, indulging its childlike love of show only as an adornment of the main course.

Such an evaluation of the limits of description could be seen as receiving classical authority from Horace's *Ars Poetica*, with its wry observation on how a purple patch of irrelevant description is the automatic recourse of every poor poet:

> lucus et ara Dianae
> et properantis aquae per amoenos ambitus agros
> aut flumen Rhenum aut pluvius describitur arcus.

> (lines describing/ Diana's grove and altar, or a stream which winds and hurries/ Along its beauteous vale, or the river Rhine, or a rainbow)[3]

Horace's lines, mimicking the unthinking language of weak descriptive poetry where all streams 'wind' (or are 'purling', as Pope proposes in line 150 of the *Epistle to Arbuthnot*) and all vales are 'beauteous', define such epithets as divorced from any experiential truth and appropriateness for the rest of the poem.

In chapter seventeen of his treatise *Laokoon*, Gotthold Ephraim Lessing cites both Horace and Pope, and adds examples closer to home in Albrecht von Haller's *Die Alpen* and Ewald von Kleist's *Der Frühling* (both poets influenced by Thomson), when parading a sequence of attestations to the inadequacy and inefficacy of descriptive poetry. Lessing's essay, subtitled 'über die Grenzen der Malerei und Poesie' ('on the Limits of Painting and Poetry'), was mostly written during his stay at Breslau in 1760–65 and completed in Berlin in 1766, where it was published in the vain hope of securing the post of Royal Librarian. Despite its somewhat arbitrary, even disorganized, structure, the publication of Lessing's work remains one of the defining moments in the history of that essentially eighteenth-century science of aesthetics.[4] Its central thesis, that poetry and painting—the celebrated Sister Arts between which, according to Pope, images reflect[5]—occupy the different categories of time and space and are thus aesthetically distinct forms of expression, has for the purposes of our present discussion the rather unfortunate effect of appearing to render invalid the very notion of descriptive poetry. For Lessing, any form of linguistic expression must be inferior to a painting in so far as it seeks to present an equivalent of an object as a visual experience. Language draws attention, not to the object described, but to the person (or the words) doing the describing: 'Ich höre in jedem Worte den arbeitenden Dichter, aber das Ding selbst bin ich weit entfernet zu sehen' ('In each word I hear the elaborating poet, but I am very far from seeing the object itself').[6]

Lessing's argument, however, is not denying that language can have a descriptive function: he does not enter a post-structuralist world of eternal and empty self-referentiality. On the contrary, his notions of language are firmly located in the Lockean perception of language as a sign system whose validity lies within a socially accepted system of referentiality.[7] Lessing repeatedly follows Locke's depiction of language as a system of 'arbitrary' ('willkürlich') signs or symbols. Lessing's limitations for language are not that it cannot refer to objects of experience, but that it cannot delineate objects in their spatial actuality. Thus language is a referential, but not a delineating, medium, its powers of depiction being therefore restricted to parts not wholes:

> ... ich spreche nicht der Rede überhaupt das Vermögen ab, ein körperliches Ganze nach seinen Teilen zu schildern; sie kann es, weil ihre Zeichen, ob sie schon aufeinander folgen, dennoch wilkürliche Zeichen sind: sondern ich spreche es der Rede als dem Mittel der Poesie ab, weil dergleichen wörtlichen Schilderungen der Körper das Täuschende gebricht, worauf die Poesie vornehmlich gehet ...

> (... I do not deny to language generally the power of depicting a corporeal whole according to its parts. It can do so, because its symbols, although consecutive, are still arbitrary; but I do deny it to language, as the means of poetry, because such verbal descriptions are entirely deficient in that illusion which is the principal end of poetry ...)[8]

Thus if a poet writes of 'The yellow Wall-Flower, stain'd with iron Brown', the parts are depicted clearly enough because we all—at least, all of us within the relevant cultural system—acknowledge and respect the differentiation of parts signified by the different words. We have no difficulty in referring the description to an example within our experience of the object itself. That we would have such difficulty if the description ran 'The emerald Wall-Flower, stain'd with iron Puce' indicates the ability of language to discriminate between probabilities. What the description cannot do, however, is to stimulate us to the illusion that we are actually looking at the object: it cannot form a total representation. We hear the poet rather than see the object, for we judge the appropriateness of the selection of words according to our consensual system of signs; and we might also notice, in this example, how the hand of the writer betrays its awareness of human processes in the use of the artistic, not natural, metaphor of staining.

The above choice of example is, of course, not arbitrary—the line is from the flower passage in 'Spring' (l. 533)—and neither is the linking of Lessing and Thomson. Lessing knew his Thomson well. He championed Thomson's plays, embarking on a translation of *Agamemnon* and writing a preface to a full German translation of the plays.[9] He also translated Shiels' *Life* of Thomson, and, in the *Laokoon* itself, refers to Thomson as a type of the descriptive poet in terms which reinforce his concern with the limitations of such writing. The painter, he says in chapter 11, who produces a beautiful landscape after a description of a Thomson (as so many did) must exert his imagination to a degree not necessary for the painter who works directly from nature, for the latter works from lively and sensible impressions whereas the former has to follow only an 'indefinite and weak representation of arbitrary signs' ('schwanken und schwachen Vorstellungen willkürlicher Zeichen').[10] Lessing would also have encountered a description of the Laocoon in the fourth part of *Liberty*, where the statue takes pride of place in Thomson's roll-call of the glories of classical sculpture. Although Lessing's essay took as its point of departure Winckelmann's description of the statue rather than Thomson's, Thomson's description of the way in which the agonies of the figure 'Seem so to tremble through the tortured stone,/ That the touched heart engrosses all the view' is interestingly similar to Winckelmann's observation that the pain is expressed through the whole posture of the suffering figure.[11]

It is Lessing's contention that the way the emotion is presented, in this case the agony of the priest Laocoon, is defined by the medium of that presentation. Whereas the poet (the example which Winckelmann compares to the Laocoon is Sophocles' dramatic version of the suffering of Philoctetes) can depict the ugly verbal shrieks which mark pain, the visual artist 'aimed at the highest beauty compatible with the adopted circumstances of bodily pain' ('arbeitete auf die höchste Schönheit, unter den angenommenen Umständen des körperlichen Schmerzes')[12] because the primary duty of art is the creation of beauty. So the sculptor did not portray Laocoon with his mouth contorted into a shriek which would have resulted in an ugly work of art, but reconciled pain with beauty by diffusing the agony in the manner described by Winckelmann and Thomson. The sculptor could not make a shriek of pain simply one element of a larger account, because he, like all visual artists, was restricted to the presentation of a single moment within an event. To have depicted Laocoon open-mouthed in pain would have produced a rebarbative image, not one which invokes compassion: the result would have been aversion, not pity. The poet, however, can make a cry of pain just one element in a longer depiction, as did Virgil in his account of the death of Laocoon in book two of the *Aeneid*. Virgil's 'clamores simul horrendos ad sidera tollit' ('the while he lifts to heaven hideous cries')[13] is but one line within a longer description of the event, which also takes its place within the context of a wider characterization of the priest as patriot and loving father; and the phrase 'clamores ... horrendos' does not evoke a visual image, so that the pain is not accompanied by ugliness.

Lessing is not concerned to assert any superiority of poetry over the visual arts or vice versa: he is attempting to define the qualities and limits of each medium. But his analysis does have a serious consequence for poetry as a descriptive medium, namely that its very nature prevents its being an effective presentation of material beauty:

Körperliche Schönheit entspringt aus der übereinstim-
menden Wirkung mannigfaltiger Teile, die sich auf einmal
übersehen lassen. Sie erfordert also, daß diese Teile
nebeneinander liegen müssen; und da Dinge, deren Teile
nebeneinander liegen, der eigentliche Gegenstand der
Malerei sind; so kann sie, und nur sie allein, körperliche
Schönheit nachahmen.

(Material beauty arises from the harmonious effect of
numerous parts, all of which the sight is capable of comprehending at the same time. It requires, therefore, that these
parts should lie in juxtaposition; and since things whose
parts lie in juxtaposition are the peculiar objects of the
plastic arts, these it is, and these only, which can imitate
material beauty.)[14]

Language, lacking this capacity for the simultaneous rendering of
forms, lines and colours, has to acknowledge that it is powerless
to render such spatial relationships and hence the very nature of
objects in their visual beauty.

Colour is a particular example of such limitations. The line
'The yellow Wall-Flower, stain'd with iron Brown', despite its
capacity to denote an object to which our experience can relate,
remains at a crude level of depiction when compared with the
variability, subtlety and interfusion which are present within
shades of colour when presented directly to the eye and which
painting is capable, at least to a degree, of imitating. A recognition of this limitation is, indeed, the very point to which
Thomson's extended flower passage in 'Spring' leads:

Infinite Numbers, Delicacies, Smells,
With Hues on Hues Expression cannot paint,
The Breath of Nature, and her endless Bloom.   (ll. 553–55)

That characteristically Thomsonian nominalization—the poet, as
it were, being absorbed into a broader notion of all those who
seek to express—generalizes the point: all who 'paint' in whatever medium, however literally or metaphorically, cannot express
adequately the boundless multiplicity and magnificence of nature
as a fully sensory experience. Humanity is unequal to the task of

comprehending the totality, the being whose source is the 'Universal Soul', the 'Essential Presence' to which the poet bends the knee in a gesture of absolute humility (ll. 556–58). Thomson is ultimately concerned with broader issues than those of aesthetics. But this does not mean that he is unaware of such issues; or that they cannot be articulated by someone writing before Lessing, before, indeed, the supposed 'invention' of aesthetics in the 1730s: the first version of the flower passage, including lines 553–55, appeared in the first edition of 'Spring' in 1728.

Thomson's lines do, indeed, anticipate one of Lessing's prescriptions for poetry which contains any kind of descriptive element. Poetry, Lessing argues in chapter 16, can only depict one property of objects (without lapsing into a ludicrous and tedious list, which even then lacks the simultaneity of visual experience), rather than the multiplicity available to those arts which can present at once shape, texture and colour. It follows that writers should restrict themselves to a moderate use of epithets. Homer, he observes in empirical justification of what he has deduced from the nature of the medium, generally restricts himself to the presentation of one characteristic at a time, a ship being 'now the black ship, now the hollow ship, now the swift ship, at most the well-rowed black ship' ('bald das schwarze Schiff, bald das hohle Schiff, bald das schnelle Schiff, höchstens das wohlberuderte schwarze Schiff').[15] This rule Thomson 'follows' by maintaining, in his list of flowers, a level of adjectival economy ('Violet darkly blue', 'broad Carnations', 'gay-spotted Pinks'), varied by such phrasal qualification as in our 'yellow Wall-Flower, stain'd with iron Brown' or by an extension into ternary form, as in 'Hyacinths, of purest virgin White,/ Low-bent, and blushing inward' (ll. 547–48). The effect is of both precise observation and (appropriately) variety and range.

To observe this is to say that Thomson is locating both the strengths and the weaknesses of his medium, and applying them both to an expressive end. It is, precisely, what poetry cannot do—provide a linguistic equivalent to the totality of the natural world—that furnishes his point about the infinite qualities of nature and its begetter; while it is the capacity of his language to render a succession of varied colours ('darkly blue ... yellow ... glowing Red ... purest virgin White') that acts as a specific empirical indication of those elements of such multiplicity which are open to human perception. Lessing observes in chapter 5 that, because of its limitations, language demands that the reader's imagination extend beyond that which is literally apparent in the text:

> Bei dem Dichter ist ein Gewand kein Gewand; es verdeckt nichts; unsere Einbildungskraft sieht überall hindurch.

> (In poetry a garment is no garment; it conceals nothing. Our imagination sees everything beneath it.)[16]

That our imagination, our capacity to form pictures to ourselves (our 'Eindbildungskraft'), is so set free to contemplate 'The Breath of Nature, and her endless Bloom', crucially stimulated by the power of what the poem does present, exactly matches Thomson's demand that we go beyond the very face of physical nature itself, to contemplate the abstractions of 'Source of Being! Universal Soul/ Of heaven and earth! Essential Presence' which are given physical expression in the scene of nature.

Language, then, provokes our visual imagination ('unsere Einbildungskraft') precisely because it lacks the visual completeness to which pictorial art can aspire. Pictorial art, on the contrary, provokes a different kind of imaginative response because its presentation of intense beauty is accompanied by stasis: by freezing the moment, painting liberates a temporal imagination in the viewer.[17] The power of imagination derives from the relative limitations of the forms of that expression: if no such limitations existed, then there would be no room for imagination. But limitation is inherent in the nature of human experience: it is our very being that demands imaginative release if we are to aspire to the highest forms of contemplation. To make each art so act requires us first to acknowledge what its specific limitations, and hence strengths, are:

> Wenn es wahr ist, daß die Malerei zu ihren Nachahmungen ganz andere Mittel, oder Zeichen gebraucht, als die Poesie; jene nämlich Figuren und Farben in dem Raume, diese aber

artikulierte Töne in der Zeit; wenn unstreitig die Zeichen ein bequemes Verhältnis zu dem Bezeichneten haben müssen: so können nebeneinander geordnete Zeichen auch nur Gegenstände, die nebeneinander, oder deren Teile nebeneinander existieren, aufeinanderfolgende Zeichen aber auch nur Gegenstände ausdrücken, die aufeinander, oder deren Teile aufeinander folgen.

(If it is true that painting and poetry in their imitations make use of entirely different means or symbols—the first, namely, of form and colour in space, the second of articulated sounds in time—if these symbols indisputably require a suitable relation to the thing symbolized, then it is clear that symbols arranged in juxtaposition can only express objects of which the wholes or parts exist in juxtaposition; while consecutive symbols can only express subjects of which the wholes or parts are themselves consecutive.)[18]

Hence descriptive poetry—in any 'pure' sense—is an aesthetic impossibility because 'the coexistence of the body comes into collision with the consecutiveness of language' ('das Koexistierende des Körpers mit dem Konsekutiven der Rede dabei in Kollision kömmt').[19]

As a consequence, any poem which seeks merely for descriptive accuracy will also face insuperable structural problems. It comes as no surprise to find Samuel Johnson, as ever capable of getting straight to the heart of aesthetic and philosophical issues, making just this point when he observes, apropos of Pope's *Windsor Forest*, that the poem's descriptive elements lack plan since 'in most descriptive poems, because the scenes, which they must exhibit successively, are all subsisting at the same time, the order in which they are shewn must by necessity be arbitrary'.[20] Spatial simultaneity of objects in a landscape cannot be equated by words' sequential movement. Thus a poet has always in some way to use features of landscape rather than simply allow them to be 'naturally' present. The writer has not only to select, but to arrange sequentially and syntactically. Not surprisingly, then, Johnson sees similar fundamental problems in *The Seasons*: 'The great defect of *The Seasons* is want of method; but for this I know not that there was any remedy. Of many appearances subsisting all at once, no rule can be given why one should be mentioned before another.'[21]

II. The Power of Description

Acknowledgement of these limitations seems naturally to lead to the purist position that description cannot function at all, or that description only has a function in relation to other, distinct and separate, literary concerns. The semantic fields associated with words lead many critics to regard literature as something which is always the subject of interpretation, of transformation, whether in terms of authorial intention or implicit or ideological meaning. Because literature is constructed of language, 'it is always possible to look at a literary work as an assertion of facts and opinions, that is, as a piece of discursive symbolism functioning in the usual communicative way.'[22] Such pursuit of meaning explicable in terms other than those of the description itself is the common fate of descriptive poetry when subjected to academic criticism. It is regularly, even routinely, seen as discourse operating within alternative, semantically related, systems. As one of the best of recent studies along these lines puts it, 'For Thomson, Cowper and Coleridge landscape-description was ... also a means of making interventions in current political debates.'[23] Because a description of a prospect cannot simply replicate that prospect (and what would be the point even if it could?), its semantic function is seen to lie elsewhere—in the confirmation or subversion of modes of ownership, control and authority; just as landscape itself, the object of artistic ordering via that quintessentially eighteenth-century art of landscape gardening, is implicit with statements of political and social theory.

This chain of reasoning recognizes and responds to the limitations of an aesthetic form by transferring its function to an alternative area of meaning. With language, that arbitrary, flexible and metaphorically luxuriant system of signs, such transference is always possible and often potent. Transference of meaning is the very essence of what language at its figurative level is about. But language is not just figurative: it actually does function very successfully at a literal level and allows us to 'read' it in spatial terms very easily. All that is required is that we do not treat language as literal in a 'pure' sense, but as a precise stimulus to our imagination.

A comparable, indeed related, issue is that of the status of artistic and literary 'Realism'. We could argue that one's perception of reality is always compromised by visual, psychological or ideological conventions. Pictorial 'realism', according to this line, attests to our capacity to believe in pictorial conventions, from perspective at the technical level to social organizations at the level of meaning. A prospect painting neatly combines both: we accept, naïvely, its 'realism' if it operates according to our unquestioned assumptions about perspective and the organization of landscape into hierarchical patterns of ownership. The more comfortable we feel with its 'realism', the more such systems of thought are demonstrated to be implicit in the modes of our thinking and perceiving.

Yet it is possible to distinguish between works of art within the terms of 'realism', which demonstrates that our perceptive faculty does operate critically; indeed, this is how we respond to most perceptions. As Crispin Sartwell points out, our familiarity with such an artistic mode as Cubism—long enough with us to be ingrained into our consciousness—has not led us to naturalize it into what we would accept as realism.[24] We do distinguish between pictorial representations on the grounds of realism; and yet we do so without falling into the naïve trap of imagining that the painting is somehow reality itself or an exact replica of it. Indeed, these two alternatives amount to the same, for an exact replica of reality could only be that reality itself. Such purism we instinctively reject. On the contrary, the degree of resemblance we trace in a work of art takes its origin from the limits of the medium of description when compared with reality. So, 'an assessment of the realism of a painting usually contains an implicit comparison to other paintings, and here three-dimensionality is left out of account as irrelevant to the comparative assessment.'[25] Three-dimensionality is released into the viewer's imagination by the stimulus of the work of art. This is what makes it a work of art and not reality: it is the work of art's plausibility, not identity, as a version of reality that creates the power which stimulates our imagination. The more plausible the painting as an account of reality, the more likely it is to stimulate our sense of imaginative likeness. But that plausibility, and hence the imaginative space created, is based on the very limits of the medium, as a black and white photograph can create in us a strong sense of the life of the people depicted: we do not reject the photograph on the purist grounds that we know that they were not in reality monochrome. We would, however, judge between two different black and white photographs on the grounds of their relative success as evocative versions of reality, and hence of their capacity to stimulate us to an imaginative re-creation of the lives of the people.

So the plausibility of poetic description does not depend on categories which are absent from the nature of the medium (obviously, and primarily, all pictorial qualities including simultaneity and juxtaposition); but rather on the qualities which are present in it. We can, and do, distinguish between 'yellow Wall-Flower' and 'emerald Wall-Flower' not because the phrase represents, still less is, visual reality, but because the denotation of the former phrase is a more plausible referent of our experience than is that of the latter phrase. Because of this, 'yellow Wall-Flower' possesses a virtual, not actual, reality which 'emerald Wall-Flower' does not.[26] This is how we distinguish between descriptions as records of visual experience: we recognize the degree to which a description intersects with our experience.

As Lessing and Johnson point out, the nature of poetic description is that it is consecutive, successive. The category of our existence, then, which language can and does implicitly contain is that of time; the category which we have to supply imaginatively when looking at a painting. Lessing's prime example of a poet's awareness of, and exploitation of, the temporal category of language is Homer's account of Achilles' shield in Book XVIII of the *Iliad*. This great showpiece, often celebrated as an instance of Homer's supreme descriptive powers, takes its energy, argues Lessing, from its presentation as process:

Homer malet nämlich das Schild nicht als ein fertiges vollendetes, sondern als ein werdendes Schild. Er hat also auch hier sich des gepriesenen Kunstgriffes bedienet, das Koexistierende seines Vorwurfs in ein Konsekutives zu verwandeln, und dadurch aus der langweiligen Malerei eines Körpers das lebendige Gemälde einer Handlung zu machen. Wir sehen nicht das Schild, sondern den göttlichen Meister, wie er das Schild verfertiget.

(Homer does not describe the shield as finished and complete, but as it is being wrought. Thus he here also makes use of that knack of art which I have commended; changing that which, in his subject, is coexistent into what is consecutive, and thereby converting a tedious painting of a body into a vivid picture of an action. We see, not the shield, but the divine craftmaster as he executes it.)[27]

The description is rendered through Vulcan's making of the shield, his fashioning of material into object. Hence adjectival writing coexists with a strongly verbal emphasis. Here is an excerpt from Pope's version, capturing this strong sense of movement:

Before, deep fix'd, th' eternal Anvils stand;
The pond'rous Hammer loads his better Hand,
His left with Tongs turns the vex'd Metal round;
And thick, strong Strokes, the doubling Vaults rebound.
    Then first he form'd th' immense and solid *Shield*;
Rich, various Artifice emblaz'd the Field;
Its utmost Verge a threefold Circle bound;
A silver Chain suspends the massy Round,
Five ample Plates the broad Expanse compose,
And god-like Labours on the Surface rose.[28]

Pope limits his use of epithets to one or two per noun-phrase. He gives emphasis to his verbs by placing them at the ends of lines and at other rhythmically strong positions, and so energizes both the act of forging and the shield being forged.

In Thomson's 'Spring' flower passage, too, the scene is created by an agent:

> Along these blushing Borders, bright with Dew,
> And in yon mingled Wilderness of Flowers,
> Fair-handed Spring unbosoms every Grace:
> Throws out the Snow-drop, and the Crocus first;
>
> (ll. 527–30)

In this epic of the natural world, the erotically creative personification—invoked in the very opening line of the whole poem—occupies the place of the divine craftsman in Homer, forging an even more vast, varied and powerful work of art. But the scene is also created by the cooperating agency of our visual responses:

> At length the finish'd Garden to the View
> Its Vistas opens, and its Alleys green.
> Snatch'd thro' the verdant Maze, the hurried Eye
> Distracted wanders; now the bowery Walk
> Of Covert close, where scarce a Speck of Day
> Falls on the lengthen'd Gloom, protracted, sweeps;
> Now meets the bending Sky, the River now,
> Dimpling along, the breezy-ruffled Lake,
> The Forest darkening round, the glittering Spire,
> Th'etherial Mountain, and the distant Main.   (ll. 516–25)

The garden is 'finish'd' in the sense that it contains a spectrum of nature suggested by the parallelism of vistas and alleys, alternative and complementary (broad and narrow) tracks for the eye to be led along. Within this perceptual structure, the eye lights upon objects in a random order, wandering from bower to sky, from dark to light; and yet, despite this apparent randomness, a further order is formed by the gradual movement from near to far, ending at the horizon of sea and mountain, the latter metamorphosed visually into the very element of distance, the sky. To trace this movement, Thomson places emphasis upon verbs of motion: 'wanders', 'sweeps', 'meets'; while creatively giving verbs adjectival or adverbial force in the past participles 'Snatch'd', 'hurried', 'protracted' and the present participles 'bending', 'Dimpling', 'darkening', 'glittering', thus identifying description with process, beauty with the action of perceiving it. This is a narrative of visual experience, its fullness of perception matching the bountiful profusion of Spring's creation of flowers.

The quality of Thomson's descriptions as forming an authentic version of experience, their capacity to create a plausible and hence effective version of visual perception, was noted early on in comments on *The Seasons*. Johnson, for all his qualifications about Thomson's overall method, recognizes that the reader 'wonders that he never saw before what Thomson shews him, and that he never yet has felt what Thomson impresses', a sharp observation of Thomson's ability to combine, as James Sambrook notes, 'novelty and familiarity'. Hazlitt, accurately if rather more prosaically, notes how Thomson's descriptions give back 'the impression which the things themselves make upon us in nature'.[29]

III. Thomson and Eighteenth-Century Aesthetics

Thomson uses the temporality of language to create landscapes which are vitally experiential, both in the sense that they are formed by visual experience and in their capacity to provoke the reader's imaginative experience through the power of their language and syntactic organization. In this, they demonstrate one of the earliest propositions of eighteenth-century aesthetics, the idea that 'beauty' is a category not so much of the object but of the act of cognition by which that object is seen and brought to life. And yet—and here again Thomson shows by example the theory as it is discursively expounded—it is in the objects themselves that some form of correlative quality must be located to act as the basis for the aesthetic perception. Beauty lies neither in the total objectivity of the object nor in the complete subjectivity of the perceiver, but in the relationship between perception and external reality.

Francis Hutcheson's *An Inquiry concerning Beauty, Order, Harmony, Design*, the first of two treatises which comprise his *Inquiry into the Original of Our Ideas of Beauty and Virtue*, was published in 1725, the year before the first version of Thomson's 'Winter'. In the first section, 'Concerning some Powers of Perception, distinct from what is generally understood by Sensation', Hutcheson explicitly identifies beauty as signifying '*the idea raised in us*', while he defines our *sense* of beauty as '*our power of receiving this idea*'.[30] Even earlier, Jean-Pierre de Crousaz' *Traité du Beau*, published in 1715 and in second edition in 1724, establishes the relationship ('le rapport') between sensation and objects as the key element in (what he does not yet call) aesthetics:

> Quand on demande ce que c'est que le *Beau*, on ne prétend pas parler d'un objet qui existe hors de nous et separé de tout autre, comme quand on demande ce que c'est qu'un Cheval, ce que c'est qu'un Arbre. Un Arbre est un Arbre, un Cheval est un Cheval, il est ce qu'il est absolument, en soi-même, et sans qu'il soit necessaire de le comparer avec quelqu'une des autres parties que renferme l'Univers. Il n'en est pas ainsi de la Beauté, ce terme n'est pas absolu, mais il exprime le rapport des objets, que nous appellons *Beaux* avec nos idées, ou avec nos sentimens, avec nos lumières, ou avec notre coeur ...

> (When we ask what the beautiful is, we do not claim to be speaking of an object which exists outside ourselves and separate from all other objects, as when we ask what a horse is or what a tree is. A tree is a tree, a horse is a horse: it is what it is absolutely, in itself, without any need to compare it with any of the other elements which the universe contains. Beauty is not like this: it is not an absolute term, but expresses the relationship between the objects which we call beautiful and our ideas or our feelings, our knowledge or our heart ...) [31]

We thus do not have to wait for Baumgarten and his naturalization of the term 'aesthetics' in Germany[32] to observe the depiction of an aesthetic theory that is centrally about the relationship between cognitive perception and the qualities of the external world so perceived. Thomson's descriptions record this interaction and so document eighteenth-century aesthetic theory in practice. Hence they themselves become aesthetic objects with which the imagination of the reader interacts to form the dynamic perception of their beauty. They are both authentic records of experience and form new objects of literary aesthetics.

Such an approach to the nature of Thomsonian description in the context of forms of eighteenth-century aesthetics leads us partly to an affective theory. Lessing's definition of the poet in chapter 17 of *Laokoon* is explicitly affective:

> er will die Ideen, die er in uns erwecket, so lebhaft machen, daß wir in der Geschwindigkeit die wahren sinnlichen Eindrücke ihrer Gegenstände zu empfinden glauben ...

> (He must awaken in us conceptions so lively, that, from the rapidity with which they arise, the same impression should be made upon our senses which the sight of the material objects that these conceptions represent would produce ...)[33]

Thomson's descriptions assert the capacity of the natural world to create vital sensations in the observer; and their language is designed to provoke like sensations in the reader, not by a vain attempt at exact representation, but by an evocation of a parallel process of imaginative sensation. 'Art', as a twentieth-century aesthetician has expressed it, 'is the creation of forms symbolic of human feeling'[34]—symbolic, because art is not itself reality or actual feeling, but is expressive of the idea of reality, of feeling as reflected in the rapport between observer and object, reader and poem.

However, de Crousaz' emphasis upon 'le rapport des objets ... avec nos idées' reminds us that such an affective theory is tempered in eighteenth-century aesthetics by an emphasis on the objectivity of the external world. Here again, we can define a remarkably consistent idea of the necessary constituents of the aesthetic object, and one which is distinctly realized in Thomson's descriptive practice. Hutcheson writes in 1725:

> The figures that excite in us the ideas of beauty seem to be those in which there is *uniformity amidst variety*.

This principle he proceeds to apply to a range of natural processes, observing that in 'every part of the world which we call beautiful there is a vast uniformity amidst almost infinite variety', as he exemplifies from the large-scale effects of light and shade upon landscape:

> how beautifully is it diversified with various degrees of light
> and shade, according to the different situations of the parts
> of its surface, in mountains, valleys, hills, and open plains,
> which are variously inclined toward the great luminary

to the high degree of uniformity he perceives within the individual species which constitute the variety of vegetation:

> In the almost infinite multitude of leaves, fruit, seed,
> flowers of any one species we often see a great uniformity in
> the structure and situation of the smallest fibres.[35]

Once again, we can find similar ideas in de Crousaz' *Traité du
Beau*. He devotes his third chapter to the 'caractères réels et
naturels du Beau' ('the real and natural characteristics of the
beautiful'), which he lists as variety, unity, regularity, order and
proportion. Variety is the infinite creation of the single God, and
is thus a principle of our experience of that creation. But within
this invigorating, stimulating variety, the human spirit finds a
quality of unity, 'sans quoi cette diversité le fatigue et l'em-
brouille, au lieu que s'il a l'une et l'autre, autant que la Varieté
l'anime, autant l'Unité le delasse' ('without which this diversity
tires and confuses it, whereas if both are present, variety enlivens
it to the same degree that unity relaxes it'). From this principle of
'la diversité, reduite ainsi à l'Unité' ('diversity so reduced to
unity') proceed the qualities of regularity, order and proportion,
which are the means by which variety is tempered by unity.[36] Out
of this process springs harmony.

These principles, stated so early in the eighteenth century and
underlying much subsequent aesthetic theory,[37] recur with
remarkable regularity in later writings on art. For example,
writing in 'An Essay on Aesthetics' in 1909, Roger Fry declares
that

> the first quality that we demand in our sensations will be
> order, without which our sensations will be troubled and
> perplexed, and the other quality will be variety, without
> which they will not be fully stimulated.[38]

These qualities, which Fry claims as essential for an aesthetically satisfying product, he also acknowledges as notably present in such natural phenomena as flowers. Within the continuity of this aesthetic theory, at root a belief in the harmonious relationship of variety and unity as the essence of our perception of the beautiful, lies the view that what is true for artistic products is so because its criteria are inherent within the natural world. Two hundred years apart, Hutcheson and Fry both appeal to nature for corroboration, indeed for the essential statement, of the aesthetic impulse: there is some definable quality in natural objects which underpins the sense of beauty that is a function of our human perception.

IV. Thomson as Descriptive Poet

Hence a poem which seeks to express truly the inherent aesthetic of nature will strive for an equivalent aesthetic in its own form. The muse, as Thomson puts it in his address to Wilmington at the beginning of 'Winter'—in a passage added for the first complete *Seasons* of 1730—has

> rounded the revolving Year:
> Skim'd the gay Spring; on Eagle-Pinions borne,
> Attempted thro' the Summer-Blaze to rise;
> Then swept o'er Autumn with the shadowy Gale;
> And now among the Wintry Clouds again,
> Roll'd in the doubling Storm, she tries to soar;
> To swell her Note with all the rushing Winds;
> To suit her sounding Cadence to the Floods;
> As is her Theme, her Numbers wildly great: (ll. 19–27)

The 'bold Description' (l. 29) with which Thomson undertakes this task is not just one of phonological mimesis, but engages an aesthetic which is formal and linguistic in the attempt to create a poem which matches the very aesthetic of its subject. The poetry of *The Seasons* strives for a formal equivalence, in the temporal mode of language, of what nature presents both simultaneously—as in a single scene of landscape—and successively in the cyclical roll of the seasons. Nature is both varied and unified, a succession and a totality: the 'varied God' of Thomson's address in 'A Hymn on the Seasons' (l. 2), the single God, the 'seul Dieu et un seul Objet' who contains 'une infinité de perfections' of de Crousaz' treatise.[39] *The Seasons* strives to be a poetic equivalent of our experience of God's world as unity within variety.

This principle underlies such a linguistic detail as Thomson's repeated use of periphrasis. At the end of 'Spring', for example, he includes in his lengthy account of the joys of contented rural retirement—an essay in the long tradition of 'beatus ille'— a description of children as 'human blossom' (l. 1147).[40] By speaking of human beings in botanical language, Thomson establishes a point of contact between different aspects of the natural world: humans' growth is analogous to that of flowers because they are both facets of one single creation. 'Human blossom' is the linguistic reverse of Thomson's frequent periphrases for natural phenomena by which they are allocated human attributes. To call the flowers of summer 'musky tribes' ('Spring', l. 546) is the mirror image of calling children 'human blossom': the noun relates each part of nature to its complementary sphere—flowers to human groups, children to young buds—while the adjective distinguishes the object as belonging to its own individual section of existence. As parts of nature reflect each other, so does Thomson's language.

This process of interconnection is pursued through other techniques, such as simple repetition, as when Thomson describes the children as blooming 'By degrees' ('Spring', l. 1146) as he had earlier described the buds of the 'juicy groves' as 'unfolding by degrees' ('Spring', ll. 90–91). The phrase echoes across 'Spring', linking its end with its beginning as it does the varied parts of the unity that is the natural principle of growth. Elsewhere, Thomson adds syntactic devices to linguistic ones. In the storm passage early in 'Winter', for example, birds and cattle are described as taking shelter:

> Thither the houshold feathery People croud,
> The crested Cock, with all his female Train,
> Pensive, and dripping; while the Cottage-Hind
> Hangs o'er the enlivening Blaze, and taleful there
> Recounts his simple Frolick: (ll. 87–91)

The 'feathery people' and the cottage-hind take their place within a continuing syntactic structure, pointed by a product of Thomson's habit of revision which happily changed a full stop in line 89 to a semicolon the better to support the conjunction 'while'. Syntax embodies the union of parts of creation within a single reaction to the tempestuous season which joins those parts together.

Descriptions also reflect across the poem's larger structure. While the animal world seeks its various shelter during the winter storm, landscape is exposed to the full force of its violence:

> Wide o'er the Brim, with many a Torrent swell'd,
> And the mix'd Ruin of its Banks o'erspread,
> At last the rous'd-up River pours along:
> Resistless, roaring, dreadful, down it comes,
> From the rude Mountain, and the mossy Wild,
> Tumbling thro' Rocks abrupt, and sounding far;
> Then o'er the sanded Valley floating spreads,
> Calm, sluggish, silent; till again constrain'd,
> Between two meeting Hills it bursts a Way,
> Where Rocks and Woods o'erhang the turbid Stream;
> There gathering triple Force, rapid, and deep,
> It boils, and wheels, and foams, and thunders thro'.
>
>   ('Winter', ll. 94–105)

The essence of this description of nature in process is movement; movement caught not simply in verbs denoting rapid movement, but also in the constantly shifting language. Language is dynamically in motion, as nature is at its most violent. First there are past participles acting adjectivally to create a feeling of full potential: 'swell'd', 'o'erspread', 'rous'd-up' (all part of Thomson's 1730 revision of the original 'Winter', whose equivalent passage—lines 133–42—launches into the violent current of the river without this sense of gathered power). Then follows a series of active verbs and strong adjectives (with 'roaring' blurring the distinction between verb and adjective), before past participles and still adjectives take over at lines 100–01. From the repeated sense of potential in 'constrain'd', the lines are freed into activity at 'bursts' and conclude with a powerful succession of actively violent verbs, the last of which ('thunders') picks up the storm which is the cause of the whole description and to whose violence the river resounds. The course of the language reflects, represents, embodies the course of the river: the passage is the poetically equivalent narrative of nature's story. Its power registers, in Hutcheson's phrase, 'our power of receiving this idea'.

An equivalent set piece of description occurs in 'Summer', the opposite season, in a passage which Thomson worked on extensively from its first version in 1727 to its final, expanded version of 1746:

> Smooth to the shelving Brink a copious Flood
> Rolls fair, and placid; where collected all,
> In one impetuous Torrent, down the Steep
> It thundering shoots, and shakes the Country round.
> At first, an azure Sheet, it rushes broad;
> Then whitening by Degrees, as prone it falls,
> And from the loud-resounding Rocks below
> Dash'd in a Cloud of Foam, it sends aloft
> A hoary Mist, and forms a ceaseless Shower.
> Nor can the tortur'd Wave here find Repose:
> But, raging still amid the shaggy Rocks,
> Now flashes o'er the scatter'd Fragments, now
> Aslant the hollow'd Channel rapid darts;
> And falling fast from gradual Slope to Slope,
> With wild infracted Course, and lessen'd Roar,
> It gains a safer Bed, and steals, at last,
> Along the Mazes of the quiet Vale.
>
> ('Summer', ll. 590–606)

As in 'Winter', this description expresses in its movement the course of nature. Adjectives and verbs are now kept distinct to present simple states and action ('Smooth ... Rolls fair, and placid'); are now merged as past and present participles to enact a similar sense of potential ('collected') and forceful movement ('thundering ... loud-resounding'); and are both grouped in series and distinguished by contrast ('fair, and placid ... impetuous ... steep'). Across the two descriptions words reflect. The final verb of the 'Winter' river turns into the adjectival present participle 'thundering' in 'Summer'; 'foams' appears as 'a Cloud of Foam'; the adjective 'rapid' becomes the adjective/adverb in 'rapid darts', as a state merges with action; 'roaring' matches 'roar'; 'sounding' echoes 'resounding'. Other words form relationships as synonyms: 'brim'/'brink'; 'silent'/'quiet'; 'gathering'/'collected'. The mirroring of the passages goes yet further as the order of the narratives is reversed. 'Winter' begins with the swollen, roused-up river orgasmically pouring over its brim; 'Summer' has the river rolling to its brink quietly, smoothly. 'Winter' ends with the most violent sequence of verbs in its passage; while 'Summer' closes with the river stealing along a quiet valley, movement at its least forceful. In 'Summer' quiet encircles violent movement, so that the energy of the river is both present and contained, controlled. In 'Winter' violent movement encircles one equivalent moment of calm ('Then o'er the sanded Valley floating spreads,/ Calm, slug-gish, silent'). Thus the same elements are present in both descrip-tions, 'Winter' containing 'Summer' within a savage, dynamic frame; 'Summer' containing 'Winter' within a quiet, calm frame— in more decent order tame. The different ordering reflects, of course, the different elements within the cycle of the year, with now violence predominating, now stillness. The variety is in the ordering; the unity in the simultaneous presence of the disparate elements of the total vision of the year. Thomson's expressive language is precisely reflecting the central aesthetic of nature, of the 'varied God': the description does not just reflect its objects, but actually re-creates them by forming its own equivalent aesthetic for the reader's imaginative engagement.

Thomson expresses the co-presence of all varied elements of nature in his description of the power of frost, added in 1730:

> The Frost-concocted Glebe
> Draws in abundant vegetable Soul,
> And gathers Vigour for the coming Year.
> A stronger Glow sits on the lively Cheek
> Of ruddy Fire: and luculent along
> The purer Rivers flow; their sullen Deeps,
> Transparent, open to the Shepherd's Gaze,
> And murmur hoarser at the fixing Frost.
>
> ('Winter', ll. 706–13)

The lines present forceful life as potential, as fostered, within apparent stasis. Frost begins and ends the description, but within lie life, power, movement; as within the appearance of wintry death lie the seeds of the new year, actually fed by winter. Within the heart of the lines, as in the heart of winter, are strength ('Vigour'), warmth ('Glow', 'ruddy Fire') and light ('luculent').

Each season is a particular ordering of the variety of creation which manifests its ultimate unity, the whole forming that proportion which is another of de Crousaz' aesthetic principles. We have seen, in Thomson's flower passage in 'Spring', the poem's expression of what de Crousaz calls 'une infinité de perfections', and Hutcheson calls 'the almost infinite multitude of leaves, fruit, seed, flowers'.[41] The other significance of this passage for us lies in its depiction of the plenitude that is an essential aspect of variety. The scene is a 'mingled Wilderness of Flowers' (l. 528), a harmonious profusion of varied creation. Within this variety lie miniature versions of a mingled profusion. The polyanthus—its very name indicates plurality (poly: many + anthus: flower)—is characterized by 'unnumber'd Dyes' (l. 532), so diverse in colour that they cannot be told; the stock is 'lavish' (l. 534) in its profusion; and the description ranges across a spectrum from blue to yellow to red and finally the 'purest virgin White' of the hyacinths (l. 547), a floral version of the 'various twine of light' which makes up 'the white mingling maze' of the rainbow ('Spring', ll. 211–12). As the colours form a mingled totality, so do the species themselves:

> No gradual Bloom is wanting; from the Bud,
> First-born of Spring, to Summer's musky Tribes:
>
> ('Spring', ll. 545–46)

Each step on the ladder of plenitude ('gradual' < Latin 'gradualis' < 'gradus': 'step'; we have met the word before in the 'Summer' river) is contained within the total ('finish'd') garden. Like the growth of flowers and humanity, the range of vegetation is set out in a plenitude of uncountable degrees ('by degrees', that recurrent phrase which we have met in the 'Summer' river as well as in 'Spring' itself). As flowers merge Spring into Summer, so our progress through this description, as through the entire

poem, is always moving in accordance with nature's own narrative. The scale of flowers ('gradual' also denotes the intervals in a
musical scale) forms the harmony of the whole, the 'Infinite
Numbers' which, like the 'Hues on Hues Expression cannot
paint', merge into the 'Breath of Nature' (ll. 533–35). The garden
at the beginning of the passage, Spring as defined halfway
through, and Nature at the end serve as expressions of comple-
tion, within which language can imply a totality and variety
beyond its literal powers of expression.

Thomson thus shapes his descriptions through an aesthetic
which reflects, and creates a linguistic version of, the aesthetic of
its object. Since poetic description operates successively, through
time, its particular function is to depict nature's process. But
process is always present in human perception, because time is a
necessary category of our existence. When we are dealing with a
painting, it is our imaginative activity which provides the
temporal axis. The same is true when we encounter apparently
stationary landscape, a prospect which seems to lie outstretched
before us. Descriptive poetry's task now is to render the nature
of that imaginative experience, to create a linguistic space
through which we can move, one which convincingly equates to
our sense of landscape as an actual object of visual experience.

Thomson's supreme capacity to shape his poetry into this kind
of aesthetic form can be gauged by contrasting the Hagley Park
passage in 'Spring' with his prose account of the same landscape
written in a letter to Elizabeth Young, dated 29 August 1743, the
year before the first appearance of the poetic version, in the 1744
Seasons:

> The Park, where we pass a great Part of our Time, is thor-
> oughly delightful, quite enchanting. It consists of several
> little Hills, finely tufted with Wood and rising softly one
> above another; from which are seen a great Variety of at
> once beautiful and grand extensive Prospects: but I am most
> charmed with it's [sic] sweet embowered Retirements, and
> particularly with a winding Dale that runs thro' the Middle
> of it. This Dale is overhung with deep Woods, and enlivened
> by a Stream, that, now gushing from mossy Rocks, now
> falling in Cascades, and now spreading into a calm Length

of Water, forms the most natural and pleasing Scene imagin-
able. At the Source of this Water, composed of some pretty
Rills, that purl from beneath the Roots of Oaks, there is as
fine a retired Seat as a Lover's Heart could wish.[42]

Even here, Thomson's habitual 'power of viewing every thing in a
poetical light'[43] is manifested not only in the diction of such
words as 'embowered' and 'purl', but in the syntactic organization of 'now gushing from mossy Rocks, now falling in Cascades,
and now spreading into a calm Length of Water'. Language is
already forming patterns of varied visual experience set into a
unified expressive pattern. That pattern, together with individual
words such as 'overhung' and 'gushing', recurs in intensified and
crucially adapted form in the poem:

> There along the Dale,
> With Woods o'erhung, and shag'd with mossy Rocks,
> Whence on each Hand the gushing Waters play,
> And down the rough Cascade white-dashing fall,
> Or gleam in lengthen'd Vista thro' the Trees,
> You silent steal;   ('Spring', ll. 909–14)

Thomson's syntax—the form of language as succession—is here
his prime means of expressing the unity which underlies the
variety within the landscape. The opening adverbial phrase,
'There along the Dale', which establishes place, is completed as a
unit by the postponed main clause, 'You silent steal', so that
Lyttelton's action, the movement of the figure in the landscape,
encircles, and rounds into a whole, the particular details of his
experience. Thomson's observation of varied effects of water in
his letter furnishes him with the precise parallelism of 'And down
the rough Cascade white-dashing fall,/ Or gleam in lengthen'd
Vista thro' the Trees', where forceful precipitation in the first line
is countered by soft horizontal light in the second, and yet both
are linked by a shared quality of light ('white-dashing ... gleam').
Further, the two lines act as reflections of one another, with a
mirror-like inversion of syntactic order in which adverbial words
and phrases encircle the central verbs, 'fall' and 'gleam'. Variety is
held within a harmony of complete unity, as Lyttelton's perception encompasses both experiences.

Thomson's imaginative walk through Hagley Park on behalf of Lyttelton culminates in the prospect from the summit of the hill:

> Meantime you gain the Height, from whose fair Brow
> The bursting Prospect spreads immense around;
> And snatch'd o'er Hill and Dale, and Wood and Lawn,
> And verdant Field, and darkening Heath between,
> And villages embosom'd soft in Trees,
> And spiry Towns by surging Columns mark'd
> Of houshold Smoak, your Eye excursive roams:
> Wide-stretching from the *Hall*, in whose kind Haunt
> The *Hospitable Genius* lingers still,
> To Where the broken Landskip, by Degrees,
> Ascending, roughens into rigid Hills;
> O'er which the *Cambrian* Mountains, like far Clouds
> That skirt the blue Horizon, dusky, rise.
>
> ('Spring', ll. 950–62)

The opening lines define the experience: the forcefulness of 'bursting' is linked to the insistent vastness of 'spreads immense around' by the specific word, 'prospect', which signifies a scale of landscape appropriate for such an overwhelming visual effect. That effect is then registered in an extended version of the technique used earlier in the flower passage, whereby the eye becomes the medium of response to the sheer dynamic power of nature which 'snatches' it into immediate reflex. As earlier in the Hagley Park passage itself, Thomson suspends his syntax so that the referent of 'snatch'd' is withheld over five lines, until 'your Eye excursive roams'. One visual experience can encompass huge variety, as the single prospect contains such diversity of scenery. That variety covers strongly contrasting elements of vertical and horizontal sights, hill against valley, trees against open ground, fruitful field against barren heath (with added colour variation in 'verdant … darkening'). The human elements of the landscape are then effortlessly harmonized into nature, the trees delicately accommodating villages, and towns being marked by strong vertical lines ('spiry … surging Columns'). As the villages are welcomed gently into the scene by nature, so in the next syntactic movement Lyttelton's personalized landscape, the hall, is characterized by appropriate hospitality, human qualities mutually reflecting those of nature as part of one creative impulse of love. This principle of harmony extends to the final, furthest point of the prospect, where the distant mountains merge vertically into the element of air. That process of merging is characterized by the familiar phrase, 'by degrees', which repeats the idea of gradualism as an essential part of the vast scale of variety held within the unified perception of the 'you' which is Lyttelton, of the poetic description which is Thomson's, and of the imaginative space which is the reader's, the other 'you'. Our senses are stimulated into a 'semblance of events lived and felt', organized to 'constitute a purely and completely experienced reality, a piece of *virtual life*'.[44] The means by which Thomson effects this is to find a poetic equivalent for the essential aesthetic of experience. This is the sense of description, purely and completely.

NOTES

1.   *An Epistle to Dr Arbuthnot*, ll. 147–48, in *The Twickenham Edition of the Poems of Alexander Pope*, vol. 4, ed. John Butt (London, 1939).

2.   *The Works of Alexander Pope* (London, 1751), IV, 19–20.

3.   *Ars Poetica*, ll. 16–18. Q. *Horati Flacci Opera*, ed. E. C. Wickham (Oxford, 1901). Translation from Penguin Classics edition, ed. Niall Rudd (Harmondsworth, 1979).

4.   On the invention and development of the term 'aesthetics', see David E. Wellbery, *Lessing's Laocoon: Semiotics and Aesthetics in the Age of Reason* (Cambridge, 1984), p. 3; Hans Reiss, 'The "naturalization" of the term "Ästhetik" in eighteenth-century German: Alexander Gottlieb Baumgarten and his Impact', *Modern Language Review*, 89 (1994), 645–58; Hans Reiss, 'The Rise of Aesthetics: Baumgarten's radical innovation and Kant's response', *British Journal for Eighteenth-Century Studies*, 20 (1997), 53–61.

5.   *Epistle to Mr Jervas*, l. 20.

6.   G. E. Lessing, *Laokoon*, ed. Dorothy Reich (London, 1965), pp. 168–69. The English version is Beasley's 1853 translation, as published by Bell (London, 1914), p. 100. Lessing's work was preceded and influenced by

a number of earlier writers, including Moses Mendelssohn in Germany and James Harris in Britain. Harris's 'A Discourse on Music, Painting, and Poetry' (1744) discriminates between form and colour as the characteristics of subjects fit for painting and actions as the proper sphere of poetry. It was Lessing's work, however, which fully developed the idea and became the *locus classicus* for such aesthetic discrimination.

7.   John Locke, *An Essay Concerning Human Understanding* (1689), bk 3, ch. 2. See also James Harris, *Hermes: or a Philosophical Inquiry Concerning Language and Universal Grammar* (1751), bk 3, ch. 3.

8.   Reich, *Laokoon*, p. 169; Beasley, *Laokoon*, pp. 100–01.

9.   See James Sambrook, *James Thomson 1700–1748: A Life* (Oxford, 1991), p. 308, n. 65. Quotations from James Thomson, *The Seasons*, ed. James Sambrook (Oxford, 1981).

10.   Reich, *Laokoon*, p. 138; Beasley, *Laokoon*, p. 75.

11.   *Liberty*, IV.185–206; Reich, *Laokoon*, p. 55.

12.   Reich, *Laokoon*, p. 68; Beasley, *Laokoon*, p. 17.

13.   *Aeneid*, II.222. Translation by H. Rushton Fairclough in the revised Loeb edition (London, 1935).

14.   Reich, *Laokoon*, p. 188; Beasley, *Laokoon*, p. 116.

15.   Reich, *Laokoon*, p. 159; Beasley, *Laokoon*, p.92.

16.   Reich, *Laokoon*, p. 99; Beasley, *Laokoon*, p.42

17.   This distinction between a painting as stasis and our imaginative perception of it as temporal was noted by Dryden in the Preface to his translation of Du Fresnoy's *De Arte Graphica*: '… I must say this to the advantage of Painting, even above Tragedy, that what this last represents in the space of many Hours, the former shows us in one Moment. The Action, the Passion, and the manners of so many Persons as are contain'd in a Picture, are to be discern'd at once, in the twinkling of an Eye; at least, they would be so, if the Sight could travel over so many different Objects all at once, or the Mind could digest them all at the same instant or point of time … yet the Eye cannot comprehend at once the whole Object, nor the Mind follow it so fast; 'tis consider'd at leisure, and seen by intervals.' *The Works of John Dryden* (Berkeley, 1989), XX, 54–55.

18.   Reich, *Laokoon*, p. 157; Beasley, *Laokoon*, p. 91.

19.   Reich, *Laokoon*, p. 196; Beasley, *Laokoon*, p. 101.

20.   Samuel Johnson, *Lives of the English Poets*, ed. George Birkbeck Hill, 3 vols (Oxford, 1905), III, 225.

21.   Johnson, *Lives of the English Poets*, III, 299–300.

22.   Susanne K. Langer, *Feeling and Form: A Theory of Art Developed from Philosophy in a New Key* (London, 1953), p. 208.

23.   Tim Fulford, *Landscape, Liberty and Authority: Poetry, Criticism and Politics from Thomson to Wordsworth* (Cambridge, 1996), p. 5.

24.   Crispin Sartwell, 'Realism', in *A Companion to Aesthetics*, ed. David E. Cooper (Oxford, 1992), p. 355.

25. Sartwell, 'Realism', p. 356. See also his essay, 'What Pictorial Realism Is', *British Journal of Aesthetics*, 34 (1994), 2–12.

26. 'Virtual' is Langer's useful term: see *Feeling and Form, passim*.

27. Reich, *Laokoon*, p. 177; Beasley, *Laokoon*, p. 107.

28. *Homer's Iliad*, bk 18, ll. 547–56. *Twickenham Edition*, vol. 8, ed. Maynard Mack (London, 1967).

29. Johnson, *Lives of the English Poets*, III, 299; Sambrook, *James Thomson*, p. 35; William Hazlitt, *Complete Works*, ed. P. P. Howe (London, 1930), V, 87–88.

30. Francis Hutcheson, *An Inquiry concerning Beauty, Order, Harmony, Design*, ed. Peter Kivy (The Hague, 1973), section 1, para. 9, p. 34. Hutcheson's analysis raises the question of the extent to which our idea of beauty resembles the quality within the object which produces the idea. His epistemological roots are in Locke's distinction between primary and secondary qualities. For Locke, our ideas of primary qualities (solidity, extension, figure, motion, number) resemble the qualities in the objects which produce them; whereas our ideas of secondary qualities (colour, sound, taste) do not. Secondary qualities are powers within the object to produce sensations in us by means of their primary qualities (*Essay*, bk 2, ch. 7). The question is not directly addressed by Hutcheson, but R. S. Downie proposes an acceptable inference, that, for Hutcheson, the 'experience of beauty is a subjective experience, like a sweet taste, but there are features of the objective situation ... which cause the idea or experience of beauty and which that idea in a way pictures or resembles' (Francis Hutcheson, *Philosophical Writings*, ed. R. S. Downie (London, 1994), p. xxvii). For more detailed discussion of the issue, see Peter Kivy, *The Seventh Sense: a Study of Francis Hutcheson's aesthetics and its influence in eighteenth-century Britain* (New York, 1976) and Emily Michael, 'Francis Hutcheson on Aesthetic Perception and Aesthetic Pleasure', *British Journal of Aesthetics*, 24 (1984), 241–55. On Thomson's knowledge of Hutcheson, particularly in relation to Hutcheson's benevolent ethics in the context of the debate between the self-love and social love theories of morality, see Mary Jane W. Scott, *James Thomson, Anglo-Scot* (Athens, Georgia, 1988), pp. 159–62.

31. Jean-Pierre de Crousaz, *Traité du Beau*, 2nd ed. (reproduced, Paris, 1985), ch. 2, para. 1, p. 22. Translation mine.

32. See note 4, above.

33. Reich, *Laokoon*, p. 165; Beasley, *Laokoon*, p. 98.

34. Langer, *Feeling and Form*, p. 40.

35. Hutcheson, *Inquiry*, section 2, paras 3, 5, 6, 7, pp. 40–43. See note 30 for the subjective/objective issue. The concept of unity in variety is of ancient origin, with its roots in Aristotle's notion of beauty as an ordered structure of parts (*Poetics*, 1450b). On the idea in Thomson's poetry, see Patricia M. Spacks, *The Poetry of Vision* (Cambridge, MA, 1967), p. 37; and

Scott, *James Thomson, Anglo-Scot*, who observes that Thomson 'took contemporary aesthetic values of "unity-in-variety," "beauty-in-diversity" set forth by Hutcheson and Turnbull, among others, to new heights in poetry' (p. 180).

36. De Crousaz, *Traité du Beau*, ch. 3, paras 2 and 3, pp. 29–30.

37. See Ernst Cassirer, *The Philosophy of the Enlightenment*, trans. Fritz C. A. Koelln and James P. Pettegrove (Princeton, 1951), p. 289.

38. Roger Fry, *Vision and Design* (London, 1928), p. 29. The essay first appeared in journal form in 1909.

39. De Crousaz, *Traité du Beau*, ch. 3, para. 1, p. 29.

40. See John Arthos, *The Language of Natural Description in Eighteenth-Century Poetry* (Ann Arbor, 1949), p. 17, on periphrasis as a mode of defining.

41. De Crousaz, *Traité du Beau*, ch. 3, para. 1, p. 29; Hutcheson, *Inquiry*, section 2, para. 7, p. 43.

42. *James Thomson (1700–1748): Letters and Documents*, ed. A. D. McKillop (Lawrence, KA, 1958), p. 165.

43. *Boswell's Life of Johnson*, ed. G. B. Hill and L. F. Powell, 6 vols (Oxford, 1934–50), III, 37. Thomas B. Gilmore, 'Implicit Criticism of Thomson's *Seasons* in Johnson's *Dictionary*', *Modern Philology*, 86 (1989), 265–73 notes that, among the large number of quotations from *The Seasons* in Johnson's *Dictionary*, many consist of 'poetic' vocabulary, such as 'azure' and 'bowery'.

44. Langer, *Feeling and Form*, p. 212.

Thomson and Shaftesbury[1]

ROBERT INGLESFIELD

Writing to Aaron Hill on 18 April 1726, shortly after the publication of the first edition of *Winter*, James Thomson expressed his gratitude for Hill's admiring comments on his poem, before launching into a short, essay-like discussion of the relation between 'Self-love' and 'Social Love'. Characteristically effusive in tone, unrestrainedly idealizing in its insistence on the power of the 'social' feelings, the discussion is obviously intended to impress Hill, whom Thomson had not yet met.[2] Hill, himself a poet as well as a periodical essayist, described in the letter as 'so bright an Example' of selfless 'Social Love' (p. 25), was 15 years older than Thomson, with a small literary circle of his own. A passionate advocate of the revival of English poetry through the pursuit of the religious 'sublime', he was to have an important influence on the young poet during the following months: the spirited and remarkably self-confident Preface that Thomson wrote for the second edition of *Winter*, published in June, is clearly influenced by Hill, and contains a passage of extravagant compliment to him.[3] The discussion in the letter reflects Thomson's familiarity and lively sympathy with the philosophical writings of Anthony Ashley Cooper, third Earl of Shaftesbury; it also suggests that he was well aware of the fierce controversy that followed the publication of Bernard Mandeville's attack on Shaftesbury in the essay 'A Search into the Nature of Society', which appeared in the second edition of *The Fable of the Bees* (London, 1723). He may also have known, at least at second hand, Francis Hutcheson's *Inquiry into the Original of Our Ideas of Beauty and Virtue*, an important attempt to develop Shaftesbury's ideas, the first edition of which appeared in March 1725. Thomson writes of 'moral Beauty and Perfection' (p. 26): the phrase 'moral Beauty' is Shaftesbury's, occurring several times in *Advice to an Author* and *An Inquiry concerning Virtue or Merit*, and is also used by Hutcheson in the *Inquiry*. The 'Excellent ones of the Earth', Thomson declares:

> in the Exercise of Social Love, feel it as much to be an orig-
> inal Impulse, as the low World that blind Affection, they
> bear themselves; nor are they, in the least, conscious of that
> forc'd, cold Reasoning, by which it is deduc'd from so mean
> an Original.
>
> How many deathless Heroes, Patriots, and Martyrs, have
> been so gloriously concern'd for the Good of Mankind, and
> so strongly actuated by Social Love, as frequently to act in
> direct Contradiction to that of Self?   (p. 26)

'That forc'd, cold Reasoning, by which it is deduc'd from so mean an Original': Thomson may well be thinking of Mandeville and his sympathizers.

Shaftesbury's influence on *The Seasons*, as well as the later poem *Liberty* (1735–36),[4] has of course long been recognized. C. A. Moore's discussion in his article 'Shaftesbury and the Ethical Poets in England, 1700–60'[5] is still useful, though some of its conclusions have been questioned, not always convincingly.[6] Alan D. McKillop touches several times, though in rather general terms, on the philosopher's influence in the first chapter ('Philosophic Views') of his invaluable *Background of Thomson's 'Seasons'* (Minneapolis, 1942). In his article '"The Friend of Mankind" (1700–60)—An Aspect of Eighteenth-Century Sensibility',[7] A. R. Humphries accurately describes Thomson as 'the most distinguished poetic disciple of Shaftesbury' (p. 209).[8] The discussion of literary 'influences' is of course always problematic, and simplification and exclusiveness are constant dangers. It is clear, however, that in Shaftesbury's writings, and particularly the remarkable dialogue *The Moralists*, Thomson found a loosely coherent pattern of philosophical ideas and attitudes with which he felt an immediate sympathy; the language and style of *The Moralists*, moreover, proved enormously suggestive. Already in the first edition of *Winter* Shaftesbury's influence is apparent in the consciously 'sublime' celebration of personified 'Nature' as a direct manifestation of divine power, and the treatment of the powerful quasi-religious feelings that 'Nature' arouses in the receptive, contemplative mind, feelings that are accompanied by a renewal and refinement of the moral and 'social' passions. The first edition of *Spring* and the 1730 text[9] of the concluding *Hymn* could without exaggeration be described as Shaftesburian poems.

The collection *Characteristicks of Men, Manners, Opinions, Times* contains most of Shaftesbury's philosophical essays and shorter pieces; it was published in 1711, though several of the essays, including the *Inquiry concerning Virtue or Merit*, had appeared earlier. A revised second edition was published in 1714, after Shaftesbury's death, and during the next 19 years four further editions appeared—some indication of the intense interest that the collection aroused. Among the best known of Shaftesbury's essays were the *Letter concerning Enthusiasm* and the notorious and much misrepresented *Essay on the Freedom of Wit and Humour*. His moral theories are most fully stated in the *Inquiry concerning Virtue or Merit*, where he argues that moral virtue originates in a natural capacity for sympathetic feeling ('social Love', 'the natural and kind Affections', *'social or natural Affection'*), which should extend to the whole of humanity, not merely those around one; he also emphasizes the need for emotional order or balance ('a due *Ballance*, and Counterpoise in the Affections'). *The Moralists* is aptly subtitled 'A Philosophical Rhapsody'—'Rhapsody' in the sense of an informal, loosely structured, apparently spontaneous composition. The dialogue was written, as Shaftesbury makes clear, with the intention of popularizing certain philosophical ideas, bringing personified Philosophy out of the 'Colleges and Cells'[10] where she had been immured; to many contemporary readers, no doubt, it seemed distinctively fresh and engaging. In *The Moralists* Theocles represents Shaftesbury's own philosophical position: he is the ideal philosopher, mild, tolerant, reasonable, though passionate in expressing the quasi-religious feelings inspired by the contemplation of the physical universe. Through him, particularly in the 'Meditations' in the third part, Shaftesbury presents an idiosyncratic, 'enthusiastic' deism (the word 'enthusiasm' is used, quite audaciously, in a strongly approving sense). The insistence on Theocles' passionate devotion to personified 'Nature', for which there was no obvious literary precedent, is very striking: "Twas

Nature, he was in love with: 'Twas *Nature* he sung' (p. 219), his companion Philocles recalls. The first of Theocles' 'Meditations' includes an invocation to 'Nature' herself, followed by an address to the deity:

> O GLORIOUS *Nature*! supremely Fair, and sovereignly Good! All-loving and All-lovely, All-divine! Whose Looks are so becoming, and of such infinite Grace; whose Study brings such Wisdom, and whose Contemplation such Delight; whose every single Work affords an ampler Scene, and is a nobler Spectacle than all which ever Art presented!—O mighty *Nature*! Wise Substitute of *Providence*! impower'd *Creatress*! Or Thou impowering DEITY, Supreme Creator! Thee I invoke, and Thee alone adore. To thee this Solitude, this Place, these Rural Meditations are sacred; whilst thus inspir'd with Harmony of Thought, tho' unconfin'd by Words, and in loose Numbers, I sing of Nature's Order in created Beings, and celebrate the Beautys which resolve in Thee, the Source and Principle of all Beauty and Perfection. (p. 345)

At the end of the long second 'Meditation' we are told that 'THEOCLES was now resolv'd to take his leave of *the Sublime*' (p. 391). Philocles, won over by the philosopher's eloquence, declares that he will now share in Theocles' delight in natural landscape, 'the rude *Rocks*, the mossy *Caverns*, the irregular unwrought *Grotto's* [sic], and broken *Falls* of Waters' (p. 393). His conversion, moreover, is marked by a new openness to inspirational feeling; all ennobling emotions, he realizes, are varieties of 'enthusiasm': '"All, all ENTHUSIASM!"—'Tis enough: I am content to be this *new Enthusiast*, in a way unknown to me before' (p. 400).

In the late 1720s and early 1730s Shaftesbury was still an extremely controversial figure, particularly on account of his deistic attitudes, which were widely considered dangerously subversive. Even Francis Hutcheson felt it necessary to include a revealing qualification in his warmly sympathetic account of Shaftesbury in the Preface to the second edition of his *Inquiry*:

How would it have moved the Indignation of that *ingenious Nobleman*, to have found a dissolute set of Men, who relish nothing in Life but the lowest and most sordid Pleasures, searching into his *Writings* for those Insinuations against *Christianity*, that they might be less restrained from their Debaucherys.[11]

George Berkeley's attack on Shaftesbury's moral theories in dialogue III of *Alciphron, or the Minute Philosopher*, published in 1732, is surprisingly bitter, ridiculing the affectation and self-indulgence of Shaftesbury's style as well as what Berkeley sees as the perversities of his intellectual position: Shaftesbury is, needless to say, seriously misrepresented. Alciphron himself, ineffectively defending Shaftesbury's views, is notably evasive and disingenuous, as for example in his reply when asked to define the term 'moral beauty'.[12] Later in the dialogue the ideas of Cratylus, representing Shaftesbury himself, are denounced with extraordinary ferocity by Crito. In *The Theory of Vision Vindicated and Explained*, published the following year, Berkeley once more attacks the morally and religiously subversive tendencies of Shaftesbury's theories. John Brown's much later *Essays on the Characteristics*, which first appeared in 1751, though much cruder in intellectual terms, is also bitterly contemptuous, the final chapter culminating in an imaginary address to Shaftesbury by members of the clergy, accusing him of '*Indecency* and *Immorality* ... in your *Manner* of attacking *Christianity*'.[13]

No doubt *Characteristicks* was widely read among Thomson's fellow students at Edinburgh, where he lived from 1715 to 1725: it is interesting to note that the Preface to the *Edinburgh Miscellany*, a volume of miscellaneous poems published in 1720 by members of one of the student societies, the Athenian Society, and actually containing three poems by Thomson, opens with a quotation from Shaftesbury's 'Miscellaneous Reflections' on 'the ingenious Way of *Miscellaneous* writing'.[14] A crude blank verse poem celebrating the manifestations of divine power in the physical universe, '*the Works, and Wonders, of Almighty Power*', probably a very early poem of Thomson's and consisting almost entirely of a paraphrase of passages in Theocles' 'Meditations', was printed in August 1724 in the London periodical *The Plain*

Dealer, published by William Bond and Aaron Hill;[15] the short essay introducing the poem is almost certainly Hill's. The only direct reference to Shaftesbury in Thomson's surviving letters occurs in a letter dated 18 September 1737, to the poet's friend and publisher Andrew Millar, requesting him to send a copy of *Characteristicks*:[16] a copy of the revised and expanded 1732 edition is listed in the sale catalogue of Thomson's library and possessions.[17] Shaftesbury's influence is, however, evident in several letters in which the poet touches on his religious beliefs: writing to Elizabeth Young, for example, on 21 January 1744, he expresses an unqualified religious optimism, declaring that 'there is no real Evil in the whole general System of Things; it is only our Ignorance that makes it appear so, and Pain and Death but serve to unfold his gracious Purposes of Love'.[18] For Thomson's friend George Lyttelton his deistic beliefs were a source of considerable anxiety, as Lyttelton makes clear in a letter to Thomson dated 21 May 1747, soon after the death of Lyttelton's wife: 'My refuge and consolation is in philosophy,' he declares, '—Christian philosophy, which I heartily wish you may be a disciple of, as well as myself. Indeed, my dear friend, it is far above the platonick'. Lyttelton goes on to mention his own recently published *Observations on the Conversion and Apostleship of St Paul*, which, he claims, he wrote 'with a particular view to your satisfaction' (p. 189). At this time Lyttelton obviously assumed, probably rightly, that his friend was not a Christian.[19]

Thomson wrote the earliest version of *Winter*, the text of the first edition, in the autumn of 1725. Though relatively short (405 lines), *Winter* set the pattern for the composite poem: with its loose reflective structure, based on more or less self-contained verse paragraphs, its carefully handled effects of climax and transition, and its combination of emotionally charged natural description and passages of invocation and moral and religious reflection, it represented, as Johnson observed, a poem 'of a new kind'.[20] *Winter* is a consciously 'sublime' poem, its language, style and versification—the blank verse strongly influenced by that of John Philips's *Cyder*—reflecting the poet's elevated conception of the emotive power of his subject matter. The influence of

'Il Penseroso' is pervasive, most obviously in the use of the emotional theme of contemplative melancholy and in the prominence of the 'I' of the poem, the solitary, contemplative poet-figure, with the accompanying use of jussive constructions such as 'Oft, let me wander o'er the russet Mead,/ Or thro' the pining Grove' (ll. 41–42). No doubt the reflective passages owe much to moralizing poems such as Parnell's 'Night-Piece on Death'—itself an 'Il Penseroso' poem, written in octosyllabic couplets—as well as to the *Spectator* and other periodical essays: for example, the entranced vision of the classical worthies, inspired by the solitary reading of Plutarch's *Lives* (ll. 258–92), is strongly reminiscent of the moralizing 'visions' of the *Spectator* essays. *Winter* seems to have been conceived partly as an expression of Shaftesburian 'enthusiasm' for 'Nature' and the refined moral and quasi-religious feelings that accompany it. A letter that Thomson wrote to his friend William Cranstoun at the beginning of October 1725, when much of the poem was already written, contains a remarkable passage in which he imagines Cranstoun walking alone in the autumn woods, responding to the inspirational power of his surroundings, 'seized w^t a fine romantic kind of a melancholy, on the fading of the Year … wandering, philosophical, and pensive, amidst the brown, wither'd groves', or enjoying stormy days when 'deep, divine Contemplation, the genius of the place, prompts each swelling awfull thought'.[21] The passage suggests something of the emotional preoccupations that lay behind the composition of *Winter*. In the same letter Thomson uses the phrase 'the lover of nature', declaring that 'Nature delights me in every form' (p. 16), before going on to describe the poem that he is writing. In *Winter* he presents himself, the poet-figure, very much as the Shaftesburian 'Nature' enthusiast: his use of personified 'Nature' is indeed directly modelled on *The Moralists*. In the opening passage he describes his own childhood, when 'nurs'd by careless *Solitude*, I liv'd,/ And sung of Nature with unceasing Joy' (ll. 8–9). The theme of the quasi-religious feelings aroused by natural surroundings is developed in the passage on the inspirational power of the autumn landscape. The autumn arouses a 'Philosophic Melancholly' in the contemplative mind:

The *Year*, yet pleasing, but declining fast,
Soft, o'er the secret Soul, in gentle Gales,
A Philosophic Melancholly breathes,
And bears the swelling Thought aloft to Heaven.
Then forming *Fancy* rouses to conceive,
What never mingled with the Vulgar's Dream:
Then wake the tender *Pang*, the pitying *Tear*,
The *Sigh* for suffering Worth, the *Wish* prefer'd
For Humankind, the *Joy* to see them bless'd,
And all the *Social Off-spring* of the Heart!   (ll. 64–73)

Elevated quasi-religious emotion is accompanied by refined, sympathetic 'social' feelings, which extend to the whole of humanity: in the slightly contrived metaphor 'all the *Social Off-spring* of the Heart' Thomson may be recalling a passage in *The Moralists* in which Theocles considers the '*Sentiments*' and other feelings, 'whatever is ingender'd in your *Heart* (good PHILOCLES!), or derives it-self from your *Parent*-MIND, which unlike to other *Parents*, is never spent or exhausted, but gains Strength and Vigour by producing … And here, as I cannot but admire the pregnant Genius, and *Parent*-Beauty, so am I satisfy'd of the *Offspring*' (pp. 409–10). The passionate invocation to 'Nature' later in *Winter* is almost certainly consciously modelled on Theocles' invocation to 'Nature' in his first 'Meditation':

Nature! great Parent! whose directing Hand
Rolls round the Seasons of the changeful Year,
How mighty! how majestick are thy Works!
With what a pleasing Dread they swell the Soul,
That sees, astonish'd! and, astonish'd sings!   (ll. 143–47)

The powerful feelings that 'Nature' inspires, described in language that may owe something to the *Spectator* essays— 'pleasing Dread', 'astonish'd'—find spontaneous expression in impassioned poetry.

The first editions of *Summer* and *Spring* were published in February 1727 and June 1728; two years later, in June 1730, the collected edition of *The Seasons* was published, in which *Autumn* and the concluding *Hymn* appeared for the first time, with revised texts of *Spring* and *Summer*, and a heavily revised and expanded

Winter. With the appearance of the collected edition *The Seasons* could be read for the first time as a composite poem. In writing it Thomson was consciously developing the new descriptive-reflective mode that he had tentatively worked out in the first edition of *Winter*: except for the *Hymn*, the individual parts are much longer, and the verse paragraphs themselves tend to be longer and more confidently and vigorously handled; there are long digressive passages, often extending over several verse paragraphs, many of them moralizing, philosophical or natural-philosophical in content, often broadly comprehensive and celebratory in style, and there are frequent passages of universalizing invocation, sometimes extending over several paragraphs; effects of climax, contrast and transition play an essential part. In terms of both general structure and moral and philosophical themes, the model of the *Georgics* was obviously very much in the poet's mind. Thomson seems in *The Seasons* to have been attempting a new depth and seriousness of moral, philosophical and religious preoccupation; to many contemporary readers the poem must have appeared in many ways distinctively individual and indeed refreshingly modern. In *The Seasons* the poet presents himself, the 'I' of the poem, as the 'enthusiastic' poet–philosopher, passionately devoted to 'Nature' in all her aspects, seeking divine truth through the philosophical understanding of the moral and physical universe. The religious attitudes that he expresses, particularly in *Spring* and the *Hymn*, are unequivocally deistic, and are accompanied by a new interest in natural-philosophical inquiry as providing evidence of the power and active benevolence of the deity. Feeling toward 'Nature' and sympathetic 'social' feeling toward humanity are to be consciously cultivated; the psychological ideal to be aimed at is one of emotional balance or harmony. Undoubtedly the pattern of ideas owes much to Shaftesbury. The 1730 revisions to the passage on the British worthies in *Summer* reflect Thomson's growing sense of personal commitment to Shaftesbury: in the 1727 text the orthodox divines Barrow and Tillotson are both included (l. 539), but three years later they are left out, and five lines on Shaftesbury are added:

> The generous ASHLEY thine, the friend of man;
> Who scan'd his nature with a brother's eye,

His weakness prompt to shade, to raise his aim,
To touch the finer movements of the mind,
And with the MORAL BEAUTY charm the heart.

(1730 text, ll. 611–15)

The use of Shaftesbury's phrase 'moral beauty', emphasized by the use of upper case, is particularly interesting; Thomson emphasizes Shaftesbury's optimistic view of man's moral nature. By 1728–29 Thomson was effectively a Shaftesburian deist, and apparently felt little hesitation in expressing his religious views in his poetry. *The Seasons* was later, of course, heavily revised for the 1744 editions. By this time Thomson had become slightly more diffident; nevertheless, in the 1744 editions and the revised 1746 edition of *The Seasons*, the last to appear during the poet's lifetime, his Shaftesburian sympathies are very much in evidence.

In the first edition of *Summer* the themes of the manifestation of divine power and benevolence in the physical universe, and the capacity of 'Philosophy' to comprehend it, are given special prominence. Near the beginning, for example, there is the passage (ll. 21–30), immediately following the invocation to Inspiration, celebrating the divine power manifested in planetary motion and the astonishing regularity of the 'vast Machine'[22] of the solar system ('With what a perfect, World-revolving Power/ Were first th' unweildy Planets launch'd along/ Th' illimitable Void!'). A little later the five-line invocation to Light (ll. 77–81) introduces the much longer invocation to the Sun (ll. 81–159), in which his 'Blessings' are celebrated at considerable length; the invocation is followed in turn by two paragraphs of passionate praise addressed to the deity (ll. 160–75), and the invocatory paragraph beginning 'To Me be *Nature*'s Volume, wide, display'd' (ll. 176–82). In the lines on planetary motion, of course, Thomson is drawing on Newtonian ideas that had been widely popularized in the periodical essays and elsewhere: he himself received instruction in the principles of the '*Newtonian Philosophy*' when writing his poem *To the Memory of Sir Isaac Newton*, which was published in May 1727, a few months after *Summer*.[23] It is likely, however, that *The Moralists* provided at least a partial model for these passages, particularly Theocles' invocation to the Sun and the impassioned celebration of the divine power manifested in planetary motion in the second 'Meditation' (pp. 371–73). Thomson's developing interest in natural philosophy is reflected in the remarkable invocation to 'PHILOSOPHY', extending over four verse paragraphs, that forms the conclusion of the first edition of *Summer*. 'Philosophy' is interpreted almost exclusively in terms of natural philosophy; she is the 'effusive Source of Evidence, and Truth!' (l. 1078), capable of comprehending, on the one hand, the '*round Complex*/ Of never-ceasing Wonders' (ll. 1128–29) revealed by the telescope, and on the other, the involved workings of the human mind, which are described in specifically Lockean terms:

> With inflected View,
> Thence, on *th' Ideal Kingdom*, swift, she turns
> Her Eye; and instant, at her virtual Glance,
> Th' obedient Phantoms vanish, and appear,
> Compound, divide, and into Order shift,
> Each to his Rank, from plain Perception up
> To Notion quite abstract.   (ll. 1131–37)

The intellectual scope of 'Philosophy' reaches, indeed, to the very edges of '*the World of Spirits*, Action all, and Life/ Immediate, and unmix'd' (ll. 1138–39).

Thomson's deistic sympathies find much more confident expression in the first edition of *Spring*. His religious optimism is reflected in the stress he places on the active benevolence of the deity manifested in the benign spring landscape, and the profound emotional influence that the season exerts on the mind of the sensitive individual. In the carefully written description of the spring shower (ll. 169–201) the approaching rain is endowed with distinct moral and emotional qualities, 'lovely, gentle, kind,/ And full of every Hope, and every Joy,/ The Wish of Nature' (ll. 179–81), and the boldly universalizing reference to 'Man', 'Man superior walks/ Amid the glad Creation, musing Praise,/ And looking lively Gratitude' (ll. 195–97), is a reminder of his place in the benevolent order of the physical universe. When the rain comes, '*Heaven* descends/ In universal Bounty, shedding Herbs,/ And Fruits, and Flowers, on *Nature*'s ample Lap' (ll. 205–07)— the universalizing language again used very deliberately. As in

Summer, natural-philosophical ideas are introduced, most star-tlingly in the passage celebrating the divine wisdom manifested in the structure and internal processes of plants (ll. 508–23), in which Thomson drew on a particular natural-philosophical work, Stephen Hales's *Vegetable Staticks* (London, 1727).[24] The opening lines, with their elevated multiple invocation to the deity, are modelled on the 'enthusiastic' invocations of Theocles' 'Meditations':

> Hail, *Mighty Being*! *Universal Soul*
> Of Heaven and Earth! *Essential Presence*, hail!
> To *Thee* I bend the Knee, to *Thee* my Thoughts
> Continual climb, who, with a Master-Hand,
> Hast the great Whole into Perfection touch'd.   (ll. 508–12)

It is not difficult to find parallels in the 'Meditations'—for example, in the invocation beginning 'O Mighty GENIUS! Sole-Animating and Inspiring Power!', in which Theocles declares that divine power operates 'as best may sute with the Perfection, Life, and Vigour of the Whole!' (p. 366); or later in the first 'Meditation' when he addresses the deity as the '*Original* SOUL, diffusive, vital in all, inspiriting *the Whole*!' (p. 370). The theme of divine manifestation in the physical universe recurs in the long verse paragraph beginning 'What is this *mighty Breath*, ye Curious, say' (ll. 795–827), which follows the account of the instinctive drives of birds and animals. The opening question is soon answered: the inspiring power that finds expression in animal instinct is the deity himself, 'What? but *GOD*!/ Inspiring *GOD*! who boundless Spirit all,/ And unremitting Energy, pervades,/ Subsists, adjusts, and agitates the Whole' (ll. 798–801). The 'informing Author' is apparent in all his works, including the most ordinary:

> In every common Instance *GOD* is seen;
> And to the Man, who casts his mental Eye
> Abroad, unnotic'd Wonders rise. But chief
> In Thee, Boon *Spring*, and in thy softer Scenes,
> The *Smiling GOD* appears.   (ll. 819–23)

A number of influences are immediately recognizable. The

opening lines of the passage were almost certainly suggested by Addison's well-known discussion of animal instinct in *Spectator* 120 and 121, which itself draws heavily on Cicero's *De Natura Deorum*, as well as recent physico-theological writings; in the first essay Addison observes that instinct is 'an immediate Impression from the first Mover, and the Divine Energy acting in the Creatures'.[25] In lines 799–801 Thomson is recalling the lines on the immanent spirit in *Aeneid* VI.724–77 ('mens agitat molem ...'), while lines 810–18, on the various awesome aspects of the natural world, are obviously modelled in part on passages in the Psalms. The passage is, however, deeply influenced by the 'enthusiastic' deism of *The Moralists*. 'All Nature's Wonders', Theocles remarks at one point, 'serve to excite and perfect this Idea of their *Author*' (p. 370). It is interesting to note that in the 1744 and subsequent editions of *The Seasons* the middle section of this passage (ll. 807–21) is omitted.

Shaftesbury's influence is most striking in the long passage later in *Spring* on 'th'infusive Force of *Spring* on Man' (ll. 828–76). The season calms the 'stormy Passions', and arouses refined feelings of benevolence and human sympathy: in lines 839–52 the poet addresses the 'generous' individuals 'in whose wide Thought,/ Of all his Works, *Creative Bounty*, most,/ Divinely burns' (ll. 839–41), and whose benevolent feelings find practical expression in the relief of suffering. The spring also inspires powerful quasi-religious feelings:

> Contentment walks
> The Sunny Glade, and feels an inward Bliss
> Spring o'er his Mind, beyond the Pride of Kings
> E'er to bestow. Serenity apace
> Induces Thought, and Contemplation still.
> By small Degrees the Love of Nature works,
> And warms the Bosom; till at last arriv'd
> To Rapture, and enthusiastic Heat,
> We feel the present *Deity*, and taste
> The Joy of *GOD*, to see a happy World.   (ll. 855–64)

Thomson describes the various 'Degrees' of emotion with characteristic explicitness; the stress on the rapturous feelings

('Rapture, and enthusiastic Heat') enjoyed by the solitary, contemplative lover of 'Nature' obviously owes much to *The Moralists*. The passage that follows in the first edition, beginning ''Tis *Harmony*, that World-embracing Power', is the most assertively deistic passage in *The Seasons*: its omission from the text of the 1744 edition may well have been at the suggestion of George Lyttelton. Thomson describes the universal 'Harmony' which, through particular aspects of the natural landscape, affects 'the Mind/ To Nature tun'd': again he suggests a special kind of sensitive responsiveness to the inspirational influence of 'Nature':

> 'Tis *Harmony*, that World-embracing Power,
> By which all Beings are adjusted, each
> To all around, impelling and impelled
> In endless Circulation, that inspires
> This universal Smile. Thus the glad Skies,
> The wide-rejoycing Earth, the Woods, the Streams,
> With every *Life* they hold, down to the Flower
> That paints the lowly Vale, or Insect-Wing
> Wav'd o'er the Shepherd's Slumber, touch the Mind
> To Nature tun'd, with a light-flying Hand,
> Invisible; quick-urging, thro' the Nerves,
> The glittering Spirits, in a Flood of Day.   (ll. 865–76)

The universal 'Harmony' is a 'Power' in itself, the activating, ordering principle of an interdependent, dynamic universe. It can, moreover, be directly apprehended through particular aspects of 'Nature', arousing rapturous quasi-religious feelings that Thomson describes in specifically physiological terms: the 'glittering Spirits' are the animal spirits, the medium of sensory perception. The underlying ideas are Shaftesburian, though it is possible that Hutcheson's discussion of natural beauty in the *Inquiry into the Original of Beauty and Virtue* was a further influence. In the opening lines Thomson is drawing partly on literary precedents: one thinks, for example, of the tradition of the St Cecilia ode, and particularly the opening of Dryden's *Song for St Cecilia's Day*, 'From Harmony, from heav'nly Harmony/ This universal Frame began'; the immediate model, however, may once again be Theocles' celebration of planetary motion in his second 'Meditation'. Again Thomson introduces the distinctively Shaftesburian conception of 'Nature'—'the Mind/ To Nature tun'd'. In the 1730 text, it is worth noting, 'World-embracing' becomes 'world-attuning', picking up the idea of musical harmony.

Addressed initially to the deity, the concluding *Hymn* is intended as an expression of inspirational religious feeling; indeed, at the end the poet becomes lost in a rapturous sense of the divine presence: 'But I lose/ Myself in HIM, in light ineffable!' (1730 text, ll. 119–20). The succession of invocations to the various aspects of the physical world that occupies much of the poem, based on extended allusions to Psalm 148, the Benedicite and, more immediately, the morning hymn in *Paradise Lost* V.153–208, represents a climactic celebration of the breadth and infinite variety of the physical universe. In the *Hymn* Thomson's Shaftesburian deism finds its most sustained expression. In the opening lines the poet declares of the seasons, 'These, as they change, ALMIGHTY FATHER! these,/ Are but the VARIED GOD'—the emphatic repetition of 'these', placed at the beginning and end of the opening line, contributing to the tone of inspired celebration, and the phrase 'VARIED GOD', emphasized by the use of upper case, bringing its own impassioned boldness and unfamiliarity. The seasons in their gradual succession form 'such a perfect whole,/ That, as they still succeed, they ravish still' (ll. 29–30); the divine power that 'wheels the silent spheres' and 'works in the secret deep' inspires 'transport' in all living things (ll. 33–39). Later, in the lines addressed to the Sun, 'Great source of day! best image here below/ Of thy creator' (ll. 69–70), the poet may be recalling Theocles' invocation to the Sun, 'Bright Source of vital Heat, and Spring of Day! ... *Mighty* Being! Brightest Image, and Representative of *the Almighty!*' (p. 371), as well as *Paradise Lost* V.95, 'Best Image of my self and dearer half'. In the final paragraph the poet emphasizes his own passionate devotion to the deity, who is 'ever present, ever felt' (l. 112):

> In all apparent, wise, and good in all;
> Since HE sustains, and animates the whole;

From seeming evil still educes good,
And better thence again, and better still,
In infinite progression.   (ll. 115–19)

This optimistic view of the ultimate unreality of evil almost
certainly reflects the influence of Shaftesbury: discussing the
unreality of evil, Philocles declares, "Tis *Good* which is predominant; and every corruptible and mortal Nature by its Mortality
and Corruption yields only to some better, and all in common to
that *best and highest Nature*, which is incorruptible and immortal'
(p. 217). In the 1744 text lines 114–16 are considerably expanded,
and the religious optimism becomes more emphatic: 'where H E
vital spreads there must be Joy', the poet asserts, adding, 'I
cannot go/ Where U N I V E R S A L   L O V E not smiles around,/
Sustaining all yon Orbs and all their Sons' (ll. 111–13). It is not
surprising that Lyttelton, when revising *The Seasons* after
Thomson's death, decided, after making one significant revision
to the second line ('the varied God' becomes 'thy varying
Power') to delete the entire *Hymn*.[26]

In the long passage in the first edition of *Summer* describing
the poet's encounter with the spiritual creatures in the 'Grove, of
wildest, largest Growth' (ll. 403–50), Thomson returns to the
theme of the inspirational power of natural surroundings. The
passage was probably suggested by Theocles' description, in his
second 'Meditation', of the dark forest in which 'Mysterious
Voices are either heard or fancy'd: and various Forms of *Deity*
seem to present themselves' (p. 390). Thomson's stress on the
quasi-religious feelings that the woodland setting arouses
('harrow'd, I feel/ A sacred Terror, and severe Delight,/ Creep
thro' my mortal Frame'; ll. 427–29) is strongly reminiscent of
Shaftesbury's passage; more particularly, the reference to ancient
inspirational religion ('These are the Haunts of Meditation,
these/ The Scenes where antient Bards th' inspiring Breath,/
Extatic, felt'; ll. 409–11) recalls Theocles' description of the
sounds and visions heard and seen in 'these sacred Silvan Scenes;
such as of old gave rise to Temples, and favour'd the Religion of
the antient World' (pp. 390–91). Thomson's spiritual creatures,
significantly, invite the poet-figure to participate in the inspired
celebration of 'Nature ... and Nature's G O D' (l. 442). The same

theme is developed in the remarkable passage on the emotional influence of the autumn landscape in the 1730 text of *Autumn* (ll. 944–77), which is a heavily revised and much expanded version of the 'Philosophic Melancholly' passage in the first edition of *Winter.* The passage is an outstanding example of the explicit, idealizing description of feeling that is characteristic of the composite poem. The gradual approach of the now personi- fied (and male) 'POWER/ Of PHILOSOPHIC MELANCHOLY', declared in the exclamations of the first two lines, arouses powerful emotional responses, even inflaming the 'imagination':

> devotion rais'd
> To rapture, and divine astonishment.
> The love of Nature unconfin'd, and chief
> Of humankind; the large, ambitious wish,
> To make them blest; the sigh for suffering worth,
> Lost in obscurity; th' indignant scorn
> Of mighty pride; the fearless, great resolve;
> The wonder that the dying patriot draws,
> Inspiring glory thro' remotest time;
> The arrousing pant for virtue, and for fame;
> The sympathies of love, and friendship dear;
> And all the social offspring of the heart.   (ll. 959–70)

'Devotion rais'd/ To rapture, and divine astonishment', 'the love of Nature unconfin'd': the language is unmistakably influenced by *The Moralists.* The relatively short enumeration of sympa- thetic feelings in the original passage in *Winter* is very much expanded, with a strong emphasis on public virtue, most strik- ingly in the reference to the inspiring power of the 'dying patriot'. The slightly awkward, but recognizably Shaftesburian, phrasing of the last line is retained. The paragraph that follows in *Winter* (ll. 74–79), describing the visionary landscape in which 'Angel-Forms are seen, and Voices heard', is also transferred in revised and expanded form (ll. 971–77): in the last lines the poet describes the 'voices more than human' that 'thro' the void/ Deep-sounding, seize th' enthusiastic ear' (ll. 976–77)—again, perhaps, recalling *The Moralists.*

The 1730 text of *Autumn* concludes with three long verse

paragraphs based on extended allusions to the second book of the *Georgics*. In the first two paragraphs (ll. 1131–73, 1174–247), based on *Georgics* II.458–74 and 493–540, Thomson celebrates the values of contemplative rural retirement, adapting Virgil's description of the innocent life of the husbandman in a characteristic way. Thomson's ideal is the retired man of refined sensibility, living, as he tells us at the end of the first paragraph, a life of 'calm contemplation, and Poetic ease' (l. 1173). In the second paragraph, beginning 'Let others brave the flood, in quest of gain', Thomson expands Virgil's account of the various extremes to which those engaged in worldly activity are driven, stressing the theme of 'inhumanity' ('Unpierc'd, exulting in the widow's wail,/ The virgin's shriek, and infant's trembling cry'; ll. 1178–79), and actually referring to the extinction of the 'social sense' (l. 1185). Thomson's ideal countryman is above all receptive to the emotional influence of 'Nature': 'To NATURE's voice attends, from day to day,/ And month to month, thro' the revolving YEAR;/ Admiring, sees her in her every shape;/ Feels all her fine emotions at his heart' (ll. 1202–05). Virgil's account of the husbandman's endless yearly round of tasks becomes an extended description of the various delights that the seasons bring to the philosophic man of refined feeling. In the autumn, for example, 'his heart distends/ With gentle throws; and thro' the tepid gleams/ Deep-musing, then he best exerts his song' (ll. 1220–22): he is himself an inspired poet—the slight paradox of 'gentle throws' effectively conveying the quality of his emotional response. Winter scenes arouse him to 'solemn thought', and he looks on the night sky with an 'astonish'd eye' (ll. 1226, 1228). He is also passionately devoted to the pursuit of philosophic wisdom: on winter evenings, 'truth, divinely breaking on his mind,/ Elates his being, and unfolds his powers;/ Or in his breast heroic virtue burns' (ll. 1232–34). Nor does he scorn simple enjoyments: 'for happiness, and true philosophy/ Still are, and have been of the smiling kind' (ll. 1242–43). It is an eminently Shaftesburian sentiment: in *The Moralists* Theocles remarks at one point, 'If PHILOSOPHY be, as we take it, *the Study of Happiness* ...' (p. 438). The last of the three paragraphs, the concluding invocation to 'NATURE' (ll. 1248–69), is based on

Georgics II.475–86, the well-known 'Me vero primum dulces ante omnia Musae' passage that Thomson had eagerly quoted, with a blank verse translation, in the Preface to the second edition of *Winter*, and which lies behind several important passages in the composite poem. Virgil's appeal to the Muses for an inspired vision of the physical universe and a penetration of its secrets provides the basis for an extended, impassioned expression of the poet-figure's aspiration to all-embracing natural-philosophical knowledge, incorporating references to contemporary notions such as the infinity of worlds and the Lockean view of the human mind. The Muses are replaced by personified 'Nature', to whom the poet professes intense quasi-religious devotion. In the opening lines of the invocation, 'Oh NATURE! all-sufficient! over all!/ Enrich me with the knowledge of thy works!' (ll. 1248–49), Thomson is again recalling Theocles' invocation to 'Nature', while the reference to 'the rising system, more complex,/ Of animals' (ll. 1257–58) doubtless owes something to Shaftesbury's discussion of 'Systems', and more particularly the '*Animal-System*', in part II of *The Moralists* (pp. 285–88). The poet looks on the wonders of the physical universe with a 'ravish'd eye' (l. 1261); Thomson presents himself once more as the poet–philosopher, passionately seeking a deeper understanding of the physical universe, and drawing powerful inspiration from 'Nature' ('From THEE begin,/ Dwell all on THEE, with THEE conclude my song;/ And let me never, never stray from THEE!'; ll. 1267–69).

In the passage on winter retirement in the 1730 text of *Winter* Thomson returns to the theme of the elevated philosophical and natural-philosophical understanding of the universe: again the 'Me vero primum dulces ante omnia Musae' passage is in the background. With his friends, the poet

> would search, if this unbounded frame
> Of nature rose from unproductive night,
> Or sprung eternal from th' ETERNAL CAUSE,
> Its springs, its laws, its progress and its end.
> Hence larger prospects of the beauteous whole
> Would gradual open on our opening minds;
> And each diffusive harmony unite,

In full perfection, to th' astonish'd eye.
Thence would we plunge into the moral world;
Which, tho' more seemingly perplex'd, moves on
In higher order; fitted, and impelled,
By Wisdom's finest hand, and issuing all
In universal good.   (ll. 471–83)

It is a rapturous, idealizing Shaftesburian vision of the universal order. Thomson's stress on the divinely maintained order of the 'moral world'—he uses the word 'impelled' metaphorically to reinforce the idea of congruence between the physical and 'moral' worlds—and his insistence on the general tendency to 'universal good' may have been suggested by discussions in *The Moralists*: in the second part, for example, Theocles remarks that if we were more concerned with achieving emotional balance 'we shou'd then see Beauty and Decorum here, as well as elsewhere in Nature; and the Order of the Moral World wou'd equal that of the Natural' (p. 294). Shaftesbury's influence is also apparent in the lines that follow, in which the poet describes how, reviewing the course of human history, he and his companions would experience an exalted sense of the divine nature of patriotic and heroic virtue (ll. 490–93).

Thomson seems to be appealing to the Shaftesburian ideal of emotional balance and harmony when, in the first edition of *Summer*, he writes of 'the virtuous Man,/ Who keeps his temper'd Mind serene, and pure,/ And all his Passions aptly harmoniz'd' (ll. 352–54), or, more definitely, when he describes the rapturous feelings of the emotionally balanced, actively benevolent man:

to th' harmonious Mind,
Who makes the hopeless Heart to sing for Joy,
Diffusing kind Beneficence around
Boastless, as now descends the silent Dew,
To Him, the long Review of order'd Life
Is inward Rapture, only to be felt!   (ll. 958–63)

In later editions, it is worth noting, 'harmonious' becomes 'tuneful'; finally, in the 1744 and later texts, Thomson refers to the 'generous still-improving Mind' (1744 text, l. 1633), perhaps recalling Theocles' discussion of 'the *improving* MIND' that 'ambitiously presses onward to Its *Source*, and views *the Original* of Form and Order in that which is Intelligent' (p. 427). Similarly, in the last lines Thomson may be remembering Shaftesbury's discussion in the *Inquiry* of the pleasures founded 'in *An easy Temper, free of Harshness, Bitterness, or Distaste*; and in *A Mind or Reason well compos'd, quiet, easy within itself, and such as can freely bear its own Inspection and Review*' (p. 114); a little later the philosopher asserts that 'every reasoning or reflecting Creature is, by his Nature, forc'd to endure the *Review* of his own Mind, and Actions' (p. 119). Shaftesbury's influence is conspicuous in the long section in the first edition of *Spring* in which Thomson describes the Golden Age and advocates vegetarianism. The two passages on vegetarianism (ll. 259–66, 380–425), are largely based on the opening of Pythagoras' speech in Ovid's *Metamorphoses* XV.75–142; in the second passage the poet stresses the human capacity for sympathetic feeling, describing man as being formed 'with every kind Emotion in his Heart', and remarking that 'the feeling Heart/ Would tenderly suggest' the cruelty of killing the hard-working ox (ll. 395, 419–20). The description in lines 267–95 of the 'glad Morning' of the human race might be seen as a Shaftesburian vision of ideal human existence, in which 'Reason and Benevolence were Law' (l. 281). The later passage describing the psychological disorder that characterizes 'these Iron Times' (ll. 324–53) probably owes something to *Metamorphoses* I.127–31, as well as *Paradise Lost* IX.1121–31; but it also recalls Shaftesbury's discussions of the ideal balance of the emotions. In modern times, the poet tells us:

> the Human Mind
> Has lost that Harmony ineffable,
> Which forms the Soul of Happiness; and all
> Is off the Poise within; the Passions all
> Have burst their Bounds; and Reason half extinct,
> Or impotent, or else approving, sees
> The foul Disorder. (ll. 327–33)

In the revised version of this passage in the 1744 text, Thomson lays greater stress on the extinction of the social feelings: love itself, he insists, has become a matter of self-interest ('sordid Interest'; l. 290), and he describes in strikingly Shaftesburian language how 'at last, extinct each social Feeling, fell/ And joyless Inhumanity pervades,/ And petrifies the Heart' (ll. 305–07). The passage might be compared to Shaftesbury's discussion in the *Inquiry* of the '*Ballance of the Affections*' on which personal happiness depends (pp. 130–39); a little later he refers to the 'Disorder and Looseness of a thousand Passions' that sensual indulgence produces (p. 154), and the destructive effect of the pursuit of '*Interest*' (pp. 155–57).

One could point to many other recognizably Shaftesburian passages in *The Seasons*. For example, in the celebration of married love in the long concluding section of *Spring*, Thomson emphasizes the harmonizing influence of refined sympathetic feeling ('Harmony itself,/ Attuning all their Passions into Love;/ Where Friendship full-exerts his softest Power,/ Perfect Esteem enliven'd by Desire/ Ineffable, and Sympathy of Soul'; ll. 1030–34). Thomson's preoccupation with the 'social' feelings reappears in the passage in the 1730 text of *Winter*, immediately after the description of the dying shepherd, where he discusses the indifference of the 'gay licentious proud' to the sufferings of their fellow human beings. If, he tells us, the rich seriously considered the sufferings of others, a moral transformation would take place:

> Vice in his high career would stand appall'd,
> And heedless rambling impulse learn to think;
> The conscious heart of Charity would warm,
> And his wide wish Benevolence dilate;
> The social tear would rise, the social sigh;
> And into clear perfection, gradual bliss,
> Refining still, the social passions work.   (ll. 327–33)

The repetition of 'social' is deliberately emphatic: 'the social tear', 'the social sigh', 'the social passions'. The exercise of the sympathetic feelings is accompanied by a gradual process of moral and spiritual refinement—culminating in a kind of moral perfection, 'clear perfection, gradual bliss': the slight strangeness of the last phrase is striking. Many contemporary readers would recognize the idea, and indeed the language, as Shaftesburian: the passage might, for example, be compared with the discussion in the *Inquiry* of the achievement of 'INTIRE AFFECTION or INTEGRITY of Mind' (pp. 113–14). The very extensive revisions incorporated in *Summer* in the 1744 edition of *The Seasons* include a passage, part of a much longer addition, on 'the soft Hour/ Of Walking', in which Thomson returns once more to the theme of the refining influence of 'Nature':

> Now the soft Hour
> Of Walking comes: for him who lonely loves
> To seek the distant Hills, and there converse
> With Nature; there to harmonize his Heart,
> And in pathetic Song to breathe around
> The Harmony to others. Social Friends,
> Attun'd to happy Unison of Soul;
> To whose exalting Eye a fairer World,
> Of which the Vulgar never had a Glimpse,
> Displays it's [sic] Charms; whose Minds are richly fraught
> With Philosophic Stores, superior Light;
> And in whose Breast, enthusiastic, burns
> Virtue, the Sons of Interest deem Romance;
> Now call'd abroad enjoy the falling Day:
> Now to the verdant *Portico* of Woods,
> To Nature's vast *Lyceum*, forth they walk;
> By that kind *School* where no proud Master reigns,
> The full free Converse of the friendly Heart,
> Improving and improv'd.   (ll. 1371–89)

It is a remarkable passage, entirely characteristic of Thomson in its idealizing preoccupation with the conscious cultivation of refined feeling and the pursuit of morally elevating philosophical truth in emotionally congenial natural surroundings; at the same time it is obviously deeply influenced by Shaftesbury. The solitary poet-philosopher, conversing with 'Nature', achieves an emotional harmony that he conveys to others through 'pathetic' poetry; the close friends of a philosophical habit of mind—the odd but deliberate phrase 'social Friends' suggesting a Shaftesburian emotional sympathy—are carefully distinguished in their refinement of moral vision from 'the Vulgar'; they display, moreover, an 'enthusiastic' devotion to Virtue (the word emphatically placed at the beginning of line 1383), which, significantly, is dismissed as illusory by those dedicated to self-interest. The 'verdant *Portico* of Woods' and 'Nature's vast *Lyceum*' provide an appropriate setting for amicable, mutually improving philosophical conversation. Again one thinks of *The Moralists*, with Theocles' passionate insistence on the inspiring and elevating influence of 'Nature': 'Can you not call to mind what we resolved concerning *Nature?*', he asks Philocles at one point, 'Can any thing be more desirable than *to follow* her? Or is it not by this Freedom from our Passions and low Interests, that we are reconcil'd to the goodly *Order* of the Universe; that we harmonize with *Nature*; and live in Friendship both with G O D and Man?' (p. 433).

NOTES

1. This chapter is partly based on 'Shaftesbury's Influence on Thomson's *Seasons*', *British Journal of Eighteenth Century Studies*, 9 (1986), 141–56.

2. *James Thomson (1700–1748): Letters and Documents*, ed. Alan D. McKillop (Lawrence, KA, 1958), pp. 25–26.

3. See Robert Inglesfield, 'James Thomson, Aaron Hill and the Poetic "Sublime"', *British Journal of Eighteenth Century Studies*, 13 (1990), 215–21.

4. Alan D. McKillop discusses Shaftesbury's influence on *Liberty* in 'Ethics and Political History in Thomson's *Liberty*', in *Pope and His Contemporaries: Essays Presented to George Sherburn*, ed. James L. Clifford and Louis A. Landa (Oxford, 1949), pp. 215–29; and *The Background of Thomson's 'Liberty'*, Rice Institute Pamphlet 38, no. 2 (Houston, 1951).

5. *Publications of the Modern Language Association of America*, 31 (1916), 264–325; reprinted in C. A. Moore, *Backgrounds of English Literature 1700–1760* (Minneapolis, 1953), pp. 3–52.

6. See, for example, Ralph Cohen, *The Unfolding of Thomson's 'Seasons'* (London, 1970), pp. 265–67; Cohen's argument is not convincing.

7. *Review of English Studies*, 24 (1948), 203–18.

8. James Sambrook's Oxford English Texts edition of *The Seasons*

(Oxford, 1981) contains a number of useful references to Shaftesbury, both in the Introduction (pp. xviii–xx, xxvi, xxviii) and notes.

9. Throughout this chapter '1730 text' refers to the 1730 collected edition of *The Seasons*, and '1744 text' to the 1744 *Seasons* (as distinct from the 1744 *Works*).

10. Anthony Ashley Cooper, third Earl of Shaftesbury, *Characteristicks of Men, Manners, Opinions, Times*, 2nd ed., 3 vols (London, 1714), II, 184; this edition is used in all references and quotations in this chapter.

11. Francis Hutcheson, *An Inquiry into the Original of our Ideas of Beauty and Virtue* (London, 1726), 2nd ed., p. xxi.

12. *The Works of George Berkeley*, ed. A. A. Luce and T. E. Jessop, 9 vols (London, 1948–57), III, 120.

13. John Brown, *Essays on the Characteristics*, 3rd ed. (London, 1752), p. 401.

14. *The Edinburgh Miscellany* (Edinburgh, 1720), p. i.

15. *The Plain Dealer*, 2 vols (London, 1730), I, 394–96; see Herbert J. Drennon, 'The Sources of James Thomson's "The Works and Wonders of Almighty Power"', *Modern Philology*, 32 (1934), 33–36.

16. McKillop, *Thomson: Letters and Documents*, p. 114.

17. *Sale Catalogues of Eminent Persons*, 12 vols (London, 1971–75), I, ed. A. N. Munby, p. 57.

18. McKillop, *Thomson: Letters and Documents*, p. 170.

19. In a letter to Dr Philip Doddridge written on 7 November 1748, a few months after Thomson's death, Lyttelton declares, 'Thomson, I hope and believe died a Christian. Had he lived longer I dont doubt but he would have openly profest his Faith' (p. 210).

20. *Lives of the Poets*, ed. George Birkbeck Hill, 3 vols (Oxford, 1905), III, 285.

21. McKillop, *Thomson: Letters and Documents*, p. 16.

22. The phrase occurs, interestingly enough, in Sir Richard Blackmore's natural-philosophical poem *Creation* (London, 1712), p. 82; it was later used by Grove in *Spectator* 635: see *The Spectator*, ed. Donald F. Bond, 5 vols (Oxford, 1965), V, 171. It also occurs in Bezaleel Morrice's poem *An Essay on the Universe* (London, 1725), p. 4.

23. James Thomson, *Works*, 2 vols (London, 1762), I, ix.

24. McKillop, *Background*, pp. 54–55.

25. Bond, *The Spectator*, I, 493.

26. Lyttelton's revisions were made in an interleaved copy of the first volume of the 1750 *Works*, which was destroyed in the Hagley fire of 1925; John Mitford's transcription of the revisions, made in a copy of the 1768 one-volume *Works*, is in the British Library.

The Seasons and the Politics of Opposition

GLYNIS RIDLEY

Whilst the last decade has seen a spate of eighteenth-century writers posthumously 'outed' as closet Jacobites, Thomson's staunchly Whig credentials have never been in doubt, the Thomson family's politics being firmly located within an established Scottish Whig tradition that inculcated vehement support for the Union and the Hanoverian cause. Yet within the Whig camp, it is now accepted that major divisions can be identified between Walpole and his supporters and the so-called 'Patriot Opposition' who had come to regard Frederick, Prince of Wales as an embodiment of their present exclusion from power and their hoped-for future greatness.[1] Thomson's Whiggism must accordingly be qualified and he has recently emerged convincingly as a Patriot in both the general and specific uses of the term. Given that all of this is accepted, it is extraordinary that Patriot readings of Thomson's poetry are to date sporadic.[2] The text which has been most extensively explained in terms of known Patriot symbols is *Liberty*. Where reference is made to a framework of Patriot Whig allusion in *The Seasons* it is to a handful of predictable passages that are cited so frequently that they must as a consequence sit uncomfortably with the surrounding text. This paper attempts a systematic examination of Patriot Whig references within *The Seasons*: returning to consideration of the most commonly cited instances of Thomson's Patriotism, but seeing these passages in the wider context of the complete text which, it will be argued, builds a systematic Patriot critique of Walpole's domestic and foreign policy, a critique in which the natural seasonal cycle may be seen to be integral, not accidental, to an understanding of Thomson's political allusions.

93

An obvious objection to any attempt to read *The Seasons* in terms of a coherent political ideology (and arguably the main reason why a sustained Patriot reading of the text has not previously been made) is that the poem's origins resist such critical impositions. From the composition and publication of the first edition of *Winter* in 1726 to the last edition of his works which Thomson saw through the press in *The Seasons* of 1746, the text has been expanded, revised and re-thought. Surely the young Scot who came to London in relative obscurity and whose literary fame gave him access to leading writers and statesmen developed politically as well as artistically throughout the two decades of revisions to *The Seasons*? Acknowledging these facts, this paper is built in part upon a conviction that Thomson's political ideology may be deduced from *The Seasons* not *despite* textual growth and revision, but *because* of it. Even had Thomson's political allegiances shifted from Whig to Tory from 1726 to 1746, rather than remaining resolutely Whig, surely the text's excisions, additions and revisions would record its author's changing convictions rather than suppressing them? In its examination of the relationship between *Summer* and the political iconography of Lord Cobham's garden at Stowe, the paper later demonstrates how an understanding of textual revisions facilitates political interpretations of the text rather than hindering such readings.

Any attempt to provide a reading of a particular text in terms of a given ideology is of course fraught with potential pitfalls. As Gerrard reminds us, an allusive framework such as the 'recreation of the past' can be 'as much an opposition Whig as a Tory theme in this period', whilst a reader's desire to find political dogma embodied in poetic description overlooks the 'subtle' but highly significant difference 'between using Gothic buildings to supply a romantic or antiquarian feature to the landscape and using them to make a statement of political principles'.[3] If a Patriot Opposition identity is apparent in the political landscape of the Walpole ministries (and this has been questioned) then the issues around which that opposition intermittently coalesced will be alluded to, and allegorized by, propagandists representing every possible factional interest.[4] 'Clear blue water' between two rival factions' use of a given image (for example, Britannia, or the sea) may be desirable for historians but is rarely a reality.

As we celebrate the tercentenary of Thomson's birth, the problem with deducing political affiliations from 'patriotic' images becomes apparent if we imagine a media historian three hundred years hence considering the British General Election of 1997. After 18 years in power under premiers Margaret Thatcher and John Major, the Conservative party found itself fighting an opposition that had been re-branded as 'New Labour'. Nowhere was the public makeover of the political image so apparent as in the readiness with which the media accepted the role of party 'spin doctors' in turning propaganda problems into opportunities. When New Labour's master of spin, Peter Mandelson, posed for the media with a bulldog called Fitz, he appropriated for New Labour an image which the electorate, by a route of Churchillian associations and anti-European professions, would more naturally associate with the Conservative Party. That Fitz was being deployed in the service of a pro-European Labour party rather than a Eurosceptic Tory one illustrates the perversity of underpinning theses with reference to decontextualized images, devoid of the frame of reference within which we can begin to recover their contemporary resonances. Accepting arguments for a Patriot Opposition to Walpole, this paper does not deny that both Walpole's supporters and Tory opponents focused upon the same issues: the economy, particularly imperial maritime trade and the state of Britain's navy; and the moral character of those in public life. It does, however, suggest that the representation of these issues *in their original context* allows a distinctive Patriot Opposition use of them to be appreciated and to be credible.

Accepting that discussion of the health of the British economy as it depended upon overseas trade was never 'exclusively "Whiggish" property', what was distinctive about the Patriot Opposition's development of images related to Britain's economic position?[5] And what evidence is there that Thomson deploys a recognisably Patriot frame of economic reference in *The Seasons*? For Walpole in the 1720s and 1730s, the surest stimulus to Britain's overseas trade appeared to be the maintenance of peace with rival French and Spanish maritime forces. The Treaty of Seville in 1729 and Treaty of Vienna in 1731 progressively distanced Britain from the threat of war with rival European powers and so held out a promise of security for her growing maritime trade. Tory polemic questioned the wisdom of an apparent retreat from involvement in the affairs of mainland Europe. Whilst many agreed with Walpole that the quantifiable profit from trade with Spain outweighed the hypothetical riches to be gained from a trade war, disaffected Whigs viewed his acceptance of the conditions of that peace as little better than appeasement.[6] Reports of the increasingly brutal exercise by Spanish forces of their right of search over British vessels in Caribbean waters at first raised unease but with each newly-reported Spanish insult the opposition cry moved resolutely towards a demand for war.[7]

When circumstances forced Walpole to accede to this demand in October 1739, the public imagination was fired with triumphalism only one month later when Admiral Vernon captured Porto Bello. The seizure of one of Spain's strongholds in the West Indies made Vernon a symbolic heir to Drake and Ralegh and in doing so rendered his inglorious campaign at Cartagena in 1741 doubly distressing. As plague stalked Vernon's ships it not merely boded ill for Britain's immediate hopes of further victories in Cuba and Panama, but also threatened a cherished belief in the inherent superiority of British navalism. As Bolingbroke insisted in *The Idea of a Patriot King*, 'like other amphibious animals we must come occasionally on shore: but the water is more properly our element and in it ... as we find security, so we exert our greatest force'.[8] When the tragic reversal in Vernon's fortunes from Porto Bello to Cartagena is understood, Thomson's rendering of the ill-fated siege is seen to have a resonance beyond the ostensible subject of 'pestilent Disease':

> ... casting down
> The towering Hopes and all the Pride of Man.
> Such as, of late, at *Carthagena* quench'd
> The BRITISH Fire. You, gallant VERNON, saw
> The miserable Scene; you, pitying saw,
> To Infant-Weakness sunk the Warrior's Arm;
> ... you heard the Groans

Of agonizing Ships, from Shore to Shore;
Heard, nightly plung'd amid the sullen Waves,
The frequent Corse ...   (*Summer*, ll. 1035–51)[9]

The antithetical construction of the passage is worth pausing over: that which towers is levelled; fire is quenched; the warrior's strength is reduced to infantile dependency; and, in a grotesque animation, corpses dive from complaining vessels into a stubbornly silent sea. Implicit in all of these reversals of fortune is Vernon's own: the victor of Porto Bello becomes in turn the vanquished. None of the images is specific to eighteenth-century naval siege warfare, rather the 'warrior's arm' and the formulation 'Carthagena' turn Britain into a second Rome, being forced to relive the imperial defeat of the first Punic war. For Vernon, a vociferous opponent of Walpole, it was clear that the cause of his wretchedness was not plague, but inept management from London and in the command of what should have been his complementary land forces under General Wentworth.[10] Whether true or not, the belief that Vernon had been betrayed by Walpole's ministry led seven constituencies to field him as a candidate in the elections of Spring 1741. He was returned by three and lost Westminster by a narrow margin only as a result of government duplicity.[11]

In choosing to illustrate the effects of 'corruption' (l. 1032) with reference to Vernon, Thomson therefore opts for a *cause célèbre* in which the chief player rejected a natural explanation of events in favour of a political one. What Thomson leaves unsaid about Cartagena does not need saying: his contemporary readers have heard Britain's defeat anatomized by every interest group and the entire episode can therefore function within the text as an extended synecdoche; the corruption to which Vernon and his crews were exposed being indicative of a perceived wider corruption in the state they serve. Lest the reader should be in any doubt that, in their opposition to Walpole's foreign policy, Vernon and Thomson are at one, the context of the passage reveals the poem's politicization of the sea.

The first named figure whom Thomson describes battling tempestuous seas is Vasco da Gama, 'by bold Ambition led, and bolder Thirst/ Of Gold' (*Summer*, ll. 1004–05). The rapacious

Portuguese explorer whose voyage is credited with buoying 'the rising World of Trade' (l. 1006) is succeeded by another Iberian, Prince Henry the Navigator, whose 'Love of useful Glory rous'd Mankind,/ And in unbounded Commerce mix'd the World' (ll. 1011–12). Whilst commerce and trade are, in principle, seen as the desirable concomitants of an increasingly civilized Europe, Thomson reminds us that Europe's commercial hegemony has been bought at the price of human suffering. Just as Spain and Portugal divided and enslaved South America so Hanoverian Britain accepts the enslaving of Africans at home and in the American colonies, making slavery 'one of the central institutions of the British empire, one of the staple trades of Englishmen'.[12] The image of Vasco da Gama and Henry the Navigator opening up Atlantic trade routes is succeeded by one of the shark feasting upon the human detritus of the slave trade:

> And, from the Partners of that cruel Trade,
> Which spoils unhappy *Guinea* of her Sons,
> Demands his share of Prey, demands themselves.
>
> (*Summer*, ll. 1019–21)

The power of this episode for eighteenth- and nineteenth-century readers contemplating the relationship of slavery to empire is attested to by Turner's reading of it and his composition of verse on the same theme as a counterpart to the famous canvas *Slavers Throwing Overboard the Dead and Dying—Typhon Coming On*.[13] The consideration of the evils of the slave trade which the passage prompts masks the fact that, for Thomson's contemporaries, the 'Tyrants and Slaves' who alike fall victim to the shark in the storm have a particular significance in the context of Iberian exploration (recalled in the image of da Gama) and the succeeding image of Vernon outside Cartagena. For Walpole's reluctant declaration of war on Spain in 1739 was the culmination of a crisis popularly believed to have originated in brutal encounters between Spanish vessels and British slavers in the Spanish West Indies.[14] The Treaty of Utrecht in 1713 had granted Britain the *asiento de negros*: 'the right (but also the duty) to furnish slaves to the Spanish overseas possessions' in addition to permission to the South Sea Company for a 500-ton ship to trade at the great annual fairs at Vera Cruz and Cartagena.[15] The right of search granted Spanish vessels was an attempted compromise to reassure the doubtful Spanish that British crews could not exploit the *asiento* for lucrative smuggling activities. In the movement of *Summer*, Thomson details how the Iberian powers map out viable trading routes, he reminds us through an image of a disastrous slaving expedition of the wider débâcle that is the *asiento*, and he builds to the image of Vernon's crews rotting outside Cartagena: in context, a direct consequence of Walpole's foreign policy.

As the text then moves to balance physical corruption at sea with an image of plague descending on the city (ll. 1052–91), Walpole seems to have fallen from Thomson's sights. The standard text of *The Seasons* gives a series of classical, seventeenth- and eighteenth-century discussions of plague as likely sources for Thomson's account.[16] This is to overlook the resonance of plague as a metaphor under Walpole's ministry. A spectacular downward spiral in the value of South Sea Company stock beginning in September 1720 implicated the government in charges of corruption and market-rigging. As 'bubbled' ministers struggled for their political survival, the health of the body politic seemed to be threatened from another quarter. Plague was reported in Marseilles and more widely in Provence, and newspapers were not slow to find analogies between the two.[17] *Applebee's Journal* from December 1720 provides one of the most succinct developments of the plague metaphor:

> In a sick body, when the mass of blood is corrupted, when the constitution of the body is subverted, and the motion of the spirit stopped and stagnated, the patient finds no benefit by medicine; he must be left to the secret operations of Nature, either for life or death. The body of the South Sea people seem to be in just such a crisis at this time; the distemper is strong upon them;—they sink under it, and 'tis in vain to offer reasons or arguments or them; the patient must be left to Nature, and to the ordinary operations of his own demented understanding.[18]

Thomson's description may therefore be seen to function on two

levels. Divorced from its context, it is merely a generic description of plague in a populous city, recalling a range of classical
antecedents even as it rehearses contemporary arguments about
the benefits of confining the infected. Returned to its immediate
context, however, that is following from the sympathetic
portrayal of Vernon as the victim of unresolved Anglo-Spanish
antagonisms, the passage exploits an early eighteenth-century
metaphorical equation whereby the infection of individuals
argues a more widespread corruption in the health of the state. In
the still wider context of *The Seasons*, the reader is reminded that
the conditions which breed pestilence are themselves subject to
cyclical change.

The poet and his earthly muse pass from contemplation of
these horrors to the calm after the storm in which a premium is
placed on innocence and virtue. The groves of Arcadia are
suddenly to be located in a telling selection of eighteenth-
century English landscape gardens. The corrupt citadel finds its
antithesis in Augusta (l. 1410), a fit civic centre for the rural idyll
envisaged as its surround. Whilst the exigencies of metre make
this appellation for London a fit choice in another sense,
Thomson's blank verse would easily bear the substitution of
'mighty London' for 'huge Augusta'. His preferred choice recalls
not only London's Roman inheritance but its Saxon one:
Thomson's own footnote to line 1408 notes that he has used 'the
old Name' of 'Shene' for Richmond, 'signifying in Saxon Shining,
or Splendor'. The importance to the Patriot Opposition of a
Saxon inheritance will be seen as Thomson's discussion of trade
moves to consider the orchestrators of that trade and hence the
virtue expected of those at the forefront of Britain's imperial
ambitions.

Just as trade is not a peculiarly Patriot topos, though Thomson's presentation of Britain's trade wars with Spain is clearly
from a Patriot perspective, so reminders of Britain's past,
present, and hoped-for future glory are not the exclusive preserve
of Patriot verse, though the symbols of that glory employed
by Thomson are of a distinctive Patriot cast. As it has
become almost a commonplace to note the 'strong Whig bias'
in Thomson's list of English worthies in *Summer*, it is worth

examining the particular cast of Whig bias within that list, and comparing it with the political preferences implicit in Thomson's homage to Lord Cobham and his estate at Stowe in *Autumn*.

The ideal vision offered by Augusta/London in *Summer* places the city at the centre of a framework of references to Walpole's political opponents. From lines 1419 to 1427 Thomson focuses upon the Ham House circle which, through a network of family, friends and patronage, embraced the Queensburys, Gay, Pope and Henry Hyde, Viscount (later Lord) Cornbury. Differences among the group were apparently outweighed by the greater common purpose of presenting a vociferous opposition to Walpole. The climax to which the verse paragraph builds begins as a celebration of Pelham enjoying the repose offered by his Claremont estate. For many readers of the 1744 edition of *The Seasons* and the 1746 issue, the great virtue of Pelham was of course that he was not Walpole, having replaced Walpole as Prime Minister in 1743. Lines 1371–1437 which build to praise of Pelham and which contain all of the references noted above to the Ham House circle were, of course, absent from editions of *Summer* from its composition in 1727 to 1738. But in the 1744 edition, the contemplation of Pelham's 'Vale of Bliss' (l. 1435) can serve many functions, making a link between the opposition to Walpole and his replacement by Pelham, and from the harmonious microcosm of Pelham's lands to the purposeful and now prosperous order of the surrounding nation. As macrocosmic harmony is achieved, the defeat of Vernon need not be repeated, the poet apostrophizing Britannia and assuring her of future naval and trading glories:

> Unmatch'd thy Guardian-Oaks; thy Valleys float
> With golden Waves ...
> And Trade and Joy, in every busy Street,
> Mingling are heard ...
>   ... Thy crouded Ports,
> Where rising Masts an endless Prospect yield,
> With Labour burn, and echo to the Shouts
> Of hurry'd Sailor ...   (*Summer*, ll. 1448–64)

As 94 per cent of a warship's timber was oak, it is not surprising to find an eighteenth-century commentary insisting that 'our existence as a nation depends upon the oak'.[19] In Thomson's image, the 'Power of Cultivation' (l. 1436) so evident at Esher radiates outwards to provide national assurance of naval supremacy. In all editions of *Summer* before 1744, lines 1438–1619, which begin with the apostrophe to Britannia and catalogue a pantheon of British heroes, appear *before* the description of da Gama, the evils of the slave trade, and the defeat of Cartagena. Thus from 1727 to 1738, *Summer* faded into a *diminuendo*: the rehearsal of past glories contrasting with an ignominious present. From the ascent of Pelham, editions from 1744 onwards build to a *crescendo*: the reader is reminded of the failings of Walpole's foreign policy only to revel more completely in the promise of a glorious future. (For readers in 1747 who saw that Anson's victory off Finisterre and Hawke's success off Belle-Île (Quiberon Bay) gave the British navy effective control of the Channel and Atlantic respectively, the assurance of *Summer* must have seemed prophetic.)

Following the praise of Pelham, Thomson's British hall of fame, which appears in all editions of *Summer* post-1744 positioned as lines 1438–1619, has a complex textual history.[20] Perhaps this fact, together with general acceptance of the pro-Frederick loyalties signalled by the homage to King Alfred with which the roll call begins, is largely responsible for a lack of detailed analysis of the list to date. Both Gerrard and Sambrook note a correlation between Thomson's list of British worthies and the shrine of that name in Lord Cobham's landscape garden at Stowe, yet examination of the relationship between the two allows a more detailed consideration of Thomson's Patriotism to be made.

In 1727 Thomson's roll call of British worthies was limited to nine: Bacon, Barrow, Boyle, Locke, Milton, More, Newton, Tillotson and Shakespeare. The choice initially appears idiosyncratic until it is appreciated that the surrounding context demands British equivalents for classical thinkers and statesmen: 'Nor cease to vie Them with the noblest Names/ Of ancient Times, or Patriot, or Sage' (*Summer*, 1727, ll. 1480–81). Only three years later Barrow and Tillotson were removed from the list: the excisions are notable as the only two Thomson ever made to what was otherwise a continually expanding catalogue of

British achievement which, in the 1744 edition, would include 13 additional names to those celebrated in 1727.[21] It is worth pausing over this expulsion to consider what in the years 1727–30 might have prompted it. In 1727 Thomson insists of both seventeenth-century divines that Britannia should glory in the thought that they are unmatched in 'Strength, and Elegance of Truth'. The truth that Barrow espoused was that of a divine with royalist sympathies and leanings towards Arminianism, which prevented his obtaining a chair of Greek and subsequently of mathematics at Cambridge until 1660 and 1663 respectively. Tillotson was likewise an ecclesiastical outsider, casting his lot with the Presbyterians at the Savoy conference and not obtaining preferment until he submitted to the Act of Uniformity in 1662. In 1727 the willingness of both Barrow and Tillotson to place belief before preferment clearly appealed to Thomson as he searched for English analogues to 'Plato, the Stagyrite, and Tully'.[22] But in that same year Dissenting congregations united in the establishment of a body that would forcibly represent their joint interests (and that would move in the 1730s towards a call for the repeal of the Test and Corporation Acts).[23] As the Dissenters threatened the exercise of a power as strong and potentially divisive as the established church, Anglican churchmen generated as much controversy as their Dissenting brethren due to what many saw as unfettered ecclesiastical ambitions. (The loathing of Edmund Gibson, Bishop of London and a staunch ally of Walpole, reached its height in the 1730s when Gibson became 'the target of numerous vehement squibs and satirical prints showing the State riding on an ass's back led by the church'.)[24] As the demarcation of roles of church and state was increasingly tested, it seems that Thomson could not brook the celebration of ecclesiastical power in any denominational guise. Perhaps Barrow and Tillotson became the Dissenting churches' equivalent of 'the purple Tyranny of Rome' (*Summer*, l. 758). What is clear from the excision of these two churchmen from all editions of *Summer* after the first is that, from 1730 onwards, Thomson's idea of a national hero was increasingly determined by his admiration for Viscount Cobham, his protégés, and their antipathy towards Walpole's administration.

Just as Thomson's praise of the Ham House circle focuses on one centre of opposition to Walpole, so his praise of Stowe recalls another. With its Temples of Ancient and Modern Virtue (the latter containing a headless statue of Walpole), the Temple of British Worthies and Temple of Friendship, the garden of Richard Temple, Viscount Cobham made visible in the landscape the political and intellectual preferences of one of Walpole's most powerful opponents. In *Autumn*, contemplation of the landscape of Stowe becomes the desideratum of the jaded poet, effusive in his praise of the 'wide-extended Walks,/ The fair Majestic Paradise' that Cobham has caused to be created in the midst of Walpole's England (*Autumn*, ll. 1041–42). It is a commonplace of commentaries on *The Seasons* to note that the catalogue of British achievement that constitutes lines 1479–1579 of the 1746 version of *Summer* shares 11 of its 28 members with Stowe's Temple of British Worthies. The possibility that the garden and Thomson's text function complementarily has not previously been pursued.

The 1727 version of *Summer* celebrates seven 'British worthies' in addition to Barrow and Tillotson: More, Bacon, Boyle, Locke, Milton, Newton and Shakespeare. With the exceptions of More and Boyle, all of the others are present in Stowe's Temple of British Worthies as 'thinkers' (being joined in that half of the Temple by Pope, Gresham and Inigo Jones). Since the Stowe Temple was not constructed by William Kent until the early 1730s, it may initially appear that Cobham borrowed most of his roll call from Thomson, or that both Cobham and Thomson had separate recourse to an established iconography of British achievement. Either assumption would surely be false. Whilst Kent did not begin work on the so-called Elysian Fields at Stowe (overlooking which the Temple of British Worthies is situated) until 1733, his designs throughout the garden incorporated statuary already in existence. In view of Thomson's interest in Saxon and Druid imagery, it is a pity that Rysbrack's series of seven Saxon Deities for the gardens are no longer in position, though Kent did retain and incorporate into his design Rysbrack's eight busts of British Worthies originally grouped around a belvedere several years before the Temple of British

Worthies was conceived, and certainly before the first composition of *Summer*. Significantly, seven of Rysbrack's original eight Worthies appear in *Summer*: Bacon, Locke, Milton, Newton and Shakespeare being present in 1727; shortly to be joined by Hampden and Elizabeth I in 1730. (The only Rysbrack 'worthy' to whom Thomson does not make explicit reference is William III.) Whilst Thomson's text seems to predate Kent's Temple of British Worthies, Kent's re-use of existing garden statuary points rather to Thomson's adoption of a Cobhamite frame of reference in *The Seasons*.[25] This established, Thomson's text may be supplemented by the epitaphs carved beneath the busts of the Worthies at Stowe.

Where *Summer* is stunned into temporary inarticulacy ('but who can speak/ The numerous Worthies of the Maiden Reign?'; ll. 1497–98), Stowe can justify Elizabeth I's inclusion in its pantheon for she 'confounded the Projects, and destroyed the Power that threatened to oppress the Liberties of Europe; shook off the Yoke of Ecclesiastical Tyranny; restored Religion from the Corruptions of Popery; and by a wise, a moderate, and a popular Government, gave Wealth, Security, and Respect to England'. If one element of the Patriots' make-up was anticlericalism, and this puts 'clear blue water' between the Whig Patriot opposition and Walpole's Tory opponents, then the reference to Elizabeth's reformation of the relationship pertaining between church and state is telling.[26] Thomson's portrait of Hampden also comes into sharper focus when seen against the backdrop of Stowe: in *Summer*, Britannia is told that he 'stem'd the Torrent of a downward Age/ To slavery prone, and bade thee rise again' (ll. 1516–17). The servitude which may be inflicted by an external aggressor is at Stowe seen to be an internal threat to the body politic: here Hampden is one 'who, with great Spirit and consummate Abilities, began a noble Opposition to an arbitrary Court, in Defence of the Liberties of his Country; supported them in Parliament, and died for them in the Field'. What unites the Stowe descriptions of Elizabeth and Hampden is that both are seen to be morally opposed to the arbitrary whims of corrupt government and to any extension of such government's power. In 1730 they were joined in *Summer* by portraits of Drake and

Ralegh. Tantalizingly, these two figures do not appear among Rysbrack's earliest worthies at Stowe; the relevant account books only allowing the certainty that these busts commissioned from Scheemakers were supplied before 1737. Since Scheemakers spent 1728–30 in Italy, and was not widely employed by the British aristocracy before this period abroad, it therefore seems evident that Thomson's decision to introduce these two British naval heroes (Drake ll. 1495–97 and Ralegh ll. 1499–1510) was a logical extension of the adoption of Elizabeth influenced by Rysbrack's busts at Stowe.

If this is true, then Thomson's poetry and Cobham's garden achieve symbiotic development by the mid-1730s. Thomson is influenced by Rysbrack's busts of British Worthies, five out of eight of whom find their way into *Summer* in 1727, whilst two of Rysbrack's remaining three are added to *Summer* in 1730 along with eight additional figures of Thomson's choosing, two of whom then appear in Kent's Temple of British Worthies, completed by 1737. The argument for such a development is strengthened by a further two additions to *Summer* in 1744, when King Alfred and a generalized reference to Britain's 'Edwards' appear for the first time. Both Alfred and Edward, Prince of Wales (eldest son of Edward III) form part of Scheemakers' commission for Kent's exedra. Given Thomson's knowledge of the iconography of Stowe, it is inconceivable that his additions of Alfred and Edward were made without an acceptance of what they symbolized for Cobham's circle.

By 1744 the identification of Alfred with Frederick, Prince of Wales was inescapable; indeed, Thomson and Mallet's masque of 1740, *Alfred*, relied upon the comparison. Alfred's epitaph at Stowe is therefore also Frederick's promise for the anti-Walpole coalition centred on Cobham: 'the mildest, justest, most beneficent of kings; who drove out the Danes, secured the Seas, protected Learning, established Juries, crush'd Corruption, guarded Liberty, and was the founder of the English Constitution'. Just as Alfred had freed Saxon England from Danish oppressors, so Frederick promised to replace his father's and grandfather's antipathy towards Britain with an apparently passionate commitment to its wellbeing. And for the anti-

Walpole coalition centred on Cobham, Britain's national health depended primarily upon its ability to prosecute its interests on a global scale. Alfred's 'securing' of the seas is, in Thomson's and Mallet's masque, a necessary precursor to imperial greatness:

> Alfred go forth! lead on the radiant years,
> To thee reveal'd in vision ...
> I see thy commerce, Britain, grasp the world:
> ... proceed, the subject Deep command
> Awe with your navies every hostile land.
> In vain their threats, their armies all in vain:
> They rule the balanc'd world, who rule the main.
>
> (*Alfred*, II.v.107–29)[27]

In context, these opening and closing lines of the Hermit's final vision have at their centre an image of the New World 'beyond the vast *Atlantic* surge' where 'towering forests' wait to 'stoop to *Britain's* thunder'. Under a truly Patriotic King, British naval power will not only discover a land of unparalleled economic possibility, but one whose trees already crowd to produce additional warship timber. This image reflects back upon the politics of *The Seasons* in an extraordinary manner. There the success of 'British Thunder' is explicitly linked to an abundance of valleys 'ribb'd with Oak' which underpin victory as 'the roaring Vessel rush'd into the Main' (*Autumn*, ll. 131–33). Scarcely does Thomson introduce a contemporary politician's estate in *The Seasons* but its yield of ship's timber is indicated: Patriotism is not just a question of political allegiance, but of provision of the raw materials of imperial conquest.[28]

Within *Summer*, the addition of Alfred to the catalogue of British worthies thus signals support for Frederick as it raises questions about Walpole's ability to prosecute a successful foreign policy: that Britain could be triumphant is implicit in the mention of Drake and Ralegh, but the fact that Elizabethan promise has been succeeded by Hanoverian apathy is recalled in Vernon's plight outside Cartagena. Yet even this does not exhaust the complexities of the web of Patriot allusion in the roll call of British worthies. The addition of Alfred in 1744 was followed within six lines by the first inclusion of an unspecified number of

'Edwards' and 'Henrys' (l. 1484): 'the First who deep impress'd/ On haughty *Gaul* the Terror of thy Arms' (ll. 1485–86). The Stowe Temple of British Worthies singles one Edward out for special commendation, his royal title having particular resonance for the pro-Frederick interest group: 'Edward Prince of Wales, the Terror of Europe, the Delight of England …'. Thus both *Summer* and the exedra at Stowe celebrate a Prince of Wales who, in safeguarding British interests, does not hesitate to counter European, and specifically French, imperial ambitions. That Thomson's first reference to a specific individual after Alfred should be to Edward makes the battle for naval supremacy between George II's Britain and Louis XV's France a Patriotic subtext for the whole catalogue. It is entirely appropriate that, this celebration of British achievement concluded, the remainder of *Summer* should build to an assertion of confidence in the will of 'Eternal Providence' (l. 1799): the present administration may seem to frustrate the sense of promise implicit in Thomson's roll call of national achievement but Thomson urges faith in a divine plan which, in his final version of *The Seasons* in 1746, still looks to Frederick's accession for its fulfilment.

A symbiosis between Thomson's text and Cobham's garden is not confined merely to the list of British worthies at the centre of *Summer*. The overt praise of Stowe previously noted in *Autumn* is there seen to be a consequence of more than Kent's landscaping initiative. Whilst 'all-beauteous Nature fears to be outdone' by Kent's 'art' (*Autumn*, ll. 1046–47), the garden is as remarkable for its statuary as its 'silvan Scenes':

> And there, O Pit, thy Country's early Boast,
> There let me sit beneath the shelter'd Slopes,
> Or in that Temple where, in future Times,
> Thou well shalt merit a distinguish'd Name.
>
> (*Autumn*, ll. 1048–51)

Thomson's own footnote to the passage informs the reader that the temple referred to is 'The Temple of Virtue in Stowe-Gardens'. Sambrook glosses this passage with the assertion that Thomson's footnote is probably wrong, since a statue of Pitt is to be found in neither the Temple of Ancient nor Modern Virtue at Stowe, and he suggests that Thomson may be referring to either Kent's Temple of British Worthies or, in 'a less extravagant compliment', to Stowe's Temple of Friendship 'which actually did contain busts of Pitt and of other opposition politicians'.[29] That Thomson is not confused about the contents of the Temple of British Worthies is clear from the preceding analysis. Why then, having displayed such intimate knowledge of Stowe's political iconography, should Thomson seem to confuse monuments and titles? Could it be that Thomson's footnote alludes not to Stowe's nomenclature, but to the chief quality held to define the Patriot opposition?

A bust of Pitt is one of four by Scheemakers that was designed for the first phase of Gibbs's Temple of Friendship in 1739:

> this, the most overtly political of all Cobham's garden buildings, was to contain classicising portraits of ten friends, all leading members of the Whig opposition. A statue of *The Borghese Gladiator* outside alluded to struggles in the larger political arena, though ironically Cobham's junto was already disintegrating by the time all were in place.[30]

Joining Pitt from the first were busts of Cobham, Chesterfield and Frederick, Prince of Wales (later to be augmented by Bathurst, Gower, Grenville, Lyttelton, Marchmont and Westmoreland). Whilst Cobham and Chesterfield had been dismissed from positions in the royal household after opposing Walpole in the Excise Crisis of 1733, Frederick had resisted their invitations to join in opposing his father's ministers at that time. Not until 1736–37 would Cobham be secure in Frederick's support: the King's reluctance to expedite the marriage of Frederick to Augusta of Saxe-Gotha in 1736, followed by the defeat of an opposition motion to award Frederick a £100,000 per annum civil list payment in 1737, perhaps crystallized matters for the Prince. Using his maiden speech in the Commons to refer to George II's tardiness in managing his son's marriage, Pitt immediately made an enemy of Walpole who, unable to bar the young and gifted orator from the House, ensured that Pitt lost his army post as cornet of horse.

The first phase of the Temple of Friendship thus recalls the means by which the key members of the opposition to Walpole came to be united against him by 1737. Dedicated to Frederick from 1744 onwards, *The Seasons* celebrates each of the other three inclusions in Stowe's Temple of Friendship by that date, Pitt and Cobham being located firmly within the environs of Stowe (*Autumn*, ll. 1048–81) whilst Chesterfield's 'Patriot Virtue' is seen against the backdrop of Court and 'Senate' (*Winter*, ll. 656–90). In locating Pitt in a 'Temple of Virtue in Stowe-Gardens', Thomson would be fully aware that no construction at Stowe bore that title. Kent's Temple of Ancient Virtue of 1734 contained statues of Lycurgus, Epaminondas, Socrates and Homer, described in Bickham's 1750 guide as 'illustrious chiefs' of antiquity 'who made Virtue their only Pursuit'.[31] The visitor's attention is then drawn by Bickham to a nearby 'Heap of artificial Ruins' which are said to symbolize the 'shattered State of Modern Virtue': a headless statue of Walpole contrasting pitifully with the classical grouping. Thomson does not, as Sambrook suggests, make a 'less extravagant compliment' to Pitt by referring to his place in the Temple of Friendship for his own footnote indicates that virtue is a necessary precondition of Patriot friendship. Nor is Thomson alone in seeing the possession of virtue as the defining quality of the opposition to Walpole.

For any group of individuals to claim a monopoly upon the possession of virtue is of course on one level absurd and Fielding points us to eighteenth-century recognition of this absurdity in his definition of both virtue and vice as 'subjects of discourse'.[32] His satirical conjoining of these binary opposites points us, however, to a feature of discourse particularly evident in elected legislatures the world over. To claim for one's own faction the possession of the moral high-ground, and to claim this loud enough and long enough, is to deprive one's opponents of power in making the like claim. The truth of this is evident in the urgency with which political parties attempt to lodge in the electorate's mind the notion that they are the party of law and order, the family or education. As political propaganda the insistence that 'we stand for that too' places the claimant on the defensive. To associate one's own faction with the possession of particular qualities and interests is to ensure that one's opponents must stake out other ground and find an alternative vocabulary with which to do so. If the (Whig) Patriot opposition made political capital out of Walpole's naval and related foreign policies, quite distinct from Tory opposition views that the Whigs were misguided in their entire maritime policy, then Patriot and Tory oppositions could at least agree that, whatever the basis of Britain's overseas policy, it should be pursued by a moral government. At the point at which Thomson recalls Pitt's placement in the Temple of Friendship, writers opposed to Walpole had secured a lexical monopoly on 'virtue'. Even were the denotation of the word merely a 'subject of discourse', it was a subject that had effectively been placed beyond the abilities of Walpole's supporters to employ in his cause.

During Walpole's ministry, his opponents' repeated denial of any virtue evident in his exercise of office resulted in the most sustained and satirically varied attack that has been mounted upon an elected politician. That a large part of the opposition's claim to virtue rested simply in the fact of opposition to Walpole has been obscured by the writing talents employed in the opposition's cause, including at various times Arbuthnot, Fielding, Gay, Pope, Swift and Thomson. Whatever ideological and material differences exist within the opposition grouping, propaganda subsumes them by emphasizing a commonality of purpose among Walpole's enemies, a purpose which is portrayed as both a definition of virtue in itself and as a necessary prerequisite for the growth of other virtues: ''Tis the first Virtue, Vices to abhor'.[33] The strength of feeling suggested by the final verb here points the reader to a further feature of opposition claims: virtue lies not in a passive acceptance of the good but rather in a conscious decision actively to pursue goodness. It is this alone that guarantees a freedom from vice:

Free as young Lyttelton her cause pursue,
Still true to Virtue, and as warm as true.[34]

Irrespective of their political allegiances and differing views on matters of policy, Walpole's critics make recourse to the same contemporary icons to illustrate active virtue. Lyttelton, for example, finds himself the subject of Pope's Tory admiration, he is celebrated in the second phase of Stowe's Temple of Friendship (as well as being responsible for the Latin epithets above statues in the Temple of Ancient Virtue) and he is the subject of a magnanimous Patriot tribute in *Spring*, ll. 904–62 (in editions after 1744). Seen walking through the patriotic oak-filled groves of Hagley Park, Lyttelton is 'conducted by Historic Truth' to survey 'the long Extent of backward Time' (ll. 926–27). Tutored in the cyclical nature of empire's rise and fall, he plans

> with warm Benevolence of Mind,
> And honest Zeal unwarp'd by Party-Rage,
> Britannia's Weal; how from the venal Gulph
> To raise her Virtue, and her Arts revive.
>
> (*Spring*, ll. 928–31)

The text insists that it is in the nature of the virtuous to wish to see an overflowing of virtue in public life. As Lyttelton contemplates the greater good as he walks about Hagley, Thomson's description shows nature mirrors back to him his own worth both in his 'lov'd Lucinda' (l. 936) and in the landscape's reflection of a benevolence and contentment which finds its bounds only in the distance of 'the blue Horizon' (l. 962). The harmonious tableau which centres upon Lyttelton finds its antithesis in the exploration of unrequited love and misplaced energies which follows, until the poem returns to the praise of 'Progressive Virtue' (l. 1164). The general celebratory climax of *Spring* therefore finds its most specific expression in contemplation of the virtues of a leading member of Cobham's circle. Whatever divides those opposed to Walpole, one principle remains constant and that is that they are 'to Virtue Only and Her Friends a Friend'.[35] When Thomson claims that Pitt 'shakes Corruption on her venal Throne' (*Autumn*, l. 1069) he claims for him the highest degree of moral probity and application of virtue for the public good; Pitt is to *Autumn* as Lyttelton is to *Spring*, as Cobham's British Worthies are to *Summer*, and as Chesterfield is to *Winter*: embodiments for the opposition (and specifically the Patriot opposition) of virtue at the centre of public life. The Temple of

Friendship has virtue as the chief condition of the friendship it celebrates: it is therefore not incredible that Thomson's reference to Pitt should locate him both spatially and linguistically within the environs of the virtuous.

Though Pitt would in later life publicly regret his opposition to Walpole and though, by the time of the 1744 edition of *The Seasons*, Walpole had moved from Commons to Lords, Thomson fixes for his contemporary readership the image of an incorruptible Patriot opposition, implacably set against the corrupt machinations of government under George II. This is not to assert that *The Seasons* is *only* Patriot propaganda, however; rather, the poem ultimately focuses upon the Patriot challenge to Walpole to pose a question that ranges beyond the bounds of factional interest. Thomson's immediate referent as he draws towards the conclusion of *Winter* may be Peter the Great's Russia, but the question he poses resonates through Hanoverian Britain and beyond:

> What cannot active Government perform,
> New-moulding Man? Wide-stretching from these Shores,
> A People savage from remotest Time,
> A huge neglected Empire ONE VAST MIND,
> By HEAVEN inspir'd, from Gothic Darkness call'd.
>
> (*Winter*, ll. 950–55)

'Active Government' must of course be informed by virtuous conduct and this, in Thomson's final analysis, spreads its influence downwards from the highest echelons of power:

> Sloth flies the Land, and Ignorance, and Vice,
> Of old Dishonour proud: it glows around,
> Taught by the ROYAL HAND that rous'd the Whole,
> One Scene of Arts, of Arms, of rising Trade:
> For what his Wisdom plann'd, and Power enforc'd,
> More potent still, his great Example shew'd.
>
> (*Winter*, ll. 982–87)

The description of Russia is remarkable for its similarities to the account of Britannia's realm in *Summer*, ll. 1457–66. There 'Drudgery' is also shaken off (as it works upon a royal commission) and the 'Sons of Art' mingle with 'Trade and Joy' in expectation of the promised expansion of empire. Even should winter overtake man's most valiant efforts (literally and meta-phorically), the text draws to the conclusion of its final verse paragraph that 'VIRTUE sole survives,/ Immortal, never-failing Friend of Man' (ll. 1039–40). If, within the context of *The Seasons*, virtue is the undeniable possession of those opposed to Walpole, then by the text's conclusion, parliamentary opposition not only has the force of divine sanction but is part of a provi-dential plan that finds cyclical expression as Winter gives way to Spring. This seasonal progression is of course one to which the text must inevitably tend on a purely naturalistic level. Yet Thomson's choice of protagonists, settings and incidents throughout *The Seasons* reveals, ultimately, that its naturalism is always informed by political ideology, and that this is for the most part of an undeniably Patriot cast.

NOTES

1.   The most systematic study of the Patriot Opposition to date remains Christine Gerrard, *The Patriot Opposition to Walpole* (Oxford, 1994). The present paper accepts Gerrard's arguments for Thomson's Patriotism and uses the term 'Patriot' after Gerrard throughout.

2.   Gerrard claims that Thomson is 'the Low-Church, pro-Union Scottish Whig at the centre of this book' who 'epitomises many aspects of the Patriot campaign' (*Patriot Opposition*, p. 17) but her text does not attempt a systematic Patriot reading of *The Seasons*.

3.   Gerrard, *Patriot Opposition*, p. 218, p. 126.

4.   Gerrard, *Patriot Opposition*, p. 13; Gerrard cites J. C. D. Clark: 'no alternative matrix of group identity arose before 1776 to challenge the monarchical one. This was true even of a system of ideas which appears on the surface to be an obvious candidate for that role … "patriotism"'.

5.   Gerrard, *Patriot Opposition*, p. 73.

6.   Jeremy Black, *British Foreign Policy in the Age of Walpole* (Edinburgh, 1985), pp. 105–06.

7.   James Sambrook, *James Thomson, 1700–1748. A Life* (Oxford, 1991), pp. 199–200.

8.   Patrick Eyres, 'Neoclassicism on Active Service: Commemoration of

the Seven Years War in the English Landscape Garden', *New Arcadian Journal*, 35–36 (1993), 62–122, cited 66.

9. Unless otherwise stated, all references are to *The Seasons*, ed. James Sambrook (Oxford, 1981) which reproduces the 1746 edition of the text.

10. Vernon's view was of course partial. Neither Vernon nor Wentworth emerge with any credit in Smollett's fictionalized account of the siege, during which Smollett was present as a naval surgeon. See *Roderick Random* (1748) ch. xxviii–xxxiv.

11. Paul Langford, *A Polite and Commercial People. England 1727–1783* (Oxford, 1989), p. 55.

12. Langford, *Polite and Commercial People*, p. 516.

13. John Gage, *J. M. W. Turner 'A Wonderful Range of Mind'* (London, 1987), pp. 193–94.

14. 'The real causes of the breakdown … were more complex, and to explain them requires more than the story of [Jenkins'] ear': Philip Woodfine, *Britannia's Glories. The Walpole Ministry and the 1739 War With Spain* (Woodbridge, 1998), p. 2 and *passim*.

15. Woodfine, *Britannia's Glories*, p. 78.

16. Sambrook (*The Seasons*) cites the descriptions of plague in Athens given in Lucretius (having its origins in Thucydides), Ovid's *Metamorphoses*, Lucan's *Pharsalia*, Defoe's *Journal of the Plague Year*, Pepys's *Diary*, and Mead's *A Discourse on the Plague*. See p. 354 fns to ll. 1055 and 1070.

17. Pat Rogers, 'This Calamitous Year', *Eighteenth-Century Encounters*, (Sussex, 1985), pp. 151–67.

18. David Nokes, *John Gay. A Profession of Friendship* (Oxford, 1995), cited pp. 309–10.

19. Eyres, 'Neoclassicism', cited pp. 16 and 18.

20. Prior to 1744 the panegyric followed on from *Summer* l. 628. It almost doubled in length between its first appearance in 1727 and 1744. Sambrook notes that panegyric aimed specifically at Scots was transferred to *Autumn* in 1730 (ll. 862–949) as the list of English worthies continued to be revised and expanded until 1744. See Sambrook, *The Seasons*, pp. 358–59 fn. to l. 1442.

21. The additions of 1730 were Ashley, Drake, Hampden, Ralegh, Russell, Algernon and Philip Sidney, and Walsingham. In 1744 were added Chaucer, Spenser, King Alfred, and a plurality of Edwards and Henrys.

22. *Summer* 1727 and *passim*: the reference appearing at l. 1542 in 1746.

23. J. C. D. Clark, *English Society 1688–1832* (Cambridge, 1985), p. 304.

24. Gerrard, *Patriot Opposition*, p. 28.

25. Ingrid Roscoe, 'Peter Scheemakers and the Stowe Commission', *New Arcadian Journal*, 43–44 (1997), 40–64. On the evidence for dating Rysbrack's commissions for the first phase of British Worthies at Stowe see Michael Bevington, *Stowe: The Garden and the Park* (Stowe, 1994), p. 92.

26. 'The associations between Patriot Whiggery and anticlericalism deserve fuller exploration': Gerrard, *Patriot Opposition*, p. 34.

27. John C. Greene, *The Plays of James Thomson 1700–1748: A Critical Edition*, 2 vols (New York, 1987).

28. Cf. *Spring*, l. 915 (for praise of Lyttelton), *Autumn*, l. 658 (for praise of Doddington) and *Autumn*, ll. 1072–73 for reference to Stowe's own 'verdant files'. See also general references to the security offered by the oak in *Spring*, l. 767, *Summer*, ll. 225 and 1448.

29. Sambrook, *The Seasons*, p. 377 fn. to *Autumn*, l. 1050.

30. Roscoe, 'Peter Scheemakers', pp. 53–54.

31. George Bickham, *The Beauties of Stow* (1750), pp. 17–20 as cited by Roscoe, 'Peter Scheemakers', p. 50. Epaminondas, Homer and Lycurgus all appear in Pope's *Temple of Fame* (1711).

32. Henry Fielding, *The Covent Garden Journal*, No. 4 (Tuesday, 14 January 1752) in *The Covent-Garden Journal and A Plan of the Universal Register Office*, ed. Bertrand A. Golgar (Oxford, 1988), p. 38.

33. Alexander Pope, *First Epistle of the First Book of Horace Imitated*, I.65–66, in *Imitations of Horace and An Epistle to Dr Arbuthnot and The Epilogue to the Satires*, ed. John Butt, vol. IV of *The Twickenham Edition of the Poems of Alexander Pope*, ed. John Butt *et al.*, 11 vols (London, 1938–68).

34. Pope, *First Epistle*, I.29–30.

35. Alexander Pope, *An Imitation of the Sixth Satire of the Second Book of Horace*, I.121, in Butt, *Imitations*.

James Thomson and the Progress of the Progress Poem: From *Liberty* to *The Castle of Indolence*

ROBIN DIX

Thomson seems to have been at odds with his readers from the very beginning in claiming that *Liberty* was his best poem. The declining print runs for the first editions of the successive parts speak for themselves, and Johnson provided a guide for posterity's verdict when he wrote in the 'Life of Thomson': '*Liberty* called in vain upon her votaries to read her praises and reward her encomiast: her praises were condemned to harbour spiders, and to gather dust'.[1] Even the wave of critical reassessments which followed the questioning of the canon seems to have come up against an effective breakwater in *Liberty*: for the vast majority of his readers, Thomson remains the poet of *The Seasons*. Those who are stimulated to read further will almost certainly choose to progress straight to *The Castle of Indolence*.

If it has proved impossible to present *Liberty* as a successful poem, it has at least become possible to see it as an interesting one, following exploration of its political and literary origins by Alan Dugald McKillop and Bertrand A. Goldgar. This research has been developed more recently by James Sambrook and Christine Gerrard, among others.[2] Their work has gone far towards enabling us to understand the intellectual, historical and aesthetic context in which *Liberty* was produced, and to see it as perhaps the most ambitious example of that form so prominent in the period, the progress poem. This essay starts from their insight that not only the political theme, but also the 'progress' structure, of *Liberty* resurfaces in *The Castle of Indolence*. It is my contention that *Liberty*, with all its warts, acted as a valuable

117

preparation for the later, artistically successful progress poem, *The Castle of Indolence.*

Although the progress poem is a form of writing which achieved its greatest prominence in the eighteenth century, it would of course be wrong to claim that this period had a monopoly on it. A genuine interest in exploring the form was bequeathed to the Romantics, and later writers such as Tennyson, Eliot and Larkin all developed it further. The form was also in existence well before the eighteenth century: indeed, William Fitzgerald has convincingly argued that Pindar's encomia can be seen as early progress poems. In these odes, the athlete, on returning from the Games, is reassimilated into his home community, which is itself modified by his victory and the poet's celebration of it. Furthermore, the encomium characteristically accentuates this motif of individual and social development by showing how the victory achieves a new element of 'continuity between a golden, or mythical, age and the present'.[3] Such a reading provides an interesting explanation of the simultaneous efflorescence of progress poetry and Pindaric odes in the eighteenth century.

Unlike Gray or Collins, Thomson did not write Pindaric odes, but in *Liberty* he did nevertheless attempt to achieve, within his progress poem, a fusion of two component traditions or ideas, namely, the *translatio imperii* and the *translatio studii*.[4] Many of the problems that readers and critics have found with the poem stem from the fact that this fusion is incomplete, and supported only by the tendentious, and highly selective, use of historical evidence. It will be convenient for the purposes of analysis to consider the two components separately; and I will begin with the *translatio imperii* or political strand.

Walpole's fall is usually said to have begun almost three years before his resignation in 1742: in 1739, he was forced to acquiesce in war with Spain, and from this point on he was fatally weakened. But if his crucial parliamentary defeat can be back-dated by three years, his defeat in the propaganda war can be backdated even further. From well before the time that Thomson was writing *Liberty*, the word he chose for the title of his poem had been effectively appropriated by the Patriot opposition.[5]

This was a major rhetorical victory, as it was clearly impossible for government writers to argue against a term which, in its broad sense, signified such generally accepted positives as freedom from oppression, a rejection of despotic and arbitrary rule, and integrity in office. The government writers, in other words, had allowed their opponents to choose one of the major weapons used in the rhetorical war, and were thus inevitably at a disadvantage. Theoretically, it might have been possible to recognize the general, uncontroversial positives suggested by the term, even to celebrate them as common ground, while at the same time denying any necessary connection between them and what the Patriot opposition stood for. But it takes a very skilled propagandist to maintain argumentative momentum after making an opponent a large concession at the outset; and it has long been appreciated that Walpole's writers were less effective than their opposite numbers. The strategy they chose instead was to challenge the historical claims on which the Patriots based their complaints against the administration. Where the Patriots claimed that Walpole's policies and practices were eroding a native tradition of political liberty, the roots of which they traced back to Saxon times, the government writers claimed (rightly) that Saxon forms of government were destroyed at the Norman Conquest, that the political liberty celebrated by the opposition in Britain really dated only from the constitutional changes of 1689, and that Walpole's administration upheld that settlement.[6]

For eighteenth-century readers, then, Thomson's allegiance to the Patriot opposition in *Liberty* would have been clear, even without the dedication or the address at the end of Part I to Prince Frederick, already a focus and figurehead for opposition activity. The fact that the work traces British liberty back to Saxon times, and is cast in the form of a progress poem, would have been enough. However, it is worth noting that the 'progress' structure, which will govern the rest of the poem, does not emerge until the poet-dreamer's petition at line 347 of the first Part. Until this point, Thomson concentrates on portraying the contrast between ancient and modern Rome, rather than on any continuous narrative. This is why, in Part III, he can return to the subject of ancient Rome when narrating Liberty's progress, without any sense that he is repeating himself.

Thomson's basic political premise, deriving ultimately from classical political theorists and historians, is that Liberty resides in countries whose constitutions allow for mixed government—that is, constitutions incorporating various checks and balances upon those in power. This division of authority, he insists, provides a people with the best safeguard against tyrannical oppression. Thus, in Part I, Liberty describes the British constitution as ensuring that '*King* and *People*' are 'equal bound/ By guardian Laws' (I.318–19). And once the narration of Liberty's progress gets under way in Part II, the very first constitution to be praised, the Spartan system supposedly set up by Lykourgos, is celebrated for its checks and balances. For a start, there were always two kings in Sparta—themselves an instance of power-sharing. In addition, there was an aristocratic assembly, or *gerousia*, and a body of free citizens, divided into tribes and smaller subgroups on the basis of an equality so strict that Spartans were known in the ancient world as *homoioi*, or 'equal ones':

> LYCURGUS there built, on the solid Base
> Of equal Life, so well a temper'd State;
> Where mix'd each Government, in such just Poise;
> Each Power so checking, and supporting, Each;
> That firm for Ages, and unmov'd, it stood,
> The Fort of GREECE! without one giddy Hour,
> One Shock of Faction or of Party-Rage.   (II.114–20)

This presentation of the Spartan constitution, probably deriving from Polybius, is idealized, perhaps most obviously because it fails to take into account the underclass of helots, who had no voice in public affairs, and whose political marginalization, coupled with their indispensable contribution to the economy, provided a real, if continuously deferred, threat to the Spartan state. The portrayal of ancient Sparta is by no means the only case where Thomson omits relevant but inconvenient material.

The Athenian constitution, too, is praised for the way political responsibility was shared between different groups. Like the earlier Lykourgan reforms in Sparta, the famed Athenian system resulted from an attempt to resolve growing social and political tensions within the previous regime. The changes were introduced by Solon after he became chief archon in 594 BC, and provided for a people's Council to act as a check on the Areopagos, or assembly of past office holders, which until Solon's reforms must have been made up entirely of aristocrats. (The Athenian Assembly, which Thomson also mentions, predates these reforms.) The footnote to II.157 illustrates the supreme importance that Thomson attributes to this feature of mixed government: he ignores all the other, far-reaching consequences of Solon's reforms, including those relating to the economy and the social structure.[7] Indeed, so convinced is Thomson of the benefits of a system of checks and balances, that he goes further, serving up to the reader Rollin's highly dubious suggestion that the rivalry between Greek states, at least in the days before Sparta's victory over Athens in 404 BC, provided a sort of supra-national check or balance that had a beneficial effect across ancient Greece.[8]

Similarly, when Liberty moves on to Rome following the victory of Philip of Macedon at Chaeroneia in 338 BC, it is the republican period, rather than the imperial, that Thomson concentrates on. Probably influenced by Livy, he presents an idealized view of the Republic, stressing the absence of civil war, which he attributes to virtuous self-restraint fostered across the class divide by republican virtue and austerity, but quietly ignoring the very real tensions between the patricians and plebeians in this period. The string of unsuccessful coups in the first century BC is bemoaned and condemned, as is Augustus' stealthy, successful arrogation of power from the Senate: Liberty leaves Rome when Brutus is killed at Philippi, and heads north into Sarmatia.

In Part III, perhaps taking his cue from Longinus now, as well as from Livy, Thomson increases the emphasis on public or civic virtue as a crucially important characteristic of politically and militarily active individuals within a successful state.[9] An ethic of public duty, involving the repression of personal desire and ambition, is seen as central to Rome's achievements. After Sulla's dictatorship,

> *Ambition* saw that stooping ROME could bear
> A MASTER, *nor had Virtue to be free.*
> Hence for succeeding Years my troubled Reign
> No certain Peace, no spreading Prospect knew.
> ...
> To these vile Wars I left ambitious Slaves. (III.460–63, 480)

The republican heroes whom Thomson seems particularly to admire, far from showing any ambition to centralize and retain power for themselves, made a point of standing down from the positions they occupied for the public good in times of crisis. Thus Cincinnatus, the republican general several times called out of retirement to lead the Roman army, is twice implicitly celebrated (I.161–62, III.143–47); Flaminius, who gave the Greek states their freedom after defeating Philip V of Macedon, is praised in an extended section (III.257–319); and in an extraordinary passage even Sulla is said to have redeemed himself to a degree by stepping down from the dictatorship he had established, despite his former cruelty, and despite Thomson's claim that his motive in doing so was vanity rather than virtue:

> In vain from SYLLA'S Vanity I drew
> An unexample'd Deed. The Power resign'd
> And all unhop'd the Commonwealth restor'd,
> Amaz'd the Public, and effac'd his Crimes.
> Thro' Streets yet streaming from his murderous Hand
> Unarm'd he stray'd, unguarded, unassail'd,
> And on the Bed of Peace his Ashes laid;
> A Grace, which I to his Demission gave.   (III.451–58)[10]

The political sections of the first 400 lines of Part IV focus mainly on Liberty's geographical progress through the northern nations unconquered by Rome, simultaneously with her chronological progress from Augustus to the end of the Renaissance. It is a complex and cramped section, drawing extensively on earlier, and largely unreliable, discussions of the Germanic or 'Gothic' attitudes to government.[11] The key political point, however, remains consistent: Liberty is to be found where mixed government obtains. The political systems referred to differ considerably from each other, but in none does the head

of state have absolute power. And it is here that the basis
becomes clear for the claim in Part I that in Britain, of all countries in all periods, Liberty's reign is 'best-establish'd' (I.316).
The mixed British constitution is itself, according to Thomson,
the product of a mixing of classical and 'Gothic' political traditions: it combines the best of both, and is thereby strengthened
further.[12]

The account of British history begins in earnest at IV.626 with
the Druids, and ends with the constitutional settlement under
William III. It is a fairly standard Whig panegyric in terms of its
heroes and villains, in the succession of whom a gradual trend
towards greater power for parliament and greater restraint of
royal prerogative can be discerned. But as the reader reaches the
end of Liberty's expansive political narrative, serious structural
and thematic problems begin to emerge.[13] As the events
described become more recent, the tone becomes more shrill: for
instance, the Wars of the Roses and the reign of Richard III are
treated briefly with an aloof 'BE veil'd' (IV.868), while James I is
treated as a tyrant of the first water,

> ... who, drunk with Flattery, dreamt
> His vain pacific Counsels rul'd the World;
> Tho' scorn'd abroad, bewilder'd in a Maze
> Of fruitless Treaties; while at Home enslav'd,
> And by a worthless crew insatiate drain'd,
> He lost his People's Confidence and Love:
> Irreparable Loss!   (IV.957–63)

And the palpable sense of outrage with which the reigns of
Charles II and James II are recounted, is so pronounced as to call
into question the very notion of a gradually increasing recognition of the claims of Liberty—that is, the notion upon which the
account of British history has been predicated.

Thomson may have been aware of this difficulty. In a brief
verse-paragraph prefacing the reign of James I, Liberty suggests
that the Stuarts should be seen as a kind of political *felix culpa*—
an eclipse from which she will emerge to shine more brightly:

> BY Means, that evil seem to narrow Man,
> *Superior Beings* work their mystic Will:

> From Storm and Trouble thus a settled Calm,
> At last, effulgent, o'er BRITANNIA smil'd.   (IV.952–55)

And yet even this attempt to overcome the inconsistency is undercut by a succession of topical references which, once identified, can be detected throughout. This is because Patriot opposition terminology is repeatedly used in describing the past, and this technique projects the sense of past political crisis into the Walpolian era. Liberty may claim that

> Nought but the felon undermining Hand
> Of dark CORRUPTION, can its Frame dissolve,
> And lay the Toil of Ages in the Dust   (IV.1189–91)

but there is an underlying sense that this corruption is already rampant, and is likely to have the same effect in Britain as it is said to have had in Rome. Corruption there is shown to have worked through luxury and through the concentration of political power in a single individual; corruption and the concentration of power in a single individual are among the charges repeatedly brought against Walpole by Patriot writers.[14] Nor is reference to these topical fears limited to general associations: there are also specific parallels with contemporary politics—for instance, the celebration of Roman generals who emerge from rural retirement to give political help at time of need (as Bolingbroke, from a Patriot perspective, could be said to have done), the hope engendered by a promising heir,[15] or the complaint against flattered heads of state manipulated by powerful, devious and corrupt ministers:

> WHEN Kings of narrow Genius, Minion-rid,
> Neglecting faithful Worth for fawning Slaves;
> Proudly regardless of their People's Plaints,
> And poorly passive of insulting Foes;
> Double, not prudent, obstinate, not firm,
> Their Mercy Fear, Necessity their Faith;
> Instead of generous Fire, presumptuous, hot,
> Rash to resolve, and slothful to perform;
> Tyrants at once and Slaves, imperious, mean,
> To Want rapacious joining shameful Waste;
> By Counsels weak and wicked, easy rous'd

To paltry Schemes of absolute Command,
To seek their Splendor in their sure Disgrace,
And in a broken ruin'd People Wealth:
When such o'ercast the State, no Bond of Love,
No Heart, no Soul, no Unity, no Nerve,
Combin'd the loose disjointed Public, lost
To fame abroad, to Happiness at home.   (IV.822–39)

This passage ostensibly applies to the Plantagenets; but each of the accusations here listed could be linked to specific events or policies of the Walpole administration. The result cannot but bring the notion of political progress once again into question. Thomson may only be doing what Bolingbroke did, in allowing the somewhat complacent progressivism of the Whig interpretation of history to stand unreconciled with deteriorationism in his work; after all, Bolingbroke's main source, Machiavelli, also adds a dash of hope to his generally bleak outlook. But neither Machiavelli nor Bolingbroke was trying to accommodate the opposing tendencies within the structure of a progress poem. This is a structure quite capable of communicating despair— witness 'reverse' progress poems such as *The Dunciad*, or indeed the ironic celebration by Liberty of the progress of Oppression, I.123–249. But in Pope, and in this passage from Thomson, the direction of the flow is perfectly clear. The structural and thematic problems begin when the direction of the flow is confused within a form that demands clarity.

If the mismatch between structure and theme in the *translatio imperii* component of *Liberty* is problematic, the problem looms much larger when we turn to the discussion of the migration of culture, or *translatio studii* tradition. The conflict between progressivism and deteriorationism here is considerably more acute. For a start, there is the fact of Thomson's preference for Grecian over Roman art. The difficulty stems from the uncompromising terms in which Liberty expresses this preference: not only is Greek cultural achievement preferred to Roman—it is preferred to all subsequent cultures:

HAIL Nature's utmost Boast! unrival'd GREECE!
My fairest Reign! where every Power benign

> Conspir'd to blow the Flower of Human-kind,
> And lavish'd all that Genius can inspire.
> ...
>   O GREECE! thou sapient Nurse of FINER ARTS!
> Which to bright Science blooming Fancy bore,
> Be this thy Praise, that Thou, and Thou alone,
> In These hast led the Way, in These excell'd,
> Crown'd with the Laurel of assenting Time.
>
> (II.86–89; 252–56)

Philhellenism was intimately linked with the trend towards primitivism in the middle and later eighteenth century; and a primitivistic aesthetic cannot be reconciled with a progressive one.[16]
This inconsistency in the attitude to the arts throws into higher
relief the similar problem that obtained in the political sections
of the work, where the Roman republican heroes are celebrated
as the acme of human moral and political achievements:

>   FOR then, to prove my most exalted Power,
> I to the Point of full Perfection push'd,
> To Fondness, and enthusiastic Zeal,
> The great the reigning Passion of the *Free*.   (III.103–06)

Despite Liberty's long residence in Britain, she admits that the
elevated notion of civic virtue which motivated a Cincinnatus or
a Cato is still sadly lacking in the modern world:

>   BUT, ah too little known to modern Times!
> Be not the noblest Passion past unsung;
> That Ray peculiar, from UNBOUNDED LOVE
> Effus'd, which kindles the heroic Soul;
> DEVOTION TO THE PUBLIC. Glorious Flame!
> Celestial Ardor! in what unknown Worlds,
> Profusely scatter'd thro' the blue Immense,
> Hast *Thou* been blessing Myriads, since in ROME,
> Old virtuous ROME, so many deathless Names
> From *Thee* their Lustre drew?
> ...
> O wilt *Thou* ne'er, in *thy* long Period, look,
> With Blaze direct, on this MY *last Retreat*?   (V.221–34)

In addition to the problems arising on both political and cultural levels from this conflict between progress and deterioration, Thomson of course also runs up against a problem faced by all poets who seek to suggest that poetic progress runs in the same direction as chronological progress—a problem memorably summed up by Swift in *A Tale of a Tub*:

> But I here think fit to lay hold on that great and honourable Privilege of being the *Last Writer*; I claim an absolute Authority in Right, as the *freshest Modern*, which gives me a Despotick Power over all Authors before me.[17]

Gray and Collins succeeded in solving this difficulty by modestly representing the English poetic tradition as in decline after a Golden Age comprising the Elizabethans and Milton. For Thomson, who is committed to the theory, described and rejected by Longinus but espoused unequivocally by Shaftesbury,[18] that art flourishes best in a free society, this is not an option: the 1689 settlement is viewed as a great step forward in terms of the liberty enjoyed by the British (IV.1115–86); and so to acknowledge the Elizabethan age as artistically pre-eminent is problematic. He skirts the paradox by the expedient of compressing Spenser, Shakespeare, and the rest into a passing reference:

> Mean-time, *Peace, Plenty, Justice, Science, Arts,*
> With softer Laurels crown'd her happy Reign.   (IV.945–46)

Such structural problems, serious as they may be, are of minor import, though, by comparison with the fact that the historical details generally simply do not fit the Shaftesburean insistence that political liberty is a prerequisite for successful art. Liberty begins her narrative in ancient Egypt, before moving through Persia, Phoenicia and the Holy Land, all of which enjoyed an early cultural efflorescence without being in any way notable for having evolved liberal political regimes.[19] Nor is Homer's work, celebrated at II.272–73 as that of the 'FOUNTAIN-BARD', credibly listed among the products of liberty. With the first political system to be described in detail, however, the difficulty is exactly the opposite: Sparta did indeed produce a stable, relatively mixed form of government, but was never notable for its artistic achievements, as Thomson is constrained to admit (II.122–24). In the lines on Athens, Thomson omits to mention that many of the most celebrated authors were either, like Thucydides, personally opposed to the democratic constitution, or, like Plato, wrote after Sparta's victory of 404 BC in the Second Peloponnesian War.

The facts of literary history remain equally unaccommodating to this theory when Liberty moves to Rome. Although Thomson celebrates Roman republican politics and ethics, he finds it impossible to prefer republican writers to those of Augustus' reign. He does what he can with Cicero, concentrating in Part III on his early career, when he was called 'the father of his country' for his 'watchful Art' during the Catiline conspiracy (III.462–70). But in Part I Thomson addresses him along with Virgil and Horace—that is, as writers whose achievements were undoubtedly admirable, but who used their talents to support the seizure of unconstitutional power.[20] At least the difficulty posed by the facts of literary chronology are admitted, though. By contrast, the inspiration for the entire framing vision of the poem is stimulated by the ancient buildings surviving in modern Rome—that is, by an architectural tradition inescapably associated with Augustus' architect, Vitruvius. Indeed, it is probable that Vitruvius did more to entrench popular support for Augustus than any of the poets did: his utilitarian projects, such as the building of aqueducts, would have had a considerable, direct impact on living standards throughout ancient Rome, while his large public buildings greatly boosted the city's image and morale. Yet Vitruvius' political affiliations escape notice and censure.

The Middle Ages and early Renaissance receive only cursory treatment: there is a rather grudging admission that learning was not entirely lost, but major cultural developments are ignored. This is perhaps because Shaftesburean theory is even less conformable to the facts of cultural history here than in the ancient world: as Johnson said in his analysis of Gray's 'The Progress of Poesy', 'in the time of Dante and Petrarch, from whom he [Gray] derives our first school of poetry, Italy was overrun by "tyrant power" and "coward vice"; nor was our state much better when we first borrowed the Italian arts.'[21] Certainly, a more detailed treatment would have necessitated a tribute to Dante's role in establishing a vernacular poetic tradition, and it may be that Thomson was particularly reluctant to discuss him, as his strongly Catholic frame of mind should, according to Whig political and religious prejudices, have been an additional factor militating against success. His achievement is recognized only in an oblique passing reference to the Arno (IV.266). Where reference to Renaissance Italy is unavoidable, as it is in sculpture, architecture and painting, Liberty claims, for no very clear reason, that the great artists were inspired by her despite the unpromising political and religious regimes under which they lived: addressing Oppression in Part I, for instance, she insists:

> *Mine* is, besides, *thy* every later Boast:
> *Thy* BUONAROTTIS, *thy* PALLADIOS *mine*;
> And *mine* the fair Designs, which RAPHAEL's Soul
> O'er the live Canvass, emanating, breath'd.   (I.246–49)[22]

The France of Louis XIV presents a similar problem: an absolute monarch who, through careful patronage, stimulates an undisputed cultural blossoming. Shaftesburean theory predicts artistic failure, but the theory is disproved here as in the Florence of the Medici or—to use a parallel which Louis preferred—the Rome of Augustus. Thomson pays full tribute to French achievements in painting, sculpture, architecture and gardening, as well as to the genius of Corneille, Racine, Molière and Boileau (V.471–548), and seeks to erase the question mark placed over the claim that political liberty fosters the best art, by claiming that these achievements would have been greater still under a mixed government. This answer, however, does not solve a second question that has been rendered more acute by the failure to celebrate the cultural achievements of the British Renaissance: why does Britain not reap the cultural rewards of its more mixed, and liberal, constitution? As Gerrard observes, Thomson adopts the strategy of prophesying a deferred renaissance, which will coincide with further political advances contingent upon stemming the flow of corruption from Walpole's administration.[23] Hume's more elegant (though also, in the last analysis, unconvincing) solution to the problem—namely, that the arts require a liberal regime to establish themselves, but thereafter can flourish under a despot, provided that he is also an enlightened patron—was not yet available.[24]

One of the things that *Liberty* succeeded in doing, then, was proving that the structural and historical problems faced by the writer of a progress poem were considerable, and that these problems increased exponentially when the focus was political and cultural progress combined on the basis of the theory that the former was necessary for the latter. Writers began experimenting with modifications to the form, with the result that one can begin to trace a progress within the progress poem tradition itself, towards a more viable structure. One solution was a drastic reduction in the amount of historical detail. This obviated the need to dwell on, or even to mention, inconvenient historical facts; and if this smaller scale progress ceased to be the prime focus of the poem, the structural difficulties posed by the form were also mitigated, while the political benefits of an allusion to the Whig interpretation of history were retained. This approach was, in fact, adopted by Thomson himself before he had the idea of writing a poem based solely on the progress of liberty and culture, and it can also be found in (for example) Akenside's *The Pleasures of Imagination* (1744), II.1–51, where a highly selective post-classical version of the *translatio* traditions appears in the context of the desirability of a union between poetry and philosophy.[25]

Another solution is to break the link between political and cultural progress noted by Longinus and adopted by Shaftesbury, and focus on one or the other. In poems focusing on culture, it is also necessary either to reverse the progress or to defer its full realization, in order to avoid the hubris of the Swiftian hack. This, in effect, is what Collins does in his verse epistle to Hanmer, where the political theme appears only in the form of audience response to Shakespeare's history plays, and 'Ode on the Poetical Character'. Gray, too, in his Pindaric progress poems, takes this route, although the linkage with politics is less rigorously suppressed here. In Collins's 'Ode on Liberty' we have a progress poem in which the main emphasis is on the *translatio imperii* tradition; and, as Paul Williamson has shown in an interesting recent analysis,[26] it is significant that Collins here modifies the normal Pindaric structure to adapt its implicit progress form to suit the theme of obstructed development that he is pursuing.

And yet it was Thomson himself who, in *The Castle of Indolence*, found the most ingenious and satisfying solution to the problems he had uncovered in *Liberty*. The relation of this most complex of eighteenth-century Spenserian imitations to the progress poem tradition has long been recognized; but it was the work of Gerrard that proved beyond reasonable doubt the existence within the allegory of political concerns topical in the 1730s.[27] As she points out, the Spenserian vogue in the eighteenth century had from its very inception engaged with political material: Prior's *An Ode, Humbly Inscrib'd to the Queen on the Glorious Success of Her Majesty's Arms, 1706*, with its modified (ten-line) Spenserian stanza, deals explicitly with Marlborough's victory at Ramillies. And while it would be a mistake to impose a political reading on every Spenserian imitation from the period, opposition poets of the 1730s could recall how Samuel Croxall, back in 1713–14, had demonstrated the value of Spenserian allegorical narrative for mounting prudent but telling attacks on those in power: he had presented Robert Harley as the enchanter Archimago,[28] and as a result, this Spenserian figure became a convenient code for shrewd political operators who were charged with deceit. It is significant, therefore, that Thomson glosses his enchanter as 'Archimage', especially as the charges he levels against him, such as encouraging corruption by persuading people to neglect their civic duties, and using the arts to gloss over the true implications of the regime he recommends, are precisely those levelled in *Liberty* against Augustus and by implication against his supposed modern parallel, Walpole. In addition, one can point to the Liberty-like westerly progress of the Knight of Arms and Industry; indeed, even his active retirement to his estate beside the River Dee, and his willingness to relinquish it when public duty demands, recall Thomson's admiration in the earlier poem for figures such as Cincinnatus, who came out of retirement at an advanced age to avert national disaster. The austerity of the Knight's lifestyle, which contrasts so effectively with the luxury of the Castle of Indolence, also suggests the Roman historians' presentation of the bracingly simple lives of the republican heroes; while the productivity of the Knight's estate recalls by contrast the barrenness of the once-fertile Campania, attributed in Part I of *Liberty* to the bad management and demoralization that results from political oppression.[29]

Already an advance on the political strand within *Liberty* is discernible. Where, in the earlier poem, a buoyant political optimism deriving from the Whig interpretation of history was often at odds with a deteriorationism born of Machiavellian theory and a sense of outrage at the corrupting cynicism and immorality of the present administration, in *The Castle of Indolence* Thomson contrives to admit both trends without contradiction. The upward movement or progress is described in the Knight's early biography (II.37–216), as he first civilizes himself, and then brings civilization to the states through which he passes. The reverse progress is located within the Castle, where an innocent-sounding relaxation leads to an irresponsible accidie, and thence to a love of luxury which in turn tempts to corruption and leads ultimately to a broken constitution and moral prostration in the castle dungeon. The opposing tendencies sit quite logically together within this poem, and the Knight's victory over the enchanter suggests that, despite the poet's residence within the Castle, the hope of amendment, which was always evident in opposition Whig writing, outweighs his pessimism. The failure of the Knight to redeem those whose degeneration is furthest advanced, however, shows that this hopefulness is contained within realistic bounds.

It is true that certain inconsistencies remain. For instance, Havens noted that Thomson's attitude towards primitive societies is ambiguous: at II.37–54 and 120–35 the primitive age is portrayed as barren and unfeeling, yet only a few lines later (II.147–62) it appears paradisal. It is even possible to find further evidence of confusion: Selvaggio, the Knight's father, is at one point described in terms reminiscent of Christ's observation on the innocent fowls of the air and lilies of the field ('he neither sow'd nor reap'd') despite his brutal rape of 'Dame *Poverty*'.[30] Yet an appreciation of the political context mitigates the effect of such confusion. It is only in Britain that the primitive age is shown as 'golden', and this strongly suggests a Whiggish allusion to the supposedly ancient native tradition of political and social liberty.[31]

As Gerrard, the uncoverer of the political undercurrent in *The Castle of Indolence*, readily admits, however, to limit the poem's significance to this political theme is to advance a reductivist view of a richly suggestive work. The echoes of attacks on Walpole's regime do not invalidate earlier interpretations, for example that advanced by Maurice Golden, who sees the poem as debating the conflict between an escapist, or purely pleasurable art, and an art that is politically and morally committed to producing useful effects.[32] It would be going too far to claim that Thomson is exploring the effect of dissolving the Horatian compound of the *utile* and *dulce*, for the Druid Bard's rousing song is not, in theory, without its own bracing, austere pleasure. It is even possible that critics' preference for the siren songs of Indolence and his cronies over the Bard's didactic stress on duty results from an entirely conscious determination on Thomson's part to force readers to appreciate at first hand the dangerous attractions of the depravity he describes. The essential point is, however, that by conveying his themes through an allegorical narrative, Thomson lights on a form which permits the simultaneous development of different ideas without generating paradoxes. It is instructive, for instance, to compare a similar contrast between the poetry of fantasy and socially committed art in *Liberty*: the earlier work, for all its celebration of political engagement, is actually framed by a dream. But whereas in *The Castle of Indolence* an interesting tension is felt between escapist and dutiful art, in *Liberty* the same issue appears as a contradiction. Furthermore, the narrative of *The Castle of Indolence* enables Thomson to dispense with the causal link between politics and culture—the link that had caused so many structural and other problems in *Liberty*. By shifting from a historical to an allegorical narrative he is also able to disburden himself of much stubborn factual material which the earlier poem had struggled to accommodate, and which was constantly in danger of undermining the general interpretation which the narrator wished to place on it.

Finally, it is perhaps worth noting that, in liberating himself from the structural and conceptual straitjacket of *Liberty*, Thomson may have been helped rather than hindered by the passage of time. The fact that the poem took fifteen years to complete has led to much humour at the author's expense; the accusation that tubby Jemmy Thomson was too indolent to complete his poem on indolence dates from his own lifetime. In fact, Gerrard's discovery of the anti-Walpole element in *The Castle of Indolence* puts a rather different gloss on the time lapse: as she observes, Walpole fell in 1742, at which point Thomson may well have lost the sense of momentum that topical reference imparts, and indeed experienced some confusion over what this poem recommending an active engagement with the world could now achieve.[33] But that is not all: it seems that Thomson was overtaken by events not once, but twice in the course of composition; for in 1744, Pope died. The identification of the Druid Bard with Pope is rendered well-nigh irresistible by the physical description of II.289–93:

> He came, the Bard, a little Druid-Wight,
> Of wither'd Aspect; but his Eye was keen,
> With Sweetness mix'd. In Russet brown bedight,
> As is his Sister of the Copses green,
> He crept along, unpromising of Mien.

His friendship with a knight who owns an estate in the country, but who abjures retirement in order to address an emergency, provides added evidence for the identification: as noted above, to a Patriot reader, the parallels between the Knight and Bolingbroke would be self-evident. They would also be reinforced by the account of the conversation between the Knight and the Bard (II.316–24), in which some of the key ideas informing *An Essay on Man* are mentioned.[34] The casting of Pope as a 'Druid' presumably reflects his attempts to write the nationalistic epic, *Brutus*, in the course of which an 'Old Druid' was to have disclosed to the hero the future history of Britain.[35] In other words, the Druid Bard's success in composing a song that counteracts the corruption engendered by Walpole's regime strongly suggests that *The Castle of Indolence* was another effort in the sporadic Patriot attempts to prod Pope into abandoning satire and completing what was to have been, from an opposition Whig point of view, his crowning glory: a non-satirical political epic.[36] Pope's death meant that on this front, too, *The Castle of Indolence* was overtaken by events.

And yet, *The Castle of Indolence* may well have benefited from the dual blows to its topicality. Thomson was able to expand the significance of the poem beyond the immediate political and literary frame, achieving in the process a suggestiveness or flexibility of significance that had previously eluded him in progress poetry. The progress of time, in other words, forced him to adapt his progress poem, and the result was that the contradictions of *Liberty* were by and large transmuted into the creative tensions of *The Castle of Indolence*.

NOTES

1. James Sambrook, *James Thomson 1700–1748: A Life* (Oxford, 1991), pp. 132–41, gives the size of the print runs as: Part I, 3,250; Parts II–III, 2,250; Parts IV–V, 1,250. For Johnson's comments on *Liberty*, see 'Life of Thomson', in *Lives of the English Poets*, ed. George Birkbeck Hill, 3 vols (Oxford, 1905), III, 289.

2. See Alan Dugald McKillop, *The Background of Thomson's 'Liberty'*, Rice Institute Pamphlet 38.2 (Houston, 1951), and his edition, *James Thomson: The Castle of Indolence and Other Poems* (Lawrence, 1961), esp. pp. 1–2, 48–52; Bertrand A. Goldgar, *Walpole and the Wits: The Relation of Politics to Literature, 1722–1742* (Lincoln, NE, 1976), pp. 141–46; Sambrook, *Thomson: A Life*, pp. 128–56; Christine Gerrard, *The Patriot Opposition to Walpole: Politics, Poetry and National Myth, 1725–1742* (Oxford, 1994), esp. pp. 132–40. See also Michael Meehan, *Liberty and Poetics in Eighteenth Century England* (London, 1986), and Philip Ayres, *Classical Culture and the Idea of Rome in Eighteenth-Century England* (Cambridge, 1997).

3. See William Fitzgerald, *Agonistic Poetry: The Pindaric Mode in Pindar, Horace, Hölderlin, and the English Ode* (Berkeley, 1987), pp. 19–21, 73–75.

4. For a definition of the *translatio* tradition, concentrating on the *translatio imperii*, see Samuel Kliger, *The Goths in England: A Study in Seventeenth and Eighteenth Century Thought* (Cambridge, MA, 1952), pp. 33–36; for the *translatio studii*, see Aubrey L. Williams, *Pope's 'Dunciad'* (London, 1955), pp. 44–48; and for their application to eighteenth-century progress poetry generally, see John R. Crider, 'Structure and Effect in Collins' Progress Poems', *Studies in Philology*, LX (1963), 57–72.

5. Bolingbroke's contributions to *The Craftsman* were particularly effective at achieving this appropriation: see e.g. nos. 123, 375.

6. For further details of this rhetorical battle, and the competing interpretations of English history that lie behind it, see Isaac Kramnick, 'Augustan Politics and English Historiography: The Debate on the English Past, 1730–35', *History and Theory*, VI (1967), 33–56.

7. For a convenient and accessible study of the political systems of Sparta and Athens, see W. G. Forrest, *The Emergence of Greek Democracy: The Character of Greek Politics, 800–400 BC* (London, 1966), pp. 123–235.

8. McKillop, *Background of 'Liberty'*, p. 46, traced this theory back to Rollin, *Histoire Ancienne des Égyptiens, des Carthaginois, des Assyriens, des Babyloniens, des Mèdes, et des Perses, des Macédoniens, des Grecs*, 13 vols (Paris, 1730–38). In fact, the achievements of fifth-century Athens (especially in architecture) were dependent for the necessary funds on the tributes exacted from other Greek states by Perikles.

9. The idea that liberty depends on constitutional forms underpinned by 'the spirit and character of the people' was also central to Bolingbroke's theories in *The Idea of a Patriot King*: see e.g. *Bolingbroke's Political Writings: The Conservative Enlightenment*, ed. Bernard Cottret (London, 1997), p. 364. Thomson and Bolingbroke are both of course working under the influence of Machiavelli, although the ideas are too common among classical and modern historians and political theorists for a single source to be credible. For Longinus' view that individual moral collapse precedes national political and cultural decline, see *On Sublimity*, XLIV.6–9. For an analysis of how the British aristocracy secured the political advantages obtained in the 1689 settlement by identifying themselves with the Roman republican tradition of disinterested public service, see Ayres, *Classical Culture*, pp. 6–7, 23–26.

10. McKillop, *Background of 'Liberty'*, pp. 56–57, cites Plutarch as the immediate source for the lines on Flaminius, and the Abbé de Vertot, *The History of the Revolutions That Happened in the Government of the Roman Republic*, 2 vols (4th ed., Paris, 1732), II, 192, as the prime source for the section on Sulla, including the key lines (III.460–63, quoted above) on the effects of his dictatorship.

11. For the complexities surrounding the word 'Gothic', see Nick Groom, 'Celts, Goths, and the Nature of the Literary Source', in *Tradition in Transition: Women Writers, Marginal Texts, and the Eighteenth-Century*

Canon, ed. Alvaro Ribeiro, SJ, and James G. Basker (Oxford, 1996), pp. 276–77, and the further references cited, p. 276n.; for details of the discussion concerning Germanic features of the British constitution, see Hugh A. MacDougall, *Racial Myth in English History: Trojans, Teutons, and Anglo-Saxons* (Montreal, 1982), pp. 31–70; for the unhistorical basis of such claims, see J. G. A. Pocock, *The Ancient Constitution and the Feudal Law: A Study of English Historical Thought in the Seventeenth Century* (Cambridge, 1957; reissued with 'retrospect', 1987), esp. pp. 30–123, 229–51.

12. In *Britannia's Issue: The Rise of British Literature from Dryden to Ossian* (Cambridge, 1993), Howard D. Weinbrot has demonstrated that British cultural self-definition in the late seventeenth and eighteenth centuries involved an assimilation of what were seen as the best characteristics of different traditions. In view of the widespread assumption that political and cultural development went hand in hand, the two processes of assimilation are likely to have been closely related.

13. See C. A. Moore, 'Whig Panegyric Verse, 1700–1760: A Phase of Sentimentalism', *Papers of the Modern Language Association of America*, XLI (1926), 362–401. The following discussion of the problems and paradoxes encountered in *Liberty* owes much to Gerrard's discussion in *Patriot Opposition*, pp. 132–34.

14. Pocock, *Ancient Constitution*, p. 367, notes that the idea of ancient liberties had been 'a means of asserting the privileges of law-courts and parliaments against the prerogative', but had by the eighteenth century 'become a means of indicting an executive government exercised through parliament, and of articulating the grievances of discontented parliamentary and extra-parliamentary oppositions'.

15. I.368–78. There are also indirect references, e.g. IV.966, V.302–03.

16. A similar conflict between primitivism and progressivism has been noted by critics of *The Seasons*. See e.g. Patricia Meyer Spacks, *The Varied God: A Critical Study of Thomson's 'The Seasons'*, University of California English Studies 21 (Berkeley, 1959), pp. 161–75, who bemoans the contradiction; John Barrell and Harriet Guest, 'On the Use of Contradiction: Economics and Morality in the Eighteenth-Century Long Poem', *The New Eighteenth Century: Theory, Politics, English Literature*, ed. Felicity Nussbaum and Laura Brown (New York, 1987), pp. 132–35, who argue that such contradictions are a price worth paying for such rich variety; and John Chalker, *The English Georgic: A Study in the Development of a Form*, Ideas and Forms in English Literature (London, 1969), pp. 100–08, who attempts a resolution of the contradiction.

17. *A Tale of a Tub*, ed. A. C. Guthkelch and D. Nichol Smith (2nd edition, Oxford, 1958), p. 130.

18. *On Sublimity*, XLIV.2–5. Longinus describes the theory as trite, and goes on to propose instead that artistic decline stems from personal moral

decline, rather than from political causes. The precedence he gives to moral considerations is reflected by Thomson in his accounts of Rome and Britain. For Shaftesbury on freedom as requisite for good art, see *Characteristics of Men, Manners, Opinions, Times*, ed. J. M. Robertson, 2 vols (London, 1900), II, 154–55.

19. McKillop, *Background of 'Liberty'*, pp. 42–43, rightly observes that Thomson had an ancient source for his claim that royal prerogative in ancient Egypt was limited: Diodorus Siculus, *Historical Library*, I.70.1–I.72.5.

20. See *Liberty*, I.268–90, where the phrase 'your flatter'd CÆSARS' (I.286) clearly continues the preceding address to Cicero, along with Horace and Virgil; see also I.86–88, which surely contains an implied reference to Cicero's support for Octavian in his final years. For an indication of the extent of eighteenth-century unease at the political complaisance of Augustan writers, see Weinbrot, *Augustus Caesar in 'Augustan' England: The Decline of a Classical Norm* (Princeton, 1978), esp. pp. 120–49 and, for Cicero, pp. 15–17.

21. 'Life of Gray', in Hill (ed.), *Lives of the English Poets*, III, 437.

22. See also IV.214–44. Akenside, who echoes Thomson's account of the Middle Ages and early Renaissance at various points in his own brief treatment of the *translatio studii* theme (*The Pleasures of Imagination* (1744), II.1–51), and also mentions Dante only in passing, differs from him in condemning the political complaisance of the Italian artists and poets, II.35–41.

23. See *Liberty*, V.549–716, and Gerrard, *Patriot Opposition*, p. 134.

24. See his 1742 essay, 'The Rise of Arts and Sciences'. Hume also comments on the failure of Longinus' theory to accord with the facts of history in 'Of Civil Liberty'.

25. Progress motifs are common in *The Seasons*, and are not limited to politics and art: the spiritual progress of the individual soul, for instance, offers another variety of the *translatio* tradition. The passage that comes nearest to what is attempted in *Liberty* is *Winter*, ll. 431–71, a shorter version of which appears in the first (1726) edition, ll. 258–92. For a critical analysis of the progress motif in *The Seasons*, and its modification by primitivistic tendencies, see McKillop, *The Background of Thomson's 'Seasons'* (Minneapolis, 1942), pp. 89–108; see also Gerrard, *Patriot Opposition*, p. 132, on why such inconsistency is less damaging here than in *Liberty*.

26. 'William Collins and the Idea of Liberty', in Ribeiro and Basker (eds), *Tradition in Transition*, pp. 257–74.

27. See Raymond Dexter Havens, 'Primitivism and the Idea of Progress in Thomson', *Studies in Philology*, XXIX (1932), 41–52, at pp. 47, 50–51; Gerrard, '*The Castle of Indolence* and the Opposition to Walpole', *Review of English Studies*, n.s. XLI (1990), 45–64, and *Patriot Opposition*, pp. 166–84.

28. See *An Original Canto of Spencer* (London, '1714', actually 1713) and *Another Original Canto of Spencer* (London, 1714), both published under the pseudonym 'Nestor Ironside'.

29. McKillop, *Background of Liberty*, pp. 34–36, traces this explanation of the condition of the Campania to Gilbert Burnet's 1686 travel book, *Some Letters, Containing An Account of What Seemed Most Remarkable in Switzerland, Italy, &c.*.

30. For the echo of Christ, see II.40, and compare Mark 6:26–28. For the rape of Dame Poverty see II.46–54.

31. The claim that the ancient Britons were undismayed by 'the *Roman* steel' (II.153), creates a context of warlike resistance to oppression, while the evocation of a context for Druidic forest rites ('A Sylvan Life till then the Natives led,/ In the brown Shades and green-wood Forest lost;' II.147–48) not only sets the scene for the redemptive Druid Bard later on, but confirms the poem's allegiance to Walpole's opponents, as Gerrard demonstrates, *Patriot Opposition*, pp. 136–45. For the similar undertones operating in the reference to deerhunting (II.150), see Gerrard, *Patriot Opposition*, pp. 215–23.

32. See Maurice Golden, 'The Imagining Self in the Eighteenth Century', *Eighteenth-Century Studies*, III (1969), 4–27, at pp. 13–18.

33. Gerrard, *Patriot Opposition*, p. 184.

34. *An Essay on Man* was of course addressed to Bolingbroke, whose influence on its composition is still a matter of controversy. For a reading which credits Bolingbroke as a significant contributor, see Brean S. Hammond, *Pope and Bolingbroke: A Study of Friendship and Influence* (Columbia, 1984).

35. For Pope's notes for *Brutus*, see *Selected Prose of Alexander Pope*, ed. Paul Hammond (Cambridge, 1987), pp. 292–96.

36. Lyttleton was especially active in these attempts. Gerrard, *Patriot Opposition*, pp. 81–82, collects much evidence from his letters, and notes the significance on his comments on Glover's *Leonidas* in *Common Sense* for 9 April 1737. For an early exhortation to Pope to abandon satire, see his 1730 *An Epistle to Mr Pope, From a Young Gentleman at Rome*. See also Sambrook, *Thomson: A Life*, p. 205.

Thomson and the Druids

RICHARD TERRY

I

On 27 August 1748, the Scottish poet James Thomson, for over 20 years a literary émigré in London, died, to be interred in the churchyard at Richmond two days afterwards. About 10 months later, his death was commemorated in a sentimental elegy written by William Collins, a fellow poet and denizen of Richmond. Entitled 'Ode Occasioned by the Death of Mr Thomson', its first stanza runs as follows:

> In yonder grave a Druid lies,
>> Where slowly winds the stealing wave!
> The year's best sweets shall duteous rise
>> To deck its poet's sylvan grave![1]

This enigmatic poem has in recent times become something of a crux in our understanding of how both Thomson and Collins alike conceived the office of poet, and of how poets generally, in the mid-eighteenth century, figured to themselves the nature of their vocation. Surprisingly, however, it was only as late as 1946, in an article by J. M. S. Tompkins, that it seems first to have been proposed that in calling Thomson a 'Druid', Collins might have been choosing his words advisedly, and in a way calculated to conjure up a quite precise set of connotations.[2] Tompkins claimed the invocation to be consistent with a composite portrait of 'the Druid' as bardic visionary, priest of nature and patriot-leader that had been built up by antiquarians like Carte, Toland and Stukeley; and in demonstration of the aptness of the sobriquet as applied to Thomson, he pointed out that the poet held a religiously heterodox belief in spiritual transmigration, a philosophy also widely credited to the Druids.[3] In 1969, however, when Roger Lonsdale glossed the poem for his authoritative Longman edition of Collins's poetry, he rebuffed Tompkins. Seeking to prune down the foliage of associations that the earlier critic had identified as surrounding 'Druid', Lonsdale posited that only 'some' of them would doubtlessly have existed in Collins's mind and these only in 'vague' form. For Lonsdale, the reference to the Druids was warranted by nothing more than that Thomson was a nature poet who, in his *Liberty* (1735–36), also wrote a long poem of a patriotic tenor.[4]

What is at issue here is the relative sharpness or inexactitude of reference implied by Collins's invocation of the term 'Druid'. In recent times, and contrary to Lonsdale, critics seem to have accorded the term a high degree of specificity. John Lucas, for example, in his *England and Englishness* (1990), asserts that 'the *only* good reason for calling [Thomson] a Druid' was that he was Scottish and therefore a Celt, the original Druids being a set of functionaries indigenous to Celtic society.[5] Yet there are two problems in construing the term in this way. To begin with, in Thomson's era, the Druids were identified with the Celtic communities of west Britain (especially Wales and Ireland) and Gaul, and until the publication of Macpherson's Ossian poems in the 1760s seem to have been associated hardly at all with prehistoric Scotland.[6] Furthermore, the very nature of Collins's poem seems to demand that the term 'Druid' be applausive, constituting a positive recommendation of Thomson as a poet; and it is hard to see how the mere specifying of his nationality (especially by the pen of a Sassenach) can generate this semantic force.

The most recent literary historian to address the crux of Thomson's designation as a 'Druid' has been Christine Gerrard in her excellent study of *The Patriot Opposition to Walpole* (1994). Gerrard claims that during the 1730s the figure of the Druid was commandeered by the emergent Patriot movement, a cross-party grouping of those entrenchedly opposed to the prime minister Robert Walpole, mainly on the grounds of his personal *hauteur*, the corruption endemic to his administration, and the pusillanimous nature of British foreign policy during his time in office. British national life, so such people believed, could only be redeemed by a resurgence of public virtue and selfless patriotism, qualities that became associated with the Druids, especially in their mythical role as leaders of British resistance to the Roman occupation. This image of patriotic resistance proved attractive to the oppositional politics of such as Thomson, Pope and Lord Bolingbroke during, what was for them, the grisly period of the Walpole ascendancy. According to Gerrard, to dwell on the sentimental association of Druids with nature worship, visionary entrancement and the like is to be distracted from the real point: when Collins introduces the word 'Druid', he lays bare and pays homage to Thomson's political affiliations.[7]

I have chosen to begin with Collins's ode because its invocation of the figure of the Druid is so tantalizing, consisting as it does of a cryptic, honorific label applied by one major poet to another; and I will return later in the essay to the fertile topic of Thomson and Druidism. My overall purpose, though, is less to haggle over the semiology of Collins's usage than to draw attention to one particular dimension of the cultural perception of Druids that may be lurking in the background of Collins's poem: this has to do, in the first instance, with the Druids being poets but, more particularly, with their being the *earliest* British poets—in effect, the founding fathers of the vernacular literary tradition. Before elaborating on this, though, it might be useful to say something about the Druids themselves and about conceptions about them prevalent in the eighteenth century.

II

Because early Celtic culture was non-literate, knowledge of the Druids has descended to us through two main sources: from classical texts that document their existence and relation to the larger Celtic community; and from archaeological evidence that has enabled the spread of Celtic culture to be charted. The Celtic world was to a remarkable degree homogeneous in terms of culture and language. It occupied much of Europe, as far east as Asia Minor, and flourished from the third century BC until, and in places beyond, the incorporation of the same land mass into the Roman empire. The unit of organization of Celtic culture was the tribe, whose leader was more of the nature of a local chieftain than a monarch. The highest echelon of society seems to have been divided between combative and non-combative élites: warriors, on the one hand, and on the other a priesthood or clerisy.[8]

As regards the structure of Celtic society, and the role within it of Druids, we are heavily reliant on the classical texts of Strabo, Diodorus Siculus, Athenaeus and Julius Caesar, writings that as well as being elliptical in nature are also in large part derivative from an even earlier, lost source: the *Histories* of Posidonius. For most lettered people in the eighteenth century, however, it was probably enough to be acquainted with just two sources, Caesar's *The Battle for Gaul* and the solitary reference to British Druids in Tacitus' *Annals*. Caesar's account accords to the Druids a prominent role as educators and shows them disseminating their 'doctrine' in the form of large numbers of verses that initiates had to commit to memory. Yet, on a condemnatory note, he also stresses their officiation at judicious and religious ceremonies, the latter including human sacrifices in which victims were sometimes immolated inside huge wickerwork figures; and a similar sense of the barbarism of the Druids is conveyed by Tacitus' description of their execrating the Roman soldiers passing through the Menai Straits. Indeed, the cultural reverence accorded to Druids in the eighteenth century (such that Collins's application of the term to Thomson can count as praise) comes about only through a process of rehabilitation, in which a blind or tolerant eye was turned to the unsavoury aspects of Druidical practices dwelt on in the classical sources. For Caesar, the privileged status enjoyed by the Druids was symptomatic of nothing so much as the inveterate savagery of early British society.[9]

It remains unclear from the classical accounts whether the Druids should be seen as a caste (in other words, set apart by birthright) or merely a set of functionaries but, in any event, their three main functions seem to have been to do with the preservation and passing down of communal lore, the administering of justice, and officiation at religious ceremonies. But a further function or propensity that became associated with them was verse-making. Some grounds for the association arise, as I have indicated, from Caesar's *Battle for Gaul*, which records how the Druids inculcated their lore through the medium of verse. This was done, however, for practical, mnemonic reasons, and Caesar offers no suggestion that the Druids wrote verses as an end in itself.[10] The equivocality of the Druids' status as poets is also evident from both Strabo and Diodorus, in whose writings they are seen as only one of three denominations of holy or learned men, these being, in loose terms, 'bards', who wrote poems of eulogy and satire; 'Druids', who were philosophers and curators of knowledge; and augurers, who interpreted sacrifices. Under this nomenclature, Druids and bards, though part of a single clerisy, form distinct categories within it.[11]

Yet from the earliest writings in English in which Druids appear, a marked feature of their representation is the tendency for the two categories of Druid and bard to be conflated. In Michael Drayton's influential *Poly-Olbion* (1622), for example, references to bards and Druids are collocated in such a way as to make ambiguous the nature of their relation. In a passage in 'The First Song', for example, Drayton petitions the ancient British bards to inspire his verse so that it might achieve a fame beyond his own death:

> Ye sacred Bards, that to your harps' melodious strings
> Sung th'ancient Heroes' deeds (the monuments of Kings)
> And in your dreadful verse ingrav'd the prophecies,
> The agèd world's descents, and genealogies;
> If, as those *Druids* taught, which kept the British rites,
> And dwelt in darksome groves, there counselling with sprites,
> ...
> When these our souls by death our bodies do forsake,
> They instantly again do other bodies take;
> I could have wish'd your spirits redoubled in my breast,
> To give my verse applause, to time's eternal rest.[12]

Although Drayton distinguishes between the two categories, it is also the case that they rise in his mind simultaneously, as if yoked together by mental association; moreover, what the bards supposedly versify (prophecies and genealogies) is material that would have formed part of the communal lore over which the

Druids supposedly exercised a curatorial role. A much more emphatic conflation of the roles of Druid and bard, however, is evident in John Milton's elegiac poem 'Lycidas' (1637). The poem's subject, Edward King, had drowned off the Irish coast, close enough to Anglesea (Mona), the legendary home of the Druids, for Milton to build an allusion to them into his lament:

> Where were ye nymphs when the remorseless deep
> Closed o'er the head of your loved Lycidas?
> For neither were ye playing on the steep,
> Where your old bards, the famous Druids, lie,
> Nor on the shaggy top of Mona high,
> Nor yet where Deva spreads her wizard stream ...[13]

The following year, in his Latin poem to Manso, Milton trumpeted England's credentials to be considered a poetical nation by again drawing attention to the Druids, as 'an ancient race' who 'were well practised in the rituals of the gods and used to sing the praises of heroes and their exemplary exploits'.[14] Such a conflation of bard and Druid was never, it might be said, strictly warranted by the classical sources on which poets like Milton depended for their familiarity with early British history. Yet even by the early seventeenth century that the Druids were hybridically both priests and poets was becoming a stock assumption, leading, in somewhat trite fashion, to their appearance in a choric role in works like John Fletcher's *Bonduca* (1618) and Thomas Carew's *Coelum Britannicum* (1634), in both of which Druids parade across the stage while chanting patriotic verses. It might be noted, however, that at this time the equation of Druids with bards did not contain the logic, as it came to do in the Romantic era, that verse-making was an intrinsically priestly and prophetic activity.[15]

That the Druids were construed as bards inevitably precipitated a further proposition: that they must be the earliest poets to have inhabited the British Isles—that they must, in effect, be the originary figures of both the English and British poetic traditions. Such a realization represented a signal departure in how the literary past was conceived. At the turn of the seventeenth century, anyone asked to nominate the begetter of the English poetic tradition could have done nothing other than cite the name of Chaucer (or perhaps Gower). For what lay before Chaucer was obscurity or, even worse, the dimly apprehended gothic age (or dark ages as we would call them) of ignorance and barbarism.[16] Indeed, the image of Chaucer's creative beam dispelling the miasma of the previous unenlightened age is a commonplace in seventeenth-century poetry, as in Sir John Denham's lines in his elegy 'On Mr Abraham Cowley's Death' which describe how Chaucer's 'light those mists and clouds dissolv'd/ Which our dark nation long involv'd'.[17]

A good snapshot of the state of literary historical knowledge obtaining in the Renaissance era is provided by William Webbe's *A Discourse of English Poetrie* (1586). Webbe is entirely candid about being at a loss to name a single English poet between Lydgate and Skelton (born c. 1370 and c. 1460 respectively) or earlier than the late fourteenth century: 'The first of our English poets that I haue heard of was *Iohn Gower*', he declares, allowing Gower temporal precedence over his contemporary, Chaucer.[18] That Webbe should have languished oblivious to any native liter-ature dating from more than a century prior to his own moment of writing could hardly have been otherwise, granted the prevailing state of knowledge in the field of literary antiquities. But twenty years later, all this was to change with the publication of a single work, William Camden's *Remaines ... Concerning Britaine* (1605). Camden's *Remaines*, as its title suggests, was a compilation of leftovers from the huge antiquarian project published as *Britannia* (1586). Unlike that work, however, it was not a county or topographical study but rather a study of selected facets of early history, organized under an assortment of heads, including languages, common Christian and surnames, money, customary apparel, military engines and so on. Most important here, however, is that Camden's *Remaines* sought to exhume a pre-Chaucerian literary tradition: in three chapters entitled 'Poemes', Epigrammes' and 'Rythmes', the work vouch-safed to subsequent literary historians a file of names of English authors from the seventh century onwards. The majority of these authors belong to what we now call the Anglo-Latin tradition; many of them, indeed, were in main part not poets at all but philosophers, theologians and historians. Such include, for example, John of Hauville, Joseph of Exeter, Geoffrey of Monmouth, Godfrey of Winchester, Gerald of Wales, Alexander Neckam, Walter Map and Michael of Cornwall.[19] But Camden also alludes to a Saxon tradition. He refers in glowing terms to Caedmon, the seventh-century poet of Whitby, whose plaque in Poets' Corner, Westminster Abbey, decorates him as the earliest Englishman ever to have written verses, and also cites Robert of Gloucester, author of a thirteenth-century metrical chronicle of England.[20]

The diffuse impact of Camden's *Remaines* was to lift a veil on what had previously been invisible, to allow subsequent poets and historians to apprehend the native literary tradition as a cultural descent from ages more remote than had previously been imagined. The influence of Camden can be gauged from two collections of authorial biography published in the second half of the seventeenth century. His roster of early authors is assimilated virtually wholesale into Edward Phillips's *Theatrum Poetarum* of 1675; and about half of the poets cited by William Winstanley, in his *Lives of the Most Famous English Poets* (1687), as flourishing prior to the late fourteenth century are lifted from Camden and Phillips.[21] By the Restoration era, it had become axiomatic that the native literary tradition, to be truly conceived, was no longer susceptible to being retrenched into a mere post-Chaucerian genealogy.

Some sense of the rupture between late seventeenth-century and earlier constructions of the native literary inheritance can be gleaned from Thomas Rymer's *A Short View of Tragedy* (1692). Rymer's work, which immediately became notorious for its critical manhandling of both Shakespeare and Jonson, balances its animus towards English tragedy by conferring an emollient accolade on English poetry: 'Since the decay of the Roman Empire this Island, peradventure has been more fortunate in matters of Poetry, than any of our Neighbours'.[22] Cited as a part of English poetry's good fortune is its comparative longevity, and in demonstration of this, Rymer cites the fact that an early British coin, catalogued in the numismatics section of Camden's *Britannia*, bears a harp on its reverse, this being a supposed sign of the flourishing of a poetic culture at the time of its minting. Whereas Webbe in 1586 could put the date of the native poetic tradition at hardly more than two hundred years, by 1693 that period had stretched itself beyond all previous measure. Indeed, in the early 1730s, when Pope's friend Joseph Spence began work on a proposed history of English poetry, he could envisage tracing the subject 'for above 2000 years': a temporal dimension that would previously have been unimaginable.[23]

Given the invariable conflation of Druids with bards, for Rymer to suppose a native poetry coeval with the 'decay of the Roman empire' was for him to predicate the Druids as its exponents. The Druidical origin of native poetry, in fact, becomes a frequent assumption made by early literary historical writers. In 1711, for example, the young Elijah Fenton wrote a verse-epistle to the dramatist Thomas Southerne in which he flattered Southerne by according him an auspicious station in a roll call of the major English playwrights. Moreover, as an auxiliary component of the poem, Fenton sought to map out a 'progress of English poesy', an account of the historical progression, and geographical translation, of the abstract principle of poetry from the Greeks to the Romans and thence to the British. Poetry, personified as a nymph, decamps to Britain after the Roman state is overrun by the Goths, there to take up residence among the Druids:

> Long in the melancholy grove she staid,
> And taught the pensive Druids in the shade;
> In solemn and instructive notes they sung
> From whence the beauteous frame of nature sprung,
> Who polish'd all the radiant orbs above,
> And in bright order made the planets move;
> Whence thunders roar, and frightful meteors fly,
> And comets roll unbounded through the sky;
> Who wing'd the winds, and gave the streams to flow,
> And rais'd the rocks, and spread the lawns below;
> Whence the gay spring exults in flowery pride,
> And autumn with the bleeding grape is dy'd;
> Whence summer suns imbrown the labouring swains,
> And shivering winter pines in icy chains:

And prais'd the Power Supreme, nor dar'd advance
So vain a theory as that of chance.[24]

Although progress-of-poesy poems are relatively common in the eighteenth century, this is the sole one with which I am familiar where the Druids are proposed as the earliest bearers of the British poetic flame. Most often, its first recipient is instead Chaucer, and where this is not the case, as in Thomas Gray's 'Progress of Poesy' (1757) where 'Poesy' flits directly from the Tiber to the Avon, the usurpation of Chaucer tends to be significant. Yet the Druids were particularly apt for Fenton's purposes since his poem is concerned to argue a close link between the flourishing of poetry and the waxing of political freedom, the successive migrations of poetry always enacting a flight from tyranny to liberty. Thus in their mythic role as opponents of Roman oppression, the Druids were well-suited to be considered as the first custodians of English poetry. As regards the *sort* of poetry practised amongst them, Fenton falls in with the Caesarean account in the *Battle for Gaul*. The Druids' poetic notes are 'solemn and instructive', which suggests that their verse-making was confined to the dissemination of lore.

The enshrinement of the Druids as the founders of the native literary tradition is completed by the middle of the eighteenth century. Joseph Spence's 'Some Historical Remarks on the English Poets', for example, composed in French in 1732–33 and unpublished until our own century, devotes an early paragraph to 'Druidical Poetry', reprising Caesar's relation of how the Druids instructed their neophytes through the mnemonic medium of verse.[25] In John Brown's *History of the Rise and Progress of Poetry* (1764), the earliest native authors are given as the ancient '*British Bards*' who, while not technically Druids as such, are described as composing a lower order in a larger clerisy of which the Druids formed a part.[26] Similarly, Thomas Gray, in his jotted draft-plan for a history of English poetry, proposes beginning with 'the poetry of the *Galic* or (Celtic) nation, as far back as can be traced'.[27] Such a project would also inevitably have involved discussion of the Druids, notes on whom (mainly deriving from Caesar and Strabo) can be found in Gray's *Common-Place Book*.[28]

Although the draft-plan of Gray's envisaged history remains undatable, his research into early British literature had certainly been long set aside when, in a letter to Thomas Warton on 15 April 1770, he enclosed his plan in the hope that it might be of use for Warton's own research on the same subject. In fact, the document was too fragmentary, and was communicated to Warton too late, for it to have had any influence on the latter's *History of English Poetry*, which eventually came out in three volumes between 1774 and 1781. Yet while Warton's *History*, in its final form, quarries back no earlier than the eleventh century, in 1753, early in his envisagement of the project, he was—like Gray—intending to begin his work with treatment of the Druids. This much is evident from surviving notebooks dating to this period, in one of which Warton has penned a thumbnail 'Plan of the History of English Poetry', in which the first of a sequence of numbered paragraphs, presumably corresponding to intended chapters, runs as follows:

> 1. The Poetry subsisting among the Druids lost: The Saxon's [sic] introduc'd it, of whom Hickes produces many Hymns: The old British Bards not yet lost: Robert of Glocester's Cronicle the Remain of them.[29]

A separate notebook contains successive drafts of 'part of a formal letter on the subject of English language and literature before the Norman Conquest', which again contains the near statutory reference to the Druids:

> It was the office of the Bards, among the ancient Britons, to sing to the Harp the Atchievements of great Men in Metre. This Institution of Men was undoubtedly dissolv'd at the Roman Invasion, as was that likewise of the Druids, Prophets, & Priests who together with the Bards were highly esteem'd, when our Island was in Possession of its original Inhabitants.[30]

What Warton might have said about the Druids, had he not retrenched the project, remains, of course, irrecuperable, but it is hard to imagine how there would have been much scope for expansion beyond the ephemeral remarks of the notebooks. The two passages quoted even show a degree of wavering over whether the Druids, strictly so called, *were* indeed poets. The latter passage, for example, keeps separate the categories of bard and Druid, and even to say, as in the first passage, that poetry 'subsists' among the Druids is to stop short of saying that the Druids were actually poets.

The truism that the Druids (or the British bards) were the originators of the English poetic tradition vied perhaps only with the equal one that none of their compositions remained extant.[31] So that when Warton writes 'The Poetry subsisting among the Druids lost', this could be read equally as an indication of what he was intending his book would include or what it would necessarily have had to exclude, given the lack of available sources. Perhaps of even greater consequence was that, in spite of the hallowed status of Druidical poetry, no scholar could point with assurance to a single exponent, let alone come to a conclusion as to the worth of the poetry that the Druids had produced. It is true that John Toland's 'Account of the Druids' (1726) enlists Merlin Silvester, Merlin Ambrosius and Taliessin as Druidical bards, but claims of this sort are in reality little more than a concoction of myth and anachronism.[32] What alone could be done with probity was to surmise that 'Druidical compositions' might have been known to poets of a later era, so that, as Thomas Gray suggests, the poems of the Druids could have 'served for a Model to Taliessin, Lhywarch, & others of the most ancient & best of ye British Poets'.[33]

Of course, the reason for the anonymity of the Druidical tradition owed less to the scattering or perishing of written sources than that such sources had probably never existed; Celtic culture was preliterate, and its verse culture described by Caesar is an entirely oral one.[34] The literary historical research of the likes of Gray and Warton, in other words, was an attempt to place on historical record the cultural achievements of a prehistoric society. The very idea of Druidical poetry was (to introduce a modern parlance) an absence that, at the same time, constituted a presence: the lack of any evidence for a Druidical poetic culture doubled up as perhaps the single circumstance most authenticating of its having existed. Indeed, the Druids in the eighteenth century, most notoriously in the case of the antiquarian William Stukeley, come to be a *tabula rasa* on to which Druidicists could map any or all of the whimsies (and perhaps tomfooleries) of their own imaginations.[35]

III

I want to return now to what might have been present in William Collins's imagination when he invoked the term 'Druid' in connection with Thomson, the way I want to address the conundrum being through the supposition that Collins, a close friend of Thomson's in the last few years of the elder poet's life, might have applied the term in fidelity to the resonances he knew it possessed for Thomson himself. Yet Thomson's conception of the term has itself been a source of dissension between critics. Thomson introduces Druids into two of his poems, *Liberty* (1735) and *The Castle of Indolence* (1748). In the first of these, he praises his native Britain as a bastion of political liberty and shows how the Druidical belief in spiritual transmigration encouraged the early Britons the more readily to sacrifice their lives in resistance to Roman tyranny. In the second, the Knight of Arts and Industry who destroys the enchanted Castle of Indolence is accompanied by 'a little Druid-Wight/ Of wither'd Aspect' (long taken, on the authority of Joseph Warton, as being a portrait of Pope), who rallies those ensnared in the castle into shrugging off their indolence: a scenario, as Christine Gerrard has recently pointed out, not unlike the campaign being conducted by Thomson's political circle for a patriotic reinvigoration of national life.[36]

As support for her argument that Thomson's references to Druids, and hence Collins's reference to Thomson *as a Druid*, are only intelligible in the context of Patriot politics, Gerrard draws attention to (in her own words) 'Thomson's failure to mention the Druids in *The Seasons*', this omission suggesting that Druids 'first entered his imaginative vocabulary not through romantic musings on contemplation, woods, and poetry, but through the more rigorous avenues of Patriot Gothicism'.[37] At

this juncture, Gerrard's argument is squarely at odds with that of
J. M. P. Tompkins, who claims *The Seasons*, albeit there are no
Druids named as such in the poem, to be Thomson's most
'druidical' work.[38] The scope for such strikingly variant readings
of the poem arises from a single, though lengthy, passage in
'Summer', originally introduced in 1727 but which I cite here
from the 1746 text:

> Still let me pierce into the midnight depth
> Of yonder grove, of wildest largest growth,
> That, forming high in air a woodland choir,
> Nods o'er the mount beneath. At every step,
> Solemn and slow the shadows blacker fall,
> And all is awful listening gloom around.
>   These are the haunts of meditation, these
> The scenes where ancient bards the inspiring breath
> Ecstatic felt, and, from this world retired,
> Conversed with angels and immortal forms,
> On gracious errands bent—to save the fall
> Of virtue struggling on the brink of vice;
> In waking whispers and repeated dreams
> To hint pure thought, and warn the favoured soul,
> For future trials fated, to prepare;
> To prompt the poet, who devoted gives
> His muse to better themes; to soothe the pangs
> Of dying worth, and from the patriot's breast
> (Backward to mingle in detested war,
> But foremost when engaged) to turn the death;
> And numberless such offices of love,
> Daily and nightly, zealous to perform.
>   Shook sudden from the bosom of the sky,
> A thousand shapes or glide athwart the dusk
> Or stalk majestic on. Deep-roused, I feel
> A sacred terror, a severe delight,
> Creep through my mortal frame; and thus, methinks,
> A voice, than human more, the abstracted ear
> Of fancy strikes—'Be not of us afraid,
> Poor kindred man! thy fellow-creatures, we
> From the same Parent-Power our beings drew,

The same our Lord and laws and great pursuit.
Once some of us, like thee, through stormy life
Toiled tempest-beaten ere we could attain
This holy calm, this harmony of mind,
Where purity and peace immingle charms.
Then fear not us; but with responsive song,
Amid these dim recesses, undisturbed
By noisy folly and discordant vice,
Of Nature sing with us, and Nature's God.
Here frequent, at the visionary hour,
When musing midnight reigns or silent noon,
Angelic harps are in full concert heard,
And voices chaunting from the wood-crown'd hill,
The deepening dale, or inmost sylvan glade:
A privilege bestow'd by us alone
On contemplation, or the hallow'd ear
Of poet swelling to seraphic strain.'

　　　　　　　　　　　　　　　　　('Summer', ll. 516–63)

The impenetrabilities here run deep, being both a matter of to
what certain phrases are actually referring and also of the
tormented articulation of Thomson's verse paragraphs. The
central, obdurate crux is the identity of the 'ancient bards', the
fact that this is withheld from us allowing for the difference of
opinion between Tompkins and Gerrard over whether they
should be identified as Druids or, alternatively, as the biblical
bards, Moses and Job. But even more knotted perhaps is the role
played by these personages (whoever they are) in the passage.
The second verse paragraph, consisting of a single sentence,
divides at the dash, with everything coming thereafter standing in
a relation of apposition to the earlier part of the sentence. But an
ambiguity arises surrounding what immediately follows the dash:
'to save the fall/ Of virtue struggling …'. For is it the ancient
bards' retirement from the world that will save the fall of virtue,
or will virtue be succoured instead by the gracious errands of the
'angels and immortal forms'? Or would this be to misconstrue
Thomson's syntax, for do the 'gracious errands' actually belong
syntactically to the 'angels and immortal forms', or should they
instead be ushered further back in the sentence to the retiring

bards? Furthermore, if there are problems enough in divining the true sense of the first part of the passage, such problems become even more recalcitrant in the final verse paragraph. The narrator becomes conscious of a 'thousand shapes' peopling the grove, but whether these correspond to the 'ancient bards' or the 'immortal forms' is left undisclosed. If the former, then Thomson (or the narrator) finds himself in a relation of creative tutelage to the bards; if the latter, then he becomes, as it were, *one of them*, joining them in being alike a poetic acolyte of the shadowy woodland deities.

Invocations of 'ancient bards' or 'bards of old' are a feature of many poems of the Augustan era, as, for example, Mark Akenside's *The Pleasures of Imagination* (1744), which encourages the novice poet to place himself under the influence of Nature, so he might 'breathe at large/ Ætherial air; with bards and sages old'.[39] The desire to recover fellowship with the old bards formed a romantic accompaniment to the more scholarly investigation of the national literary past, but part of the convention of conjuring up such dusky figures, observed by both Thomson and Akenside, was that they remain unnamed. Evidence, however, does exist for supposing that Thomson had Druidical poets in mind, if not perhaps *exclusively* so, in his passage in 'Summer'. In the Augustan era, there were two aspects of the Druidical myth that had gained currency independently of the classical sources. These were that the Druids belonged to a particular sort of locale, that of dingy woodland recesses, and that they were wont to hold communion with a pantheon of rural spirits and semi-deities. Both of these truisms are to the fore in a passage from Drayton's *Poly-Olbion* cited earlier, in which the Druids are described as dwelling 'in darksome groves, there counselling with sprites'.[40] Such a coming together of Druids and woodland deities may have been driven by the felicitous near-homophone of 'Druid' and 'dryad' (wood spirit), interest in which class of creatures seems to have been accelerated in the eighteenth century as a result of the influential passage in the Earl of Shaftesbury's *The Moralists: A Philosophical Rhapsody* (1709), in which Theocles and Philocles pay an early morning visit to the 'sacred Groves of the *Hamadryads*'.[41] Only four years later, William Diaper's *Dryades* (1713), a weird and fanciful disquisition on 'daemons', 'genii' and natural deities, showed Druids and dryads actually consorting together. Diaper allocates his spirits to hierarchical categories, detailing the behaviour of the lower sort in the following terms:

> Inferiour Orders have a meaner Home,
> And here in wilds, and woody mazes roam,
> To learned *Magi* we strange Spells impart,
> Myst'ries disclose, and tell the *Secret* Art.
> With Sacred *Miselto* the *Druids* crown'd
> Sung with the Nymphs, and danc'd the pleasing Round.[42]

Although there is no evidence for Thomson's being familiar with the poem, *Dryades* does seem to have influenced the treatment of Druids in Samuel Garth's 'Claremont', published a year later (1714).[43]

These beliefs, that the Druids lived in secluded groves and fraternized with spirits, are often invoked, either singly or in tandem, in connection with the otherwise faceless 'ancient bards'. In Sir John Denham's *Cooper's Hill*, for example, the poet, enjoying his hill-top panorama, speculates about the stories 'Of Fairies, Satyrs, and Nymphs' that would have been heard had 'some bold Greek or British bard' beheld the scene.[44] Moreover, the same ingredients occur in a poem that probably provides the most immediate analogue to the passage in Thomson's 'Summer', Richard Glover's 'Poem on Sir Isaac Newton', written in 1726, though only published two years later, as prefixed to Henry Pemberton's *A View of Newton's Philosophy*. In this work, the poet imagines himself venturing out beneath a 'silver-tressed moon', searching for a solitary enclave amidst the 'darksome woods' (a phrase that may recollect the 'darksome groves' inhabited by Drayton's Druids). Here he will watch in his mind's eye as the 'fairy elves/ Dance o'er the magic circles', or alternatively behold,

> In thought enraptur'd with the ancient bards,
> Medea's baleful incantation draw
> Down from her orb the paly queen of night.[45]

Although Glover's 'ancient bards' here include Euripides, it seems improbable that he did not intend the category to be sufficiently generic to include Druidical bards as well, especially since the entire *mise en scène*, including the accompanying activity of 'fairy elves', had already acquired an overriding association with bards of the native British tradition.

Glover must have written his 'Poem on Sir Isaac Newton' close to the period of Thomson's composition of 'Summer', but I want now to turn to two poems, germane to Thomson's possible association of his 'ancient bards' with Druids, that were written some years later, and that give the impression of being revisitings of the original passage in *The Seasons*. Joseph Warton's 'The Enthusiast' (1744), written during the period of the author's developing friendship with Thomson, preserves the fundamentals of Thomson's scenario, with the poet exhorting 'green-rob'd Dryads' to lead him to the inner recess of a shadowy copse, whereupon his thoughts turn to his poetic predecessors:

> The bards of old,
> Fair Nature's friends, sought such retreats, to charm
> Sweet Echo with their songs; oft too they met
> In summer evenings, near sequester'd bowers,
> Or mountain nymph, or muse, and eager learnt
> The moral strains she taught to mend mankind.[46]

That Warton retains here the established collocation of 'bards of old' with rustic spirits (dryads and mountain nymphs) is in keeping with the bards of Thomson's 'Summer' who converse with 'angels and immortal forms'. Moreover, Warton's passage possesses the same sense of vista that is such a pronounced, albeit confusing, aspect of 'Summer', ll. 516–63: in 'The Enthusiast', the poet takes counsel of the bards of old who, in a recessive manner, themselves take counsel of 'a mountain nymph, or Muse'.

The year following the appearance of Joseph Warton's poem, his brother, Thomas, began composition of a work along very similar lines, to be published anonymously in 1747 as 'The Pleasures of Melancholy'. Once more the poet imagines himself wandering in 'solemn glooms/ Congenial with my soul', and

conjures up a succession of melancholy incidents and subjects.
This line of development is consummated, close to the poem's
end, with a direct apostrophe to 'Melancholy, queen of thought',
which then itself gives way to an invocation of the goddess
'contemplation':

> Then ever beauteous contemplation, hail!
> From thee began, auspicious maid, my song,
> With thee shall end; for thou art fairer far
> Than are the nymphs of Cirrha's mossy grot;
> To loftier rapture thou canst wake the thought,
> Than all the fabling poet's boastful pow'rs.
> Hail, queen divine! whom, as tradition tells,
> Once, in his ev'ning walk a Druid found,
> Far in a hollow glade of Mona's woods;
> All piteous bore with hospitable hand
> To the close shelter of his oaken bow'r.
> There soon the sage admiring mark'd the dawn
> Of solemn musing in your pensive thought;
> For when a smiling babe, you lov'd to lie
> Oft deeply list'ning to the rapid roar
> Of word-hung Meinai, stream of Druids old.[47]

In 'Winter', the 'ancient bards' are shown dwelling in 'haunts of
meditation'; in Thomas Warton's 'Pleasures of Melancholy', the
very concept of contemplation, or meditative withdrawal, is
revealed as having been invented by the Druids, whose
harbouring of the goddess contemplation 'mark'd the dawn/ Of
solemn musing'. Both Joseph's and Thomas's poems seem to me
to represent retrospective glossings of the original Thomsonian
passage, in which the invocation of Druids, cryptically subdued
in Thomson, is drawn out in more pronounced relief. It remains
true, of course, that Thomson's reference to his shadowy bards
may not refer *singly* to Druids, in the sense of categorically
excluding the biblical and classical poets, but it seems unlikely
that Druids did not form at least part of his conception.
Moreover, by the mid-eighteenth century, the collocation of
Druids with dim, moonlit groves, woodland spirits such as
the ubiquitous dryads, and a prevailing spirit of melancholy

contemplation had turned into what was at once both a rural and a poetic myth.

If Thomson's 'ancient bards' can be taken as Druids, what was Collins saying about the poet in his elegiac 'Ode' when investing him with the same label? For one thing, he may have felt he was endorsing the autobiographical dimension of 'Summer', ll. 516–63, in which the Thomsonian narrator (in one particular construction of the passage) follows in the footsteps of the Druids in placing himself beneath the creative tutelage of the 'immortal forms' frequenting the forest. But Collins would almost certainly also have been familiar with a tradition of enshrinement of the Druids not just as poets but as the founding fathers of British poetry. The consecration of any author to the literary tradition necessarily involves some rite of nomination, and Collins would have understood that the identification of Thomson as a Druid constituted just such a rite. To be of the genealogy of the ancient, poetic Druids was, in a very real sense, to be assimilated to the oaken trunk of the family tree of native literature. For Thomson to be 'of the Druids' was for him to stand in a rich line of canonical literary inheritance. It is not that this resonance of the term necessarily negates alternative ones that critics have claimed for it. Rather it complements them, while also perhaps helping us see why (as the poem seems to insist) the word 'Druid', in its application to Thomson, is not merely a predicate but an accolade.

NOTES

1.   *The Poems of Gray, Collins and Goldsmith*, ed. Roger Lonsdale (London, 1969), pp. 488–89.

2.   J. M. S. Tompkins, 'In Yonder Grave a Druid Lies', *Review of English Studies*, 22 (1946), 1–16.

3.   John Toland, *A Critical History of the Celtic Religion and Learning*, published posthumously in *A Collection of Several Pieces by John Toland* (1726); William Stukeley, *Stonehenge: A Temple Restor'd to the British Druids* (1740), and *Abury, a Temple of the British Druids* (1747); Thomas Carte, *A General History of England* (1747).

4. Lonsdale, *Poems of Gray*, pp. 487–88.

5. John Lucas, *England and Englishness* (London, 1990), p. 47.

6. For the Druids as part of Welsh historical identity, see Prys Morgan, 'From a Death to a View: The Hunt for the Welsh Past in the Romantic Period', in *The Invention of Tradition*, ed. Eric Hobsbawm and Terence Ranger (Cambridge, 1983), esp. pp. 62–66.

7. Christine Gerrard, *The Patriot Opposition to Walpole: Politics, Poetry, and National Myth, 1725–1742* (Oxford, 1994), esp. pp. 136–49. The meaning of Collins's elegy is discussed in A. L. Owen, *The Famous Druids* (Oxford, 1962), pp. 173–78.

8. For general information about the Druids, I am indebted to Stuart Piggott, *The Druids* (London, 1968). See also T. D. Kendrick, *The Druids: A Study in Keltic Prehistory* (London, 1927); and Owen, *The Famous Druids*.

9. For Tacitus, see *Annals*, XIV, 30. For Caesar, see *Battle for Gaul*, VI, 13–16. The relevant classical sources are available in Kendrick.

10. Caesar, *Battle for Gaul*, VI, 14.

11. See Kendrick, *The Druids*, pp. 82–83.

12. Cited from *The Complete Works of Michael Drayton*, ed. Rev. Richard Hooper, 3 vols (London, 1876), I, 2–3.

13. Cited from *The Poems of John Milton*, ed. John Carey and Alastair Fowler (London, 1968), pp. 243–44. For a comment on Milton's introduction of Druids here, see Joseph Warton, *An Essay on the Genius and Writings of Pope*, 2 vols (1756, 1782; 1806), I, 7: 'The mention of places remarkably romantic, the supposed habitation of Druids, bards, and wizards, is far more pleasing to the imagination, than the obvious introduction of Cam and Isis, as the seats of the Muses'.

14. *The Poems of John Milton*, p. 266.

15. See William Cowper's 'Table Talk' (1782) for how in former times 'the graceful name/ Of prophet and of poet was the same' and how 'ev'ry druid was a bard'; see *The Poems of William Cowper*, ed. John D. Baird and Charles Ryskamp, 3 vols (Oxford, 1980–95), I, 254. For William Blake's interest in Druids, see Owen, *The Famous Druids*, pp. 224–36. Also Marilyn Butler, 'Druids, Bards and Twice Born Bacchus: Peacock's Engagement with Primitive Mythology', *Keats–Shelley Memorial Bulletin*, 36 (1985), 57–76; and John Mee, *William Blake and the Culture of Radicalism in the 1790s* (Oxford, 1992), pp. 89–100.

16. Grisly evocations of the dark ages are common in late seventeenth- and eighteenth-century poetry. Book II of Mark Akenside's *The Pleasures of Imagination* (1744) opens with a lurid vision of how the 'iron-swarms' 'swept the works/ Of liberty and wisdom down the gulph/ Of all-devouring night'. See *The Poetical Works of Mark Akenside*, ed. Robin Dix (London, 1996), p. 111. Also Pat Rogers, 'Thomas Warton and the Waxing of the Middle Ages', in *Medieval Literature and Antiquities: Studies in Honour of*

Basil Cottle, ed. Myra Stokes and T. L. Burton (Cambridge, 1987), pp. 175–86.

17. Cited from *The Works of the British Poets*, ed. Robert Anderson, 13 vols (1795), V, 678.

18. Cited from *Elizabethan Critical Essays*, ed. G. Gregory Smith, 2 vols (Oxford, 1904), I, 240–41, 242.

19. For information on the Anglo-Latin tradition, see A. G. Rigg, *A History of Anglo-Latin Literature 1066–1422* (Cambridge, 1992).

20. See 'Certaine Poemes or Poesies, Epigrammes, Rythmes, and Epitaphs of the English Nation in former Times', in William Camden, *Remaines of a Greater Worke Concerning Britaine etc* (1605).

21. These seventeenth-century discussions of authorial biography are discussed in René Wellek, *The Rise of English Literary History* (Chapel Hill, 1941).

22. *The Critical Works of Thomas Rymer*, ed. Curt A. Zimansky (New Haven, 1956), p. 119.

23. See James M. Osborn, 'The First History of English Poetry', in *Pope and his Contemporaries: Essays Presented to George Sherburn*, ed. James L. Clifford and Louis L. Landa (Oxford, 1949), pp. 230–50, 238.

24. Anderson, *British Poets*, VII, 661.

25. See Osborn, 'The First History of English Poetry', p. 241.

26. John Brown, *History of the Rise and Progress of Poetry &c* (1764), p. 201.

27. Letter from Gray to Thomas Warton, 15 April 1770, in *The Correspondence of Thomas Gray*, ed. Paget Toynbee and Leonard Whibley, 3 vols (Oxford, 1935), III, 1122–25.

28. *Thomas Gray's Common-Place Book*, 3 vols, Pembroke College Library, Cambridge (unclassified), I, 310.

29. Cited from David Fairer, 'The Origins of Warton's *History of English Poetry*', *Review of English Studies*, New Series 32 (1981), 37–63, 42.

30. Fairer, 'Origins of Warton's *History*', p. 52.

31. See Jonathan Swift's fragment, 'An Abstract of the History of England': 'Their [the early Britons'] priests were called Druids: These lived in hollow trees, and committed not their mysteries to writing, but delivered them down by tradition, whereby they were in time wholly lost'. Cited from *The Prose Writings of Jonathan Swift*, ed. Herbert Davis *et al.*, 14 vols (Oxford, 1939–68), V, 3.

32. *A Collection of Several Pieces of Mr. John Toland*, 2 vols (1726), I, 191.

33. *Gray's Common-Place Book*, II, 799.

34. Caesar, *Battle for Gaul*, VI, 14.

35. Stuart Piggott, *William Stukeley: An Eighteenth-Century Antiquary* (London, 1950; rev. and enlarged 1985).

36. *Liberty*, IV.624–33; *The Castle of Indolence*, Canto II. XXXIII.

Thomson's poetry is cited from *The Seasons*, ed. James Sambrook (Oxford, 1981) and *Liberty, The Castle of Indolence and Other Poems*, ed. James Sambrook (Oxford, 1986).

37. Gerrard, *Patriot Opposition*, p. 141.

38. Tompkins, 'In Yonder Grave' p. 13.

39. Dix, *Works of Akenside*, p. 92.

40. Hooper, *Works of Drayton*, I, 2.

41. Third Earl of Shaftesbury, *Characteristicks of Men, Manners, Opinions, Times*, 3 vols (fifth edn. corrected, 1732), II, 343.

42. *The Complete Works of William Diaper*, ed. Dorothy Broughton (London, 1951), p. 67.

43. Anderson, *British Poets*, VII, 108.

44. Anderson, *British Poets*, V, 675.

45. Anderson, *British Poets*, XI, 545.

46. Cited from *The Three Wartons: A Choice of their Verse*, ed. Eric Partridge (London, 1927).

47. Anderson, *British Poets*, XI, 1079.

James Thomson and Eighteenth-Century Scottish Literary Identity

GERARD CARRUTHERS

I

Eighteenth-century Scotland produced two poets of lasting influence: James Thomson and Robert Burns. Indeed, of all Scottish poets, these two are probably the most important in international terms. However, while Burns, elevated by both popular and critical accord, has endured as Scotland's national bard, Thomson has seen his poetic stock in his native country sharply decline since his lifetime. Through the eighteenth century, Scotland was as enthusiastic about Thomson as anywhere and, indeed, the country's penchant for public celebration of its poetic progeny was lavished upon him. In 1791 Burns penned his 'Address, To the Shade of Thomson, on crowning his Bust, at Ednam, Roxburgh-shire, with Bays' to be read at the event described in the poem's title which was sponsored by David Steuart Erskine, the eleventh earl of Buchan, a man who fancied himself a great patron of Scottish literature. Feeling oppressed by the pompous earl and his proposed occasion and having recently read, by way of preparation for his poetic task, William Collins's finely-crafted and intimate 'Ode occasion'd by the death of Mr Thomson' (1749), Burns sensed a disjunction between the set-piece ceremony and the payment of proper tribute to Thomson. As a result he produced a piece which, while sincere in its homage to a poet he read voraciously, is somewhat limp.[1] It ends:

> So long, sweet Poet of the Year,
> Shall bloom that wreath thou well hast won;
> While Scotia, with exulting tear,
> Proclaims that *Thomson* was her son.[2]

Privately, Burns vented a less stylized emotion against Buchan and his kind in a piece that in addressing Thomson is horribly prescient of his own posthumous cultic elevation:

Dost thou not rise, indignant Shade,
    And smile wi' spurning scorn,
When they wha wad hae starv'd thy life,
    Thy senseless turf adorn.–

They wha about thee mak sic fuss
    Now thou art but a name,
Wad seen thee d–mn'd ere they had spar'd
    Ae plack to fill thy wame.–

Helpless, alane, thou clamb the brae,
    Wi' meikle, meikle toil,
And claught th' unfading garland there,
    Thy sair-won, rightful spoil.–[3]

In another instance of ostentatious celebration two decades earlier, the Cape Club of Edinburgh (including among its membership Burns's great predecessor in Scots poetry, Robert Fergusson) was wont patriotically to mark Thomson's birthday.[4] Into the early nineteenth century, Thomson continued to be seen as very special Scottish property, as John Wilson ('Christopher North') claimed approvingly that the poet was beloved by the nation's peasantry so that his work 'lies in many thousand cottages'.[5] By the end of the nineteenth century, however, the wide-reaching admiration for Thomson in Scotland had all but evaporated.

Thomson's fall from favour was assured with the development of the modern Scottish literary critical tradition. The roots of this tradition lie in the musings of Matthew Arnold in the 1860s over the racial pedigree of English poetry. Arnold speculates that this is informed by an 'honesty' which is fundamentally 'Saxon' and an 'energy' taken from 'Celtic' and 'Roman' sources.[6] Famously, Arnold also suggests a Celtic component in English poetry's 'turn for natural magic, for catching and rendering the charm of nature in a wonderfully vivid way'.[7] From the 1880s writers of literary histories of Scotland take Arnold's cue and

emphasize the 'Celtic' spirit of Scotland. The tendency begins
with John Ross's *Scottish History and Literature* (1884) which
points to the 'Celtic fervour and enthusiasm' lying behind
Scotland's national and literary identities.[8] Increasingly, with the
passing of the Victorian age and a renascent cultural nationalism
in Scotland, literary commentators widen their net in the
identification of the 'Celtic' strain and separate the alien 'Saxon'
influence which sometimes is seen inevitably (given Scotland's
problematic, entangled relations with its southern neighbour) to
pollute the Celtic–Scottish psyche. An example of this sleight-
of-hand process is found in George Douglas's *Scottish Poetry*
(1911). Appropriating for the Scots vernacular poets of the
eighteenth century, Allan Ramsay, Robert Fergusson and Robert
Burns, the neo-Celtic qualities of 'native energy, simplicity and
spontaneity', Douglas contrasts an opposing tendency in the
work of cultural émigré James Thomson, whose poetry is held to
take too much of an unfortunate studied or 'academic' turn
which is associated with 'Saxon' England.[9] It is ironic that
Thomson should lose out on his claim to a Celtic poetic gene
given his contemporaneously recognized role in the formation
of the idea of the culture of the ancient Celt/Briton in the
eighteenth century and, clearly, he fails also to be Celticized on a
second count as Arnold's notion of Celtic sensitivity to nature
does little to reinvigorate interest in his work in Scotland. The
irony continues to heap up as, at the beginning of the twentieth
century, several eighteenth-century Scottish Gaelic poets begin
to find renewed favour for their supposedly very 'Celtic' treatment of nature. These include Duncan Ban Macintyre (1724–
1812), Alexander MacDonald (c.1695–c.1770) and Dugald
Buchanan (1716–68) and it is very apparent that all three of these
poets at times draw heavily on Thomson in their detailed description of flora and fauna and in their didacticism.

The crude reading of a natural Celtic/unnatural Saxon bifurca-
tion has formed the basis of Scottish literary canonicity
throughout the twentieth century. To this infirm foundation
critics have added a series of related essentialist co-ordinates
against which James Thomson flounders to prove that he really is
one of 'Scotia's sons'. Indeed, Thomson begins to be seen as one

of the progenitors of an eighteenth-century Scottish anti-canon, whose writers in their iniquity perform one or more of eschewing the Scots language, residing in England, and seeming comfortable with, rather than feeling oppressed by, the 1707 union of Scottish and English parliaments. Damningly, Thomson's emigration to England comes to be seen not simply as an accidental rubbing off of his Celtic–Scottish potential as a writer, but as a deliberate act of materialistic opportunism under the dispensation of the shiny new British state, a motivation in which many other Scots (according to popular English prejudice at the time and much Anglocentric historiography since) were to follow Thomson. This portrayal gains its most forceful recent expression in Andrew Noble's analysis of *The Castle of Indolence*:

> This, to say the least, is a paradoxical creation. It is a poem by a Scotsman written in Spenserian stanzas with an equally contrived archaic vocabulary in praise of British social and political progress extending itself into the realms of a right-eous imperial destiny. Hence the activity of the hero, 'The Knight of Arts and Industry':
>
> > Then towns he quicken'd by mechanic arts,
> > And bade the fervent city glow with toil;
> > Bade social Commerce raise renowned marts,
> > Join land to land, and marry soil to soil,
> > Unite the poles, and without bloody spoil
> > Bring home of either Ind the gorgeous stores;
> > Or, should the despotic rage the world embroil,
> > Bade tyrants tremble on remotest shores.
> > While o'er th' encircling deep Britannia's thunder roars.
>
> Imperial prosperity without guilty blood on its hands certainly belongs more to the world of romance than reality. Thus Thomson's deliberate choice of his medium. Aided by abandoning the tough specificity of his own Scottish language, his 'mythic' poetry veers towards propaganda as it insinuates that the desires of the establishment, of the prop-ertied classes and the economic and social theoreticians, are the reality of eighteenth-century Britain.[10]

The charges of prostituted culture and artistry come no bigger and what follows here in the description of Thomson's Scottish background and his relationship to the poetry of his native land in the eighteenth century is an attempt to counter the claims of Noble and many other hostile Scottish critics. As we shall see, Thomson illuminates, negotiates and works fruitfully with the complex possibilities in the Scottish cultural and literary identity of his day and influences substantially the much approved-of Scots poetry tradition of the eighteenth century. In short, Thomson is both very deeply and very creatively Scottish and offers a challenge to much of the dominant, modern canonizing of Scottish literature and culture.

II

Let us consider the cultural and literary background from which James Thomson emerged.[11] At the beginning of the eighteenth century the Scottish poetic compass was uncertain. Aside from Scottish folk-poetry and ballads (which many commentators, without much evidence, have suggested as influencing the young Thomson), four sites of literary production, together embodying some of the most profound tensions in Scottish culture, can be identified: a Scottish Latinist/humanist intellectual heritage, Scots vernacular verse, Augustan verse in English mimicking the taste south of the border, and a mode of poetry, usually in English, which might be described as Calvinist pietism.[12] This was the bewildering Scottish poetic palette which the young James Thomson would know in his years at Edinburgh College (1715–25).

The Scoto-Latin or humanist strain was propagated by cultural activists across a wide political spectrum, including the pro-Unionist, Hanoverian-supporting, patrician Sir John Clerk of Penicuik (1676–1755) and the anti-Unionist, Jacobite, publisher Thomas Ruddiman (1674–1757). In spite of glaringly different political allegiances, such men had in common a cultural nationalism in which they sought to perpetuate a traditional Scottish commitment to the classic languages and ideas of the West, while asserting the distinctive and unconquerable independence of

the Scottish nation.[13] If Clerk seems ambidextrous in his combination of Unionism and Scottish patriotism, Ruddiman, an
Episcopalian, was no less accommodating of a variety of possibilities in the Scottish identity. He is the producer both of an
edition of George Buchanan, Scotland's great Renaissance
Latinist and a Presbyterian stalwart, and of the *Aeneid* (1710),
which had been translated into middle Scots by the last of the
great 'makars', Gavin Douglas, the early sixteenth-century
Catholic bishop of Dunkeld. Thomson's Latinisms, which were
later to become so notorious, no doubt originate in the very wide
and dedicated context of Scottish humanism, and it may even be
that the aureate texture often pointed to in Thomson's verse
derives in part from his reading the very aureate Scots of Douglas.[14]

More importantly, Thomson drew from the Scoto-Latinist
context an emphatic sense of ancient Scottish racial virility. It was
a common claim in the antiquarian and literary work of Clerk
and in the poetry of pro-Jacobite, anti-Unionists such as Allan
Ramsay (1684–1758) (who was published by Ruddiman and who
had Clerk for his patron), that the Romans had been unable to
overcome the ancient Caledonians. For instance, in a thinly-
disguised medieval 'forgery', 'The Vision' (1724), Ramsay's
narrator moves from contemporary complaint to historical boast,
'Throch feidom our freedom/ Is blotit with this skore,/ Quhat
Romans or no mans/ Pith culd eir do befoir' (ll. 11–14).[15] In a
number of places in his mature career Thomson grafts this
Scottish *mythehistoire* onto the life of an ancient Briton who is
located unspecifically at large in a greater Britannia. For instance,
in *The Castle of Indolence* (1748):

> ... Sir Industry then spread
> The swelling sail, and made for Britain's coast.
> A sylvan life till then the natives led,
> In the brown shades and greenwood forest lost,
> All careless rambling where it liked them most—
> Their wealth the wild-deer bouncing through the glade;
> They lodged at large, and lived at Nature's cost;
> Save spear and bow withouten other aid;
> Yet not the Roman steel their naked breast dismayed
>
> (II, xvii)[16]

Thomson here invests the wider (modern) British nation with an ancient Scottish pedigree of indomitablity and purity. This allows the implication that ancient 'Britannia' was never really part of the Roman world and so not subject to the cultural corruption which was held eventually to consume it. The idea dovetails with the theme of the moral superiority of Britain's commonwealth over that of ancient Rome, prosecuted by Thomson in tandem with a number of contemporary writers (it is especially marked in Thomson's *Britannia* (1729) and *Liberty* (1735–36)).[17] Thomson, then, bolsters from his Scottish mindset the mythic, worthy primitivism in which Britain liked to cloak itself from the beginning of the eighteenth century and this represents a huge act of racial ecumenicalism. 'Sir Industry' arrives in the nation on the basis of a sound moral framework and, while this narrative of rightful British progress can be read as (and certainly later in the hands of others becomes) part of a ferocious strain of imperious and imperial British superiority, in Thomson's hands, well in advance of the worst excesses of the Industrial Revolution or British overseas expansion, it stands for a strongly moral exhortation to honesty, hard work and fairness.[18] Thomson has to be understood as emerging from a variegated cultural background where his beliefs are predicated upon the enmeshing of a confident Scottish humanism and a Real Whig outlook (which is strongly informed by the charitable, communitarian tendencies of Scottish Presbyterianism).[19] Thomson is the new British Virgil as he hails from a far northern part of the commonwealth and brings from there a strongly independent voice proclaiming the 'liberty' which his people had safeguarded in the face of assaults by ancient Rome and, indeed, later by the 'Roman' church. It is an inward-looking moral voice also, which seeks to recognize the concerns of the labouring masses, the backbone of the indomitable nation, as Thomson's anxieties about the vicissitudes suffered by the lower orders throughout his poetry make clear.[20]

The seemingly very different careers of Allan Ramsay and James Thomson are frequently pointed to as indicative of the choices taken by Scots at the beginning of the eighteenth century. Ramsay is the father of the eighteenth-century Scots poetry revival (the second site of literary impetus mentioned above) and an important part of this position is comprised by his famed mock-elegies which combine a scurrilous sexual and toilet humour with a critique of the rapaciously commercial and culturally iconoclastic Britain which Tories accused Whigs of creating. Fleetingly, the young Thomson dabbled in the form in his one known Scots-language work, 'An Elegy upon James Therburn in Chatto'. In this lame piece Thomson ventures a slightly salacious depiction of Therburn, but his heart seems not to be in the kind of bawdy detail so enjoyed by Ramsay and he also evades the larger sociocultural comment which is such a feature of Ramsay's mode. In his mature poetry Thomson's satirical voice is a conventional (even hackneyed) and impersonal one, and from all biographical accounts this would seem to be in keeping with the conventionally moral and rather gentle nature of the man. There is an erotic undercurrent in *The Seasons* which suggests that Thomson was no prude but neither the explicit, full-bodied exploration so beloved by Ramsay in his work nor his pessimistic, high Tory, anti-Calvinist frame of reference would have been likely to appeal to the sincerely Presbyterian Thomson. It is worth adding that Thomson, who would sometimes speak a very broad Scots, would have been much more used to reading (and so writing) literary English and probably even Latin than either the medieval Scots or Ramsay's new-minted Scots poetic idiom which he was becoming aware of in his Edinburgh years.

We have already glimpsed a point of contact between Ramsay and Thomson in their use of Scottish humanism's primitivist patriotism. It is not only Thomson, however, who feeds this stance into a discourse of Britishness. Ramsay, the anti-unionist, also does so. We see this in his Horatian ode, 'To John, the second Duke of Argyll' (1720), celebrating a staunch Hanoverian military commander who fought against the French with the Duke of Marlborough at Malplaquet in 1709. Ramsay yokes Argyll together with one of the greatest of all Scottish heroes, 'Wha can at Bannockburn bauld Bruce display,/ Or thee at Mallplackae forcing thy way?'[21] This poem directly influenced Thomson in one passage in *Autumn* (1730) when he portrayed another great Scottish patriot, Wallace, as the typological ancestor of Argyll.[22]

For both Ramsay and Thomson, then, the martial proclivities of ancient Scotland and modern Britain operate in a continuum.

The points of difference and contact between Ramsay and Thomson are revealing of their national context. Early eighteenth-century Scottish culture and literature are polyphonic and experimental. Ramsay and others writing poetry in Scots are confident innovators rather than marginalized revivers. They often assert the pure and *traditional* nature of their poetry 'revival' (Ramsay to the extent of even fabricating its roots in 'The Vision') but the literary choices they make result in a new poetic confection. Stitching together the patriotic ideals of Scottish humanism, Jacobite and Tory ideology, contemporary Scots *patois*, elements of the literary language and modes of pre-Reformation Scotland (often only half-digested) and elements from Scottish folk-poetry, Ramsay and others fabricated a new 'national' literature. For many Scots (including James Thomson), though, the vehicles and ideology of this mode would not necessarily seem authentically or naturally the only way of being Scottish. Indeed, Ramsay's own espousal of a pan-British identity in 'To Argyll' and elsewhere shows that Scots, particularly those cradled by Scottish humanism, were prone to try some of the different options of identity open to them in the early eighteenth century. Modern Scottish criticism has tended to deal with this fact in the case of Ramsay with the diagnosis of an 'identity crisis' (which has tended to obscure Ramsay's polyglossic literary abilities) and in the case of Thomson's more harmonious-seeming Britishness with the inflexible conclusion that he treacherously assimilates himself to an unScottish identity. We see this when Thomson is berated by Scottish critics for utilizing the archaic and 'English' Spenserian stanza in *The Castle of Indolence*, but his use of this stanza form can be defended, not only on the grounds that it is a very good medium for the musical effects of his poem, but also because he is a Scot. Like Ramsay, Thomson, devoid of any enduring, authoritative, distinctively national Scottish model, is free to indulge in acts of literary retrieval. He turns to Spenser for his model, however, not in a simple act of gratuitous eclecticism but because reading *The Faerie Queene* was part of his formative literary experience, comprising as it did a seminal part of the British Protestant cultural canon.[23] In common with a number of other poets, such as William Shenstone and Gilbert West, Thomson, in *The Castle of Indolence*, repopularizes the Spenserian stanza, but it is the last of these who makes it resonate through British literature in a large-scale production. His chivalric allegory, used as a vehicle for the exploration of the primitive co-ordinates of nationality, feeds the celebration of and anxieties over agrarian life (*The Seasons* is also influential here) in Robert Fergusson and Burns, in William Wordsworth and, later, influences the medievalism of John Keats and others. Thomson, then, encourages a substantial manoeuvre of mythic and sociocultural reappraisal in Britain. Its hallmark is an examination of British roots antecedent to the sectarian strife of the seventeenth century and it is no accident that the plural sensibilities of an early eighteenth-century Scotsman should precipitate such a re-examination.

Thomson's *The Seasons* (1726–30) can also be discussed in the light of its author's Scottish origins. Leaping to the defensive against those who would see this work as too Anglocentric in its setting, some have asserted that Thomson's depiction of landscape is crucially informed by the location of his Scottish borders upbringing. From Thomson's nineteenth-century editor, J. Logie Robertson, to Mary Jane Scott such claims have been pressed, but, apart from several places where the borders locale is explicitly mentioned, these arguments are forced.[24] His landscape is construed from a wide but catholic range of classic Greek and Roman ideas about nature which are set in a largely Miltonic field of rhetoric and theocentricity and intensified by a Newtonian awareness. Thomson's classicism is thoroughly grounded in the Scottish humanist tradition and is not some English affectation. He is steeped in Milton owing to the fact that, for 200 years, an increasingly English-speaking Scotland had lacked any great writers of its own and the views of the dissenting Milton were (like those of Spenser) in large measure in keeping with the Scottish Presbyterian background from which Thomson emerged. And, as John MacQueen has observed, Thomson's scientific precision, which is found in so much of his natural depiction, is partly the result of a Scottish university education much more receptive to Newtonian empiricism in the early eighteenth century than the academies of England.[25] None of these features point to Scottish cultural purity but this is hardly Thomson's fault. He *does* emerge from a culturally problematic (though far from culturally disabled) national background and assembles the materials which are to hand to create his particular poetic vision. Some brief attention to two other sites of eighteenth-century Scottish literary production throw further light on Thomson's emergence from his native context.

Among the less successful attempts at cultural promotion by the multifarious Sir John Clerk was his attempt to propagate a very mainstream type of Augustan poetry in English in Scotland. His *The Country Seat* (1726) is the most fully-flexed attempt of his own and a number of other writers in this area in early eighteenth-century Scotland.[26] James Thomson and David Mallet were asked for their appraisal of the piece in London in 1726 and were rather lukewarm to it, though Thomson in a letter to Clerk, in dealing with this powerful and worthy cultural entrepreneur, can be seen choosing his words carefully.[27] *The Country Seat* delivers 1,600 lines of detailed advice on how to construct a country house and attendant park. It represents a blandly assured rehearsal of urbane Augustan values and preoccupations of a kind which Thomson in his poetry (or indeed any major English Augustan in theirs) was never so complacent about. Thomson is obviously much wider in his poetic treatments of 'improvement', paying attention, for instance, to the difficult transitions in the progress of civilization and the condition of man. (He shows, too, an intense empathy with the plight of animals hunted by country gentlemen and this also indicates his distance from Clerk.) In short, Clerk's poem represents the kind of urbane, arcadian fantasy that undiscriminating Scottish critics have never been slow to attribute wrongly to Thomson in *The Seasons* or *The Castle of Indolence* in evidence of his supposed alien, reality-evading, English Augustan cultural pollution.

A fourth literary site, Calvinist pietism, was the predominant genre of published poetry for much of the eighteenth century in Scotland. Mostly written by Scottish divines, such work was concerned to enjoin either melancholy attention to the condition of man or sentimental attachment to God. (Representative

examples of the maudlin and doom-laden genre include Samuel
Arnot's *Eternity, A Poem* (1711) and James Craig's *Spiritual Life,
Poems* (1727).) Poetry had struggled in Scotland since the
Reformation due to the nation's puritanical Calvinist church, but
in the early eighteenth century a change in attitude was slowly
happening. Against this background, poetry of Calvinist pietism
arises, and against this background Thomson's early mentor and
a man whom he acknowledged as a seminal influence upon the
composition of *Winter*, church-licensate Robert Riccaltoun
(b.1691), wrote poetry. Riccaltoun is far from being as lachry-
mose as most Scottish theologians writing poetry in this period,
but in his work we find a typically anxious attention to the
external world:

> On the cold clift I'll lean my aking head,
> And, pleas'd with winter's waste, unpitying see
> All nature in an agony with me!
> Rough, rugged rocks, wet marshes, ruin'd tow'rs,
> Bare trees, brown brakes, black heaths, and rushy moors,
> Dead floods, huge cataracts, to my pleased eyes
> (Now I can smile!) in wild disorder rise:
> And now the various dreadfulness combin'd
> Black melancholy come to doze my mind.[28]

As James Sambrook has rightly observed of *The Seasons*, 'none of
the interspersed passages of moral reflection has a Scottish [i.e.
Calvinist] cast', but Thomson's close-focus attention to natural
detail emanates perhaps as much from the Newtonian influence,
as from a (usually) more positive reworking of the morbid attention to the external world found in Calvinist pietism.[29] There are
also various points in *The Seasons* where there is a darker underlying note comprising sudden reversals for dumb creatures and
for man, and there is more than a hint that the world is not
entirely to be trusted. In this connection we might compare the
work of Thomson's early colleague in the poetry anthology the
Edinburgh Miscellany (1720), Rev. Robert Blair (1699–1746). His
hugely popular *The Grave* (1743) is a melancholy meditation on
the transience of the physical world which is as luxuriously
painted in its own way as *The Seasons*.

I have been trying to assemble some sense of the variegated and problematic national culture which shapes Thomson's poetic genesis. He draws on a store of primitivist patriotism and classical learning, both things taken from the repository of Scottish humanist scholarship and successfully transported to the south when he emigrates. As a classically-educated Scot he is able to make his important contribution to an Augustan age which is more truly *British* than is often thought. (It is unfortunate that both Scottish and English scholarship has been blind also to Allan Ramsay the Scottish Augustan, since with Thomson, he comprises an important Scottish–British corridor to the ages of neoclassicism and modern British culture.) Thomson's choice of literary materials is also informed by the fact that he is a Presbyterian, an identity that has been frowned upon by Scottish criticism in its recourse to a crude version of the Weber–Tawney thesis, where Scottish Protestantism is read as putting itself at the service of British progress and in the process helping to obliterate indigenous Scottish cultural expression. The fact is, however, that what might look like more genuine Scottish cultural expression at the beginning of the eighteenth century (most notably, the Scots vernacular revival in poetry) is as synthetically-placed as any other strand of the country's literary creativity at this time. To Thomson the Whig, and later the Real Whig, antipathy to the authoritarian high Tory and pro-Stuart principles expressed by a Thomas Ruddiman or an Allan Ramsay was a sincerely held position of more vital importance to what he took to be the central planks of his Scottish culture than the coincidental championing by the Jacobite, anti-Unionists of a Scots-poetry revival. (The triumphalist Whig–Protestant version of British history which essentially postdates Thomson, but appropriates some of his rhetoric of Britishness, tends equally to obscure Thomson's concerns about constructing a moral and socially just commonwealth and to encourage the view that he is an unmitigated optimist with regard to the trajectory of British civilization.) Part of a politico-religious culture, one of several historically aged strands of 'Britishness' (often a dissenting, liberalizing one), Thomson's English language, and his Spenserian and Miltonic frames of reference were unaffected literary choices associated with this culture. At the same time, Thomson's cultural background does present him with at least one problem. The Calvinist hostility to poetry and profane literature is something that provides a warped mode of dominant religious poetry in eighteenth-century Scotland—a culture which accounts for Thomson's emigration to England—but even here Thomson manages to extract from a native influence something to utilize to his own ends. It is from a Scottish culture which is both manifestly plural and problematic that James Thomson emerges.

III

Thomson's influence on eighteenth-century Scottish literature has been seen as largely unhelpful. For some modern commentators he encourages later Scottish writers, by his successful example, to mimic shamelessly the mores of English literature. Even worse, he is seen as a seminal inspiration to a loose line of eighteenth-century Scottish literary creativity which, in its supposed neglect of contemporary Scottish reality, is held to open the door for those notorious nineteenth-century literary vacuums of irresponsible fantasy, 'tartanry' and 'kailyard'. It is true that Thomson's sensitive landscape-painting helps precipitate the close and sometimes cloying treatment of Scottish natural surroundings in the likes of John Home's drama, *Douglas* (1756), James Macpherson's 'Ossian' poems (1760–63) and James Beattie's poem, *The Minstrel* (1771–74) but, like the work of Thomson, none of these texts represents simply a scenic escape route *out of* the real Scotland. Each is motivated by the concern that the primitive (or 'uncivilized') moral and aesthetic sensibilities (things in their formulation which again show the influence of Thomson) ought to be properly regarded in the headlong rush toward 'development' in contemporary Britain. For instance, as Howard D. Weinbrot has shown, the Ossian poems can be read as very much a post-Culloden phenomenon, cautioning against losing wholesale the 'primitive' culture of the Scottish highlands.[30] These texts, born out of a sensitive awareness to the delicacy of Scottish–British culture, are precursors of Romanticism's reservations about modern society. The conservation of a particularly Thomsonian espousal of a primitive sensibility is more particularly seen, however, in the work of the two greatest Scots-language poets of the century, Robert Fergusson and Robert Burns.

Robert Fergusson (1750–74), a member of the Cape Club which held Thomson in such high esteem, and a Scots poet who, but for his tragically early death, might well have eclipsed Robert Burns, left behind him a clutch of truly excellent poems. Strong features of his work include a very sharp eye for climatographical detail and a celebration of peasant life and the pleasant rudiments of this existence. Traditionally, Scottish commentators have seen such 'realistic' concerns as entirely natural given their assumption of the strong roots of eighteenth-century Scots vernacular poetry in a direct and earthy folk tradition and other demotic sources, and it is only in comparatively recent years that the wider *literary* origins of the work of Fergusson and others have begun to receive a more studied attention. F. W. Freeman has pointed in greater detail than anyone to Fergusson's indebtedness to the Scottish Latinist/humanist tradition as part of a wider network of the British Tory mentality.[31] Given the highlighting of this Tory *Weltanschauung*, however, what Freeman underplays is the wider range of ideological strands participating in the Scottish humanist project and so 'Whigs' such as James Thomson receive scant attention as disseminators of the largely conservative ideals of eighteenth-century humanism. This is an oversight which dovetails with a long-standing distinction in eighteenth-century English literary studies which crudely opposes Tory humanists and optimists, usually Whigs, who welcome new trends of economic and cultural progress with much less reservation.

Thomson's influence on Fergusson, including an impetus toward Fergusson's finely drawn details of the natural environment and his portrayal of peasant life, has been undervalued. A number of key depictions frequently associated with the ideals of Tory humanism are to be found in a beautiful passage of *Winter* (1726) and this passage, clearly, had a particular impact upon

Robert Fergusson. Lines 572–645 encompass, in a wide panoramic sweep (a poetic movement in which Fergusson also specialized), the themes of sheltering in human company from the elements, looking for the underlying harmony of the world, patriotism, peasant virtue and the city swarming with folly and foppery. These themes comprise a compendium of Fergusson's major poetic themes, but to take only one area of influence, part of the passage informs the fabric of one of Fergusson's greatest pieces, 'The Farmer's Ingle' (1773) (a poem which is the major inspiration for Burns's 'The Cottar's Saturday Night'). Lines 617–20 of *Winter*, where the narrator looks on with enjoyment on the titillating telling of ghost stories in the village, stand behind the telling of similar sensational stories in the homely cottage in Fergusson's poem (ll. 59–63). (It is interesting to contrast Thomson's generally indulgent treatment of the supernatural traditions of the country with the man who is more obviously Fergusson's antecedent in the attention to the culture of the lower classes, Allan Ramsay. Ramsay in respect of the supernatural is much more of a rationalist than Thomson and is usually dimissive of it.) Of larger importance to the anthropological exploration and cultural commitment of 'The Farmer's Ingle' is the influence of *The Castle of Indolence*. Thematically Fergusson takes from Thomson (*cf.* Canto II, Stanzas LIII–LVIII) the notion of the farming labourer as living the life of the healthy body and the healthy mind and forming the nation's martial backbone:

> Frae this lat gentler gabs a lesson lear;
>> Wad they to labouring lend an eidant hand,   [busy
> They'd rax fell strang upo' the simplest fair,   [grow
>> Nor find their stamacks ever at a stand.
> Fu' hale and healthy wad they pass the day,
>> At night in calmest slumbers dose fu' sound,
> Nor doctor need their weary life to spae,   [foretell
>> Nor drogs their noddle and their sense confound,
>> Till death slip sleely on, and gi'e the hindmost wound.
>
> On sicken food has mony a doughty deed
>> By Caledonia's ancestors been done;

By this did mony wight fu' weirlike bleed
   In brulzies frae the dawn to set o' sun: [broils
'Twas this that brac'd their gardies, stiff and strang,   [arms
   That bent the deidly yew in ancient days,
Laid Denmark's daring sons on yird alang,   [earth
   Gar'd Scottish thristles bang the Roman bays;
   For near our crest their heads they doughtna raise.[32]

Fergusson also takes the Spenserian stanza from Thomson and this represents an interesting cultural 'interchange'. He makes it the vehicle for a new 'high' Scots poetic production with his highly serious attention to the peasant theme and a rather Miltonic syntax which is something else he imbibed from Thomson. What we see, then, is part of the programme of the regeneration of Scots vernacular poetry in form and theme which Fergusson was accomplishing almost single-handedly at this time. In a nice circle, the idea of the virtuous primitive patriot which Thomson had taken with him to England is re-imported to Scotland along with an 'English' poetic technology and these things are used to re-energize a strand of Scottish literature which some commentators have claimed to stand in complete antipathy to the literary and cultural sensibilities of James Thomson.

As we have seen already, Robert Burns (1759–96) expresses himself with great feeling over the poetic career of James Thomson and it is surely because of his own painful realization of the enduring difficulties of being a poet in Scotland (financially, with a disapproving church looking on, and having to make sense of a range of possible literary directions) that he sees his predecessor's émigré achievement as 'helpless' and 'sair-won'. Burns, for his own part, was very well aware of the greater poetic help, at least, at hand to him by the late eighteenth century, comprising not only the great Scots-poetry impetus of Ramsay and Fergusson, but also the artistic sensibility of James Thomson himself. (Along with Pope, these three Scottish writers make up the four poets whose influence is felt most largely in Burns.) Indeed, it is the Thomsonian influence which presides over Burns's most important early written attempts to articulate his creative self. In a letter to his former tutor, John Murdoch, in June 1783, Burns locates his imaginative propensities, primed by his favourite reading, as a counterpoint to the humble reality he inhabits:

> ... the man whose heart distends with benevolence to all the human race—he 'who can soar above this little scene of things'—can he descend to mind the paultry concerns about which the terrae-filial race fret, and fume, and vex themselves? O how the glorious triumph swells my heart! I forget that I am a poor, insignificant devil, unnoticed and unknown, stalking up and down fairs and markets when I happen to be in them, reading a page or two of mankind, and 'catching the manners living as they rise', whilst the men of business jostle me on every side, as an idle encumbrance in their way.[33]

Burns quotes *Autumn* (l. 966) and associates Thomsonian 'soaring' with both benevolence and objectivity of vision, though the appropriation of these qualities for himself is clearly delivered with a conceited pride. He is both adopting a Thomsonian persona in this passage (the use of the manneristic 'terrae-filial race', so typical of Thomson, confirms this), and, at the same time, he casts himself almost as a country character in *The Seasons* as he views himself at fairs and markets being jostled by the 'men of business'. What we have here is a very good identification of the significance of one of Thomson's master poetic strategies (casting a sympathetic eye widely over the world), an identification which may have been helped by Burns's reading of Adam Smith in *The Theory of Moral Sentiments* (1759) where Smith saw Thomson as overwrought in his attention to the misfortunes of others.[34] Looking with a minutely sympathetic eye at the world is something that Burns is very much drawn toward by Thomson. His most obviously Thomsonian work is 'The Vision' (1784).[35] The poem is an attempt to make sense of the heritage of Scottish culture and Burns's own poetic vocation as it combines the 'standard habbie' stanza which he had picked up from Ramsay and Fergusson as indicating a Scottish cultural signature, Ramsay's visionary topos found in his poem of the same name, and a panoramic and quasi-mystical view of the topography and achievement of Scotland which represents, more than anything, an importation of the methodology of the Thomsonian poetic eye. The narrator, alone after a hard day's farm-labouring and cursing his useless propensity for writing verse, goes into a dwam and is awakened by Coila (the spirit presiding over Burns's native Kyle) who shows him in her robe a vision of the beauties of the Scottish landscape, some hints of its ancient Pictish and English-resisting history and its contemporary British martial, political, philosophical and poetic heroes. Coila shows him 'the great Genius of this Land' (l. 145), its 'Arts' and 'Arms' (l. 149), so that Scotland is seen as a place of both thought and action. Its lush land is fertile in producing philosophers, poets (including Thomson), politicians and soldiers who contribute, clearly, to the wider British good. Scotland is presented, then, as a repository of staple cultural values which balance its material underdevelopment where the narrator is 'half-fed, half-sarket' (l. 29). The narrator is assured also of his poetic role by Coila. In a Thomsonian flourish—*The Seasons* in miniature as Carol McGuirk has observed[36]—Coila says that she has been watching over him:

'I saw thee seek the sounding shore,
'Delighted with the dashing roar;
'Or when the North his fleecy store
        'Drove thro' the sky,
'I saw grim nature's visage hoar,
        'Struck thy young eye.

'Or when the deep-green-mantl'd Earth,
'Warm-cherish'd ev'ry floweret's birth,
'And joy and music pouring forth,
        'In ev'ry grove,
'I saw thee eye the gen'ral mirth
        'With boundless love.

'When ripen'd fields, and azure skies,
'Call'd forth the Reaper's rustling noise,
'I saw thee leave their ev'ning joys,
        'And lonely stalk,
'To vent thy bosom's swelling rise,
        'In pensive walk.   (ll. 211–28)

This sets the scene for the narrator to be told not to despair because he too is part of the nation's cultural fabric; he is a 'rustic bard' (l. 196) whose role is to sing of the ways of the Ayrshire countryside.

Burns's facility to oversee and bring together the cultural landscape of his country in 'The Vision' is analogous to the overview of the British cultural landscape, and its integral primitive elements in particular, which is such a hallmark of all Thomson's long poetry. Burns's synthesis of diverse poetic elements is a lesson which he also takes from Thomson in an act of instinctive logic while synthesizing diverse thematic elements. Burns the bard is observed by Coila in a Thomsonian seasonal landscape and this is a sly manoeuvre—perhaps more conscious than in the letter cited above—where Burns both soars above and looks down upon himself. His role as peasant-poet is contextualized with direct recourse to Thomson (along with several other poets cited in the poem who promulgate the treatment of nature as a central concern) and so Burns constructs his location for himself in a curiously literary gambit. Burns is in reality a peasant farmer but his poetic status as widely received rustic bard is largely allowed by the sympathetic attention to nature and the primitive sensibility precipitated so pre-eminently by Thomson. Clearly, it is with some slyness that Burns manipulates the movement toward nature in British literature. In a sense he takes advantage of his identity as a countryman to produce poems which are for the most part sophisticated literary works and it is Thomson who helps him to do this.

Numerous incidental and several larger examples show the substantial Thomsonian input to Burns's peasant sensibility. One of his earliest songs, 'Song, composed in August' (c.1776) draws on Thomson's sympathy for hunted animals, most especially on one passage in *Autumn*, as an integral part of a piece which makes plain the ambidextrous relationship of man as both pastor and exploiter of nature:

> Thus ev'ry kind their pleasure find,
>   The savage and the tender;
> Some social join, and leagues combine;
>   Some solitary wander:

Avaunt, away! the cruel sway,
　Tyrannic man's dominion;
The Sportsman's joy, the murd'ring cry,
　The flutt'ring, gory pinion!　　　　　(ll.17–24)[37]

Burns's treatment of the country often echoes very directly the
phraseology and the sensibility of Thomson. Burns's sharp
country eye, which is frequently adduced by critics and by the
legion popular commentary on Burns, often turns out to come
from a Thomsonian source. For instance, 'The Holy Fair' (1785)
has a small example of this detail-painting of Burns which is so
heavily schooled in Thomson.[38] The narrator pictures a morning
where 'The hares were hirplin down the furrs' (l. 7) and this
is directly drawn from *Summer*: 'And from the bladed field
the fearful hare/ Limps awkward' (ll. 57–58). In one of many
examples of Burns imbibing what he took to be the essential
Thomsonian spirit of 'philosophic melancholy', a very fine use of
nature contextualizes the heavy circumstances of human life.[39]
As Carol McGuirk has pointed out, perhaps the finest and
certainly the most famous stanza in Burns' song, 'Man was made
to Mourn, A Dirge' (1785):

Many and sharp the num'rous Ills
　Inwoven with our frame!
More pointed still we make ourselves,
　Regret, Remorse and Shame!
And Man, whose heav'n-erected face,
　The smiles of love adorn,
Man's inhumanity to Man
　Makes countless thousands mourn!　　(ll. 49–56)[40]

is based on some lines from *Winter*, which if made by Burns into
something better, share a very similar sensitivity toward
humanity:

How many feel, this very moment, death
And all the sad variety of pain;
How many sink in the devouring flood,
Or more devouring flame; how many bleed,
By shameful variance betwixt man and man　　(ll. 327–31)

The Thomsonian spirit of attending to the common man helps feed a strong anthropological technique in both Fergusson and Burns (which is not found in Ramsay) and is integral to some of Burns's most famous poems about his immediate environment. 'The Cotter's Saturday Night' (1785–86) features a sharply-drawn portrait of the most humble but dignified and philosophical human activity amid a difficult natural environment.[41] Perhaps less directly drawn from Thomson but even more importantly owing to his seminal influence, the notion of the Scottish peasantry as the moral and patriotic backbone of the country which Fergusson, in 'The Farmer's Ingle' had taken from Thomson's treatment of the British peasantry, is here passed to Burns and so a strong line of Scottish writers attending to popular culture is drawn right through the eighteenth century and plays a major part in the encouragement to the new focus of Romanticism. The intense sentimental sympathy with one's fellow man and even one's fellow creatures which Adam Smith found overdone in Thomson, was something which Burns had no such qualms about. Indeed, Burns can pursue such sympathy to an injudicious degree of a kind which is found nowhere in Thomson, when he writes 'To a Mountain-Daisy' (1786), ludicrously lamenting the fact that his plough has destroyed a very common flower.[42] Much more happy effects of a generally Thomsonian impetus are 'To a Mouse' (1785) and 'To a Louse' (1785).[43] The first of these poems features a very unpeasant-like attitude to dumb beasts, which we have already seen Burns imbibing from Thomson, and a completing of the circle so that the plight of an animal registers the plight of man (the drawing out of what Ruskin would term pathetic fallacy which is so famously absent in Thomson). The mouse has lost his house under an unthinking plough and the poet reflects upon the thoughtless actions of distant landlords who can equally ruin the tenant farmer. Thomson, then, feeds Burns's sensibilities of political protest and also, as we have seen in several examples above, a rather melancholy, morbid outlook, which, present in Thomson, is cranked up in Burns. If 'Man was made to Mourn' represents a feeling rendition of the fragility of the natural condition and 'To A Mountain-Daisy' provides a silly version of it, 'To a Louse' is one of Burns's most deeply thoughtful and deeply felt treatments of mortality. The sympathy in the poem is extended, in mock-fashion, to the conceited and unknowing woman upon whom the louse crawls while she is at church and, in an equally empty gesture, the presumption of the louse is berated. The poem resolves itself, however, with the sombre contemplation of the fact that the human world is simply part of the natural world and that it is humanity in its airs and graces which is presumptuous in attempting to separate itself off from this world. As is often pointed out, the most famous lines of the poem, 'O wad some Pow'r the giftie gie us/ To see oursels as others see us' (ll. 43–44) are a version of Adam Smith's philosophical recommendation to objectivity and placing ourselves in the position of others. However, the very melancholy frame of reference in the poem which accompanies such cool judgement derives from a line of sentimental engagement with nature which has its origins in the poetry of James Thomson more than anyone else.

Thomson's influence upon the canonical Scots poets of the eighteenth century is much more telling than is usually thought to be the case. The critical purblindness of his native land, however, has meant that we are only now in the early days of seeing Thomson's centrality to the poetic project and persona of Burns and the cultural vision of Fergusson. Equally, Thomson's complex and easily misunderstood identity as both a Scot and a Briton must be appreciated if we are to restore the poet to his proper native context and to understand his stature as the first truly British poet in modern history. In this sense, Thomson now presents an urgent challenge to the literary historians of both Scottish and English poetry.

NOTES

1. See *The Letters of Robert Burns*, vol. II (Oxford, 1985), ed. J. De Lancey Ferguson; 2nd ed. G. Ross Roy, pp. 102, 106 & 442. Hereafter referred to as *Burns's Letters*.

2. *The Poems and Songs of Robert Burns* (Oxford, 1968), ed. James Kinsley, poem no. 331. All subsequent citations are from this edition.

3. Burns, *Poems*, no. 332.

4. See *Poems of Robert Fergusson*, ed. Matthew McDiarmid (Edinburgh & London, 1954), I, p.55.

5. Quoted in Mary Jane Scott, *James Thomson, Anglo-Scot* (Athens & London, 1988), p. 7.

6. Matthew Arnold, *On the Study of Celtic Literature* (1867) in *The Complete Prose Works of Matthew Arnold*, vol. 3: 'Lectures and Essays in Criticism' (Ann Arbor & Toronto, 1962), ed. R. H. Super, p. 341.

7. Arnold, *Celtic Literature*, p. 361.

8. John Ross, *Scottish History and Literature* (Glasgow, 1884), p. 2.

9. George Douglas, *Scottish Poetry* (Glasgow, 1911), pp. 66 and 155.

10. Andrew Noble, 'Urbane Silence: Scottish Writing and the Nineteenth-Century City' in *Perspectives of the Scottish City*, ed. George Gordon (Aberdeen, 1985), p. 66.

11. James Sambrook in *James Thomson 1700–1748, A Life* (Oxford, 1991) and Scott, *James Thomson*, both provide good accounts of Thomson in his formative years; the diverse cultural context of Scotland in this time, however, especially with regard to poetry, remains under-analysed.

12. My identification of these modes, in particular, is based on research into the poetry collections at the National Library of Scotland and, especially, *The Catalogue of the Scottish Poetry Collection*, vols I & II, for the Mitchell Library, Glasgow.

13. Details of the career of John Clerk of Penicuik are to be found in Iain Gordon Brown, 'Modern Rome and Ancient Caledonia: The Union and the Politics of Scottish Culture' in *History of Scottish Literature Volume 2: 1660–1800*, ed. Andrew Hook (Aberdeen, 1987), pp. 33–48; for Thomas Ruddiman, see Douglas Duncan, *Thomas Ruddiman, A Study in Scottish Scholarship of the Early Eighteenth Century* (Edinburgh, 1965).

14. The connecting of Thomson and Douglas has been a battleground through the years for those arguing over the essential continuities in the Scottish literary tradition. The two most extreme positions are represented by John Speirs and Mary Jane Scott. Speirs writes: 'It may not have been an accident that the poet of the *Seasons* was like the poet [Douglas] of these Prologues [Douglas' prefatory material to his translation of the books of the *Aeneid*], a Scotsman, but though a Scotsman Thomson was not a Scots poet. That in itself sets Thomson and Douglas so far apart as to make the comparison between them, sometimes recommended, of little help. Unlike Thomson's Miltonic English, the unScottish elements in the literary language Douglas inherited could not prevent him from being a Scots poet even in his summer.' (*The Scots Tradition in Literature: An Essay in Criticism* (London, 1962), 2nd ed., p. 75).

Scott, *James Thomson*, has argued most closely for the linguistic influence of Douglas on Thomson, see pp. 100–01 and *passim*, and, indeed, for a

Scots cadence, generally, in Thomson's poetry, see especially pp. 182–203. If Scott's argument is sometimes forced, Speirs is too dismissive of the cultural connection. It seems implausible to me that Douglas's adoption of the mantle of Virgil, a poet of the rustic north in relation to Rome (and from a region on the fringes of the Celtic world in Romanocentric ethnic theory), did not point the way to Thomson's deeply Virgilian poetic master-persona in *The Seasons*. This choice would be especially resonant in the climate of classically-informed cultural nationalism in early eighteenth-century Scotland, given the nation's relations with a more powerful, allied southern culture.

15. *The Works of Allan Ramsay*, ed. A. M. Kinghorn and Alexander Law (Edinburgh & London, 1961), III, p. 81.

16. All quotations and citations of Thomson's poetry are taken from the Oxford University Press editions edited by James Sambrook.

17. For an excellent account of this tendency, see Howard Weinbrot, *Britannia's Issue: The Rise of British Literature from Dryden to Ossian* (Cambridge, 1993), pp. 237–75.

18. Thomson's patriotic and moral mode begins to change in the hands of others within a few years of his death. This is particularly true in Scotland, where imitators welded to his themes and style a xenophobia and a Protestant triumphalism alien to Thomson; see, for instance, Rev. Robert Dysart Colvill, *Britain, A Poem* (Edinburgh, 1757).

19. Thomson's allegiance to the 'Real Whigs' and the Scottish background to this is inadequately understood. One scholar who has an appreciation of this context, but who places Thomson in it only in passing, is Caroline Robbins. See her *The Eighteenth-Century Commonwealthman* (Cambridge, MA, 1961), pp. 220 and 258–59.

20. See *Winter*, ll. 276–388.

21. Kinghorn & Law, *Works of Allan Ramsay*, III, p. 341.

22. See *Autumn*, ll. 894–938.

23. James Sambrook, *James Thomson 1700–1748, A Life* (Oxford, 1991), p. 264.

24. See Scott, *James Thomson*, esp. pp. 113–45.

25. See John MacQueen, *Progress and Poetry: The Enlightenment and Scottish Literature* (Edinburgh, 1982), pp. 56–65.

26. 'The Country Seat' is to be found in several manuscript versions in the 'Clerk of Penicuik Papers', West Register House, Edinburgh.

27. See *James Thomson (1700–48) Letters and Documents*, ed. A. D. McKillop (Lawrence, KA, 1958), pp. 58–60.

28. Robert Riccaltoun's poem, 'A Winter's Day', which may have been the poem Thomson alludes to as a particular inspiration, is helpfully reprinted in Scott, *James Thomson*, pp. 297–99.

29. Sambrook, *Thomson, A Life*, p. 36.

30. Weinbrot, *Britannia's Issue*, pp. 526–41.

31. F. W. Freeman, *Robert Fergusson and the Scots Humanist Compromise* (Edinburgh, 1985).

32. Robert Fergusson, 'The Farmer's Ingle', in *Poems by Allan Ramsay & Robert Fergusson*, ed. A. M. Kinghorn and A. Law (Edinburgh, 1985), pp. 161–64.

33. *Burns's Letters*, I, 17–18.

34. Adam Smith, *The Theory of Moral Sentiments*, ed. D. D. Raphael & A. L. Macfie (Indianapolis, 1976), p. 139.

35. Burns, *Poems*, no. 62.

36. Carol McGuirk, *Robert Burns and the Sentimental Era* (East Linton, 1997), p. 40.

37. Burns, *Poems*, no. 2; see *Autumn*, ll. 360–79.

38. Burns, *Poems*, no. 70.

39. Burns highlights the phrase (used by Thomson in *Autumn*, l. 1005, in a rather different way), in a letter of January 1788 to Agnes McLehose, to indicate what he takes to be sensitivity to the fragility of human happiness: *Burns's Letters*, I, 209.

40. McGuirk, *Sentimental Era*, p. 168. McGuirk picks up a strong Thomsonian influence which had hitherto gone unnoticed despite James Kinsley's excellent commentary volume, *The Poems and Songs of Robert Burns*, vol. III (Oxford, 1968). Kinsley picks up many Thomsonian echoes across around 40 poems but it seems that even he fails to be anything like exhaustive and many influences are missed; for instance, to take one very small example which I have noticed, 'Tam o' Shanter' (Burns, *Poems*, no. 321) pictures Tam's wife Kate 'Gathering her brows like gathering storm,/ Nursing her wrath to keep it warm'; *cf.* 'Of driving tempest is for ever heard:/ Here the grim tyrant meditates his wrath' (*Winter*, ll. 897–98).

41. Burns, *Poems*, no.72.

42. Burns, *Poems*, no.92.

43. Burns, *Poems*, nos. 69 and 83.

Britannia's Heart of Oak:
Thomson, Garrick and the Language
of Eighteenth-Century Patriotism

TIM FULFORD

Immediately before the battle of Trafalgar, the sailors of Nelson's fleet were mustered to their stations as the drums beat out the rhythm of a song written by David Garrick for an earlier war:

> Hearts of Oak are our ships, jolly Tars are our men
> > We ever are ready
> > Steady boys, steady
> We'll fight and we'll conquer again and again.[1]

Singing 'Hearts of Oak' was a communal declaration of courage in Nelson's navy. So was the performance of Thomson's 'Rule Britannia', which confidently declared that foreign 'strokes' served only to strengthen Britain's 'native oak'.[2] Both songs were made part of the ceremonial of war by officers keen to foster self-confidence in the crew. Sung by men whose oaken ships were about to face gunfire at close quarters, they voiced their belief in themselves, in their vessels, and in their nation.

That 'Hearts of Oak' was sung was a testament to the enduring power and popularity of the oak as a symbol in eight-eenth-century Britain. Nelson's sailors were bonding themselves to a myth of national character in which the navy, and the oak from which its ships were made, were seen as the embodiment of British manliness. Their hearts, as well as their ships, would be of oak, if the song had its intended effect. And they would be of British oak, which British naval historians thought stronger than European oak:

> It is a striking, but well-known fact, that oak, the growth of other countries, though lying under precisely the same

latitude with Britain, has been invariably found less service-
able, in a degree almost incredible, than that of the latter, as
though nature itself, if it were possible to indulge so
romantic an idea, had forbad that the national character of a
British ship should be suffered to undergo a species of
degradation by being built of materials which were [not]
indigenous to it.[3]

If the sober and empiricist John Charnock thought himself
'romantic' in indulging the idea, he nevertheless found reasons to
believe in its truth. The strength of British oak stemmed from
the fact that it was not usually grown in tightly planted woods,
but in more isolated situations where it had weathered
'tempests', acquiring 'the power of long defiance to those ravages
of time which would ... prove destructive to the upstart plant'.[4]
Nelson agreed, but worried that his nation was no longer
producing the close-grained timber necessary if his fleet was to
triumph over the huge ships of France and Spain. In 1803 he
compiled a report on the Forest of Dean, drawing its 'deplorable'
state to 'the serious consideration of every lover of his country'.
He recommended that government 'form a plan to purchase ...
the growing oak' on gentlemen's estates, to save it from being
felled early.[5] Nelson had good reason: the gentry were clearing
their parks and woods to raise cash to meet the burden of
wartime taxation. Felled too young, their oaks were of little use
for the massive and crooked timbers needed for naval construction (and a ship of the line consumed between two and three
thousand oaks).[6] The navy became so short of timber that
Nelson was only able to muster sufficient ships at Trafalgar by
virtue of last minute repairs using imported fir rather than British
oak. He did not live to see it, but nineteenth-century govern-
ments responded by instituting a determined planting drive
specifically geared to the needs of the navy.

Nelson and Charnock were expert on the material properties
of oak. In giving it symbolic properties as well, they were perpet-
uating a myth which was not only nationalist but conservative. It
was a myth dating from Charles II's escape, via the sheltering
branches of an oak tree, after the battle of Worcester. Garrick and
Thomson helped to popularize it but Nelson, in life and death,

placed it at the heart of Britons' beliefs about themselves and their history. In his last days in England before rejoining his fleet, Nelson went to hear the tenor John Braham sing the songs that had made him popular: 'Hearts of Oak' and 'Rule Britannia'.[7] In 1811 Braham returned the compliment by singing 'The Death of Nelson' to great acclaim. This song celebrated Trafalgar as a victory of native growth, despite the irony that Nelson's ships were patched with imported wood: 'We scorn'd the foreign yoke,/ Our Ships were British oak,/ And hearts of oak our men'.[8]

By 1814 the oak was firmly rooted in popular perceptions about Britain's military history and national character. Celebrations of Napoleon's defeat in the seafaring village of Clovelly involved decorating the houses with oak branches as well as singing 'God Save the King' and 'Rule Britannia'. Yet, as the villagers' choice of Thomson's song indicates, the oak-symbol had already enjoyed a considerable life by the time that Nelson popularized it again. It was a life that cannot be separated from what Gillian Russell has called the 'struggle for the meaning of patriotism' in the eighteenth century.[9] In that struggle the oak came to be used as a political icon by Patriot politicians, by the Whig gentry, and by reformers and radicals. The oak was a contested symbol: when reformers used it to define the people as a whole it had already been associated with Stuart monarchs and then with gentlemanly government. Nurtured by Jacobites, it later grew under the hands of Hanoverian Whigs into a symbol of the Britain that was thought to have resulted from the constitutional settlement of 1688—a Britain of rooted traditions which changed slowly and organically, a Britain strong and independent, capable of resisting sudden shocks. For Edmund Burke in 1790 the tree symbolized a Britain rightly dominated by its aristocracy and gentry, on whose estates the oak grew. Land, passed down the generations, gave gentlemen the capacity to take the long and disinterested view of the national benefit that fitted them for rule. Burke depicted Britain's form of government as tree-like, of ancient growth: it 'moves on through the varied tenour of perpetual decay, fall, renovation and progression' in 'the method of nature'.[10] The people were 'great cattle reposed beneath the shadow of the British oak'—protected by a constitution rooted enough to resist revolutionary disturbances like that occurring in France.[11]

Others made the nationalism and the conservatism of the tree still more explicit. For the shipwright Roger Fisher, warning of the looming timber crisis in 1763, 'the welfare of our king and country, our religion, laws and liberty depend[ed] upon' the propagation of oaks.[12] Robert Southey, Tory apologist and Poet Laureate, wrote of order depending on men 'whose names and families are older in the country than the old oaks upon their estates'.[13] He also wrote an idealizing biography of Nelson which lauded the admiral for his strength of character. Oak-like Nelson and his oaken ships had become the heroic embodiments of a Britishness made possible by a constitution that fostered gentlemanly resolution and paternalism.

At least, that was the myth which Burke, Southey and Nelson himself helped to propagate. It was first defined, however, much earlier in the eighteenth century. In 1744 Thomson politicized the oak, along with the gentlemanly landscape in which it stood, as he paid tribute to his patron Lyttelton sitting in Hagley Park

> beneath the Shade
> Of solemn Oaks, that tuft the swelling Mounts
> Thrown graceful round by Nature's careless Hand
> ('Spring', ll. 914–16)[14]

The oaks give seriousness to the philosophizing of their owner; they shelter his patriotic concern for his country for he is

> Planning, with warm Benevolence of Mind
> And honest Zeal, unwarp'd by Party-Rage,
> BRITANNIA's Weal; how from the venal Gulph
> To raise her Virtue and her Arts revive.
> ('Spring', ll. 928–31)

Lyttelton's views are made to ascend through the landscape of Britain from which they spring: from the oak nursery the patriot rises to ever wider prospects of his nation. He stands on the hilltop, seeing his countrymen sheltered as he himself was in 'villages embosom'd soft in Trees' (l. 953).

In his description of Hagley, Thomson was naturalizing the

politics of the Patriot opponents of Walpole and George II who
had been grouped around the Prince of Wales. This grouping
included several suspected of Jacobitism. And one of the
emblems of the Stuart dynasty had been the oak, which
continued as late as 1750 to appear on Jacobite tokens of loyalty
to Charles Edward Stuart.[15] But Thomson eschews any Jacobite
reference, instead converting the oak into a symbol of non-
factional loyalty to the native land. This was in line with the
attempt by the Patriot Whigs and Tories to refute acccusations of
Jacobitism and of self-interest by presenting their opposition to
Walpole as motivated by a loyalty to their country which
subsumed party affiliations. They had explicitly offered this
loyalty to the Hanoverian Prince of Wales, rather than the
Stuarts over the water. He had publicly accepted its non-factional
patriotism by patronizing both Whigs and Tories at his court.
Lyttelton, one of the courtiers, is here portrayed as a natural
patriot, because his political views seem simply part of the scene.
In Thomson's verse they are views springing from a recognizably
British landscape, in which the oak shows the statesman's desire
to protect the land and its people to have grown naturally from
his British nature. What had been a symbol of the Stuart
monarchs' paternal strength is now conferred upon the
gentleman landowner and politician, so that he too seems strong,
paternalist and disinterested. The Royal Oak becomes the gentlemanly oak.

In *The Seasons* oaks were the natural protectors of Britain's
rural heart: 'the grey-grown Oaks/ (That the calm Village in their
verdant Arms,/ Sheltering, embrace)' ('Summer', ll. 225–27).
They were also the guardians of its commerce. Thomson was
excited by the strength and power of the warships being built on
the Thames: they were monarchs of a forest of shipping.

> On either Hand,
> Like a long wintry Forest, Groves of Masts
> Shot up their Spires; the bellying Sheet between
> Possess'd the breezy Void; the sooty Hulk
> Steer'd sluggish on; the splendid Barge along
> Row'd regular, to Harmony; around,
> The Boat, light-skimming, stretch'd its oary Wings;

While deep the various Voice of fervent Toil
From Bank to Bank increas'd; whence ribb'd with Oak
To bear the B R I T I S H   T H U N D E R, black, and bold,
The roaring Vessel rush'd into the Main.
                                        ('Autumn', ll. 123–33)

The Patriot politicians were critics of Walpole's reluctance to
make full-scale war on Spain despite its interference with British
merchant shipping. This portrait of warships as protectors of the
forest suggests that a failure to use them to defend trading vessels
was an offence against the natural order. In *Liberty* (1735–36)
Thomson made the accusation explicitly, fearing ministerial
corruption and sloth would let Britannia's '*Naval Oak* be basely
torn,/ By such as tremble at the stiffening Gale' (V, 313–14).[16] In
Britannia (1729) he declared it Britain's destiny to 'on the sea be
terrible, untam'd,/ Unconquerable still' (ll. 179–80) in order to
teach other nations to respect its power and wealth. Nature had
ordained it:

For this, your oaks, peculiar harden'd, shoot
Strong into sturdy growth; for this your hearts
Swell with a sullen courage, growing still
As danger grows; and strength, and toil for this
Are liberal pour'd o'er all the fervent land.
Then cherish this, this unexpensive power,
Undangerous to the publick, ever prompt,
By lavish Nature thrust into your hand.   (ll. 200–07)

Here Thomson formulates the myth that both Nelson and
Charnock were to take up. British courage is inspired by visions
of naval power and founded on British nature: the stubborn resolution of the men grows just as the uniquely hard and sturdy
native oaks do. From here it was only a short voyage to Trafalgar
and the singing of 'Hearts of Oak' on deck.

If the voyage was short, this particular oaken vessel was not
yet ready to sail. What Thomson had not achieved in his poetry
which espoused the arguments of the anti-Walpole Patriot politicians was a genuinely popular vision of British character. *The
Seasons* found public success as a loco-descriptive, rather than
political, poem: Thomson's endorsement of patriotism appeared

uncontroversial because it seemed to grow naturally from the landscapes that were described in detail. In *Liberty*, however, he made political points at the expense of particularized portrayals of landscape. And he identified patriotism closely with politicians grouped around the Prince of Wales who were suspected of jockeying for power. When, after Walpole's political demise, some of those politicians abandoned the Prince and accepted places in a ministry led by men they had formerly attacked as corrupt and self-interested, their former protestations of patriotism seemed hollow. So did Thomson's poetic praise of them. The poem flopped, critically and commercially.

Out of the failure of his Patriot writing came one success— 'Rule Britannia!', which appeared in *Alfred: A Masque*, the play Thomson co-authored with Mallet in 1740. Like 'Hearts of Oak', this song took on a life beyond its original context and beyond the printed book. *Alfred* was revived in 1745 by the composer of its music, Thomas Arne, with 'Rule Britannia' repositioned as the grand finale. 'Rule Britannia' was sold in the streets in broadsides and was performed, as it still is, in concerts. It was sung in theatres by actors and audience, uniting the gentlemanly occupants of boxes with the common people watching from the gods. It formed the climax of dramatic entertainments designed to commemorate naval successes. In 1794 Admiral Howe's victory was celebrated at Drury Lane with *The Glorious First Of June*, a 'spectacular' in which the battle was recreated using model ships and a water tank. 'The conclusion was a brilliant display of Fireworks, one of which exhibited the words RULE BRITANNIA in capital characters, a shower of fire descending from each letter, while the Song was given by the performers in full chorus'.[17] Here singing the song made the actors and theatregoers like the victorious sailors who sang 'Rule Britannia' on their ships—the theatre united in the patriotic image (or rather voice) of the navy. Conversely, Howe's and Nelson's sailors, when they sang Thomson's and Garrick's words between decks, made their ships into theatres in which a communal patriotic role was assumed and enacted. The sailors translated songs sung about them in the theatres of Britain into songs by which they defined their role in the theatre of war. They would act for the nation as actors had sung of them acting, consciously matching their deeds to the words of the songs. After a complicity of ideology and action as close as this it is not surprising that the very title 'Rule Britannia' became shorthand for British imperialism and naval dominance.[18]

It was the song's verbal and syntactical simplicity that made its generalities memorable and persuasive. It did not involve its audience in convoluted sentences and tendentious party politicking, as did *Liberty*. It presented imperial aspirations as if they were already attained:

> Still more majestic shalt thou rise,
> > More dreadful from each foreign stroke;
> As the loud blast that tears the skies
> Serves but to root thy native oak.
> > 'Rule, Britannia, rule the waves;
> > Britons never will be slaves.'   (ll. 13–18)[19]

Here the symbol of the oak is deployed with new immediacy. Presented starkly, with no surrounding argument, it works directly on the emotions, giving prejudices about British resilience and naval power apparent root in the ruggedness of its native tree. The poem naturalizes patriotism, disguising its arguments as facts about British nature. It is successfully ideological because it is insidious: its 'facts' are accepted as such because they are presented simply enough to stick in the mind. And when sung, the poem calls its audience together in an enactment of patriotic feeling which itself engenders the emotion of communal solidarity that Thomson identifies as peculiarly British.

After the popular success of 'Rule Britannia!' and 'Hearts of Oak', the oak symbol was well-enough established in the national imagination for it to become a powerful weapon in political rhetoric. Eighteenth-century patriotism, as Gillian Russell has reminded us, was a performance, an assumption of a role.[20] Thomson's popular song allowed all ranks—whether on shipboard or in the theatre—to unite beyond their social divisions in a performance in which all shared the language of loyalty. As they sang of the oak, they ensured that patriotic symbols were no longer chiefly associated with an anti-Walpole opposition composed of noblemen and gentry. Indeed Roger Fisher's *Heart of Oak* chided the gentry on behalf of his fellow artisans for failing to cultivate 'the ancient and natural defence' on which Britain's national security depended. Taking his evidence from shipwrights and timber contractors, Fisher showed tradesmen to be more alert to the timber shortage and its consequences for the nation than the governing classes who were supposed to nurture Britain's interests on their estates and in parliament. He criticized the gentry for failing in a patriotic duty that their social inferiors appreciated. But he was not a radical: he did not demand that the gentry share power with their inferiors, only that they return to their historic duty—a duty that he presented in nostalgic and idealized terms:

> Formerly the grandeur of our noblemens and gentlemens seats was much increased by the vast quantity of woods, parks, and groves of timber growing all around them. So that, properly speaking, they appeared at a distance, as in the midst of a wood, and were only to be seen through the avenues leading to them. A vacant space of ground round the mansion house for their sumptuous gardens, meadows, &c for family use, was deemed sufficient. Thus situated they were sheltered from storms and tempests, and had the pleasure of viewing from every apartment the progress of their labours; still keeping in view the grand design, the naval power of Britain.
>
> When a little cloyed with enjoyment, or to retire from business, or for the sake of meditation, a walk for the space of a furlong, or little more, leads the wealthy inhabitant into a spacious wood. The variety of the scene revives his drooping spirits. On the branch of a full topt oak, at a small distance, the blackbird and thrush warble forth their notes, and, as it were, bless their benefactor. A little further, the turtle dove, having lost his mate, sends forth his mournful plaint, till, by means of echo from a neighbouring wood, passing through the silent air, the happy pair are again united. Variety of changes draw on the pleasing hour amongst the massy bodies of the full-grown oaks and thriving plants. The prospect of his country's good warms his heart. He returns and beholds his little offspring round

his board, satiated with the views of the provision made for
their defence in the thriving nurseries all around. He enjoys
it a while, and in a good old age lies down and dies in
peace.[21]

As Thomson had done when describing Hagley Park, Fisher here
makes oak woods into a landscape symbolizing gentlemanly
patriotism. Echoing Jonson's 'To Penshurst' and Pope's 'Windsor
Forest', he suggests that nature rewards with peace and compla-
cency the gentleman who plants for his country. By virtue of the
oak, the actual prospect of natural plenty is identical with the
metaphorical 'prospect' of national good. The gentleman gains
pastoral peace as he surrounds himself with the oaks that
make his country strong in war: self-interest and national interest
coincide on the gentleman's estate. But Fisher, unlike Jonson and
Pope, places this idyll in the past. Contemporary gentlemen had
fallen from their former disinterested love of British nature to
their own and their country's detriment. Despite this criticism,
Fisher would have seemed, to later radicals who did demand that
the landowning classes share their dominance of political power,
thoroughly complicit with the Georgic propaganda by which that
dominance was presented as a natural extension of a lifestyle
lived chiefly for the nation's good. And many of those radicals
were, like him, artisans and tradesmen.

Radicals were to transform the Georgic when they felt that the
people, on the basis of their conduct, had a better claim to the
language of patriotism than did the gentry. Songs which allowed
the people to perform that language enabled them to lay claim to
it. So did popular broadside verse which used the symbols associated with gentlemanly patriotism to criticize gentlemen for
neglecting the national interest in their public capacities as well as
on their private estates. Topical verse attacked ministers who
were reluctant to engage in war, as Thomson had attacked them
in *Britannia* and *Liberty*. The target is Henry Pelham rather than
Walpole in 'The Wonder of SURRY! The Wonder of SURRY! Or
the genuine Speech of an old BRITISH OAK; being a true and
faithful Narrative or what passed between an OAK, and a certain
Great Minister':

When a Voice Majestic issued,
    From a Reverend BRITISH OAK
'Twas an ancient *British* Druid
    Who to trembling P-LH-M spoke,
'On that Turf thou liest dejected
    Full five hundred years I've stood,
Every Neighbouring Shrub protected,
    King of all the Neighbouring Wood.
Full of Honour, full of Glory,
    [Till] thy Hatchet thin'd the Grove
Through thy Power, O fatal Story!
    FOREIGN Trees with *Native* strove
Mighty EDWARD once reclining
    Near this Branch that sweeps the ground
Call'd his blooming offspring to him,
    Princes, Nobles, standing round.
Hear my son thy Aged Father,
    BRITISH Valour *France* has won,
Trust thy faithful Subjects ever,
    FOREIGN Troops and *Vassals* shun
EDWARD bow'd, and view'd his Nobles,
    Generous Tears ran trickling down,
Native Courage warm'd each Feature,
    And his Face was Mercy's Throne.
Heaven forbid, my vertuous Sire!
    I disclaim these valiant Bands
Or, like former Tyrants, venture,
    BRITAIN'S fate in *Foreign* Hands
'Twas beneath my spreading Branches,
    MARY mourn'd her CALAIS lost:
DUNKIRK, lavish CHARLES lamented,
    Now the dread of ENGLAND'S Coast
But within these Woods resounded
    Ne'er till now such horrid Cries,
Ne'er till now our *Fleets* retreated:
    Fatal Sight to *British* Eyes![22]

The anonymous poet is attacking Pelham (Walpole's successor as Prime Minister) for British failures in the Seven Years' War. In

1755 Pelham had incurred the wrath of his cabinet and his country by agreeing to the employment of 8,000 Hessian troops to serve anywhere in British dominions at a cost of £300,000. Pitt the Elder was dismissed for failing to support the agreement; he then attacked Pelham when in 1756 Admiral Byng failed to relieve a French siege of Minorca. After an indecisive engagement with a French fleet commanded by de la Galissonnière, Byng had ordered his ships to retreat to Gibraltar. In the ensuing scandal Pelham made Byng the scapegoat, but Pitt accused him of planning the loss of Minorca in order 'to justify a bad peace'.[23] For Pitt, Pelham's policy was one of unpatriotic cowardice and dishonour.

The poem takes Pitt's view. Pelham's preference for diplomacy over battle is shown to be a betrayal of native tradition. In letting the fleet retreat and in employing Hessian troops he was, the oak symbolism suggests, undermining the tradition of native self-reliance passed down through monarchy and nobility since King Edward's time. The oak is a living—and speaking—reminder of the legacy from history which is embodied in the constitution. It is a legacy of xenophobia as well as courage, in which foreigners are untrustworthy and Britishness is an organic growth as native as an ancient oak and as a medieval king. The tree is itself 'King of all the Neighbouring Wood' and it speaks for the native King it once sheltered against gentlemen-ministers who neglect their patriotic duty as defined by history.

It was an oak of this political species that Burke described in his 1790 defence of the British constitution against gentlemen who supported the French revolution. And it was a similar tree that William Cowper portrayed in his poem of 1791 or 1792,[24] 'Yardley Oak' (a poem influenced by readings of both Thomson and Burke).[25] Hollow and aged yet 'still erect' (l. 119) Yardley oak stands for England—diseased by corruption yet sustained by its rootedness in history: 'So stands a kingdom, whose foundations yet/ Fail not, in virtue and in wisdom laid,/ Though all the superstructure, by the tooth/ Pulveriz'd of venality, a shell ...' (ll. 120–23). Cowper speaks on its behalf for an organic constitution, ancient and slow to grow and change—unlike the sudden innovations of the French revolution. And he then turns an actual local event into a symbolic instance: the threat that Yardley oak will be felled symbolizes the corruption of that constitution and the landowners' neglect of their duties to the land: 'in those thriftier days/ Oaks fell not, hewn by thousands, to supply/ The bottomless demands of contest wag'd/ For senatorial honours' (ll. 100–03).[26]

By 1792 Britain's constitution was under threat from radicals as well as from corrupt and profligate landowners. And the radicals had behind them a tradition of verse in which the language of patriotism was as much used to criticize the governing classes for neglecting their duties as it was to praise them as natural guardians of the national interest. And the radicals also knew that popular songs had made patriotic symbols available to all Britons. The anxiety about the contemporary gentry expressed by Cowper and Fisher became outright opposition to landowners' domination of power when a people brought up to sing of themselves as 'hearts of oak' heard Burke call the lower orders a 'swinish multitude'. Radical opposition was expressed not least through songs which took exception to Burke's image of a swinish people grazing on acorns below the sheltering boughs of the aristocratic constitution. Many of these songs used a tree of their own, grown from revolutionary America and France, as a counter-symbol to the oak which Burke had tried to appropriate exclusively to an aristocratic government. 'The Tree of Liberty. A New Song Respectfully Addressed to the Swinish Multitude, By Their Fellow Citizen, William England' is one example:

> Brave Washington the MAN WAS HE,
> Who nourish'd up fair Freedom's Tree,
> Which brought forth fruit abundantly:
> A noble treat, delicious, sweet
> And PAINE declared it was complete,
> So wish'd it universal.[27]

Another song, also entitled 'The Tree of Liberty', was sold by 'Citizen T. G. Ballard'. It portrayed the radicals' struggle for constitutional reform as a clearing of the forest of corruption:

> Ye Trees of Corruption, in Courts ye abound;
> The fruits ye produce are a curse to the ground;
> In the soil where ye flourish no others can grow;

But now see the axe at your roots aim the blow
All shall yield to Freedom's fair tree;
Bend to thee
Blest Liberty
Heroes are they now planting thee,
And all their great names immortal shall be.[28]

The Liberty trees had French as well as American origins: young rather than old, symbols of rejuvenation rather than tradition, they were planted on village greens and town squares all over revolutionary France in 1791. Around them would dance the inhabitants, all ranks participating in one fraternal circle.[29]

Those who wished to plant French-style liberty in Britain were opposed by Gagging Acts, by trials for sedition, and by propaganda. The propaganda revealed the persistence of the oak symbol in British political language, but it gave that symbol a newly reactionary twist. It also revealed conservatives' appreciation of the power of patriotic song. 'The Contrast. 1792' was to be sung to the tune 'Hearts of Oak':

Rise up hearts of oak, honest Britons free born,
The arts of designing seducers we scorn,
United and steady in Liberty's Cause
We'll ever defend both our king and our laws
Hearts of Oak, &c.[30]

Not only Garrick but Thomson provided the language by which conservatives sought to show radicals to be unBritish enemies of the nation. The broadside verse of 'Church and King' was intended to be sung to the tune of 'Rule Britannia'. Its anti-Jacobin language gained strength from the shadowy presence behind it of Thomson's well-known words, which the tune keeps in the singer's mind:

The Gallic lilies droop and die
Profan'd by many a *patriot knave*;
Her clubs command, her nobles fly,
Her Church a martyr—king a slave
CHORUS While Britons still united sing
Old England's glory—Church and King.

Yet Priestley, Faction's darling child,
    Enjoys this sanguinary scene,
And celebrates, with transports wild,
    The *wrongs*, miscall'd the *Rights of Men*.
     CHORUS But Britons still united sing, &c.[31]

Such 'united' singing had its effect: Joseph Priestley went into exile in America after a mob chanting 'Church and King' burnt his laboratory to the ground in 1791.

Attitudes hardened further as the prospect of invasion by Napoleon's army loomed. In 'Old England for Ever!', 'Hearts of Oak' and 'Rule Britannia' inform, at the levels of quotation and allusion, the poet's effort to call Britons to arms:

I

Let BRITONS attend, and unite in the cause,
To save their Religion, THEIR KING, and their Law,
Against an Usurper, whose treacherous blow
Has laid throughout Europe all Potentates low!
                      Hearts of Oak

II

'Tis his wish and intention this land to invade,
To ruin our Commerce, and Credit degrade—
Our Birthright he threatens at once to enslave—
But BRITONS have e'er been courageous and brave!
                      Hearts of Oak

...

IV

In a moment of danger let's rally around
TRUE LIBERTY'S STANDARD ON OLD ENGLISH GROUND!
Should Neptune take charge of the Consul at sea,
BRITONS may boast, they STILL LIVE—and ARE FREE!
                      Hearts of Oak.[32]

Under pressure in the early 1790s from the radical symbols of the French Revolution, by 1798 conservatives had succeeded in stigmatizing radicals as unpatriotic, disloyal and traitorous. The radical liberty-tree proved too easily portrayable as an import from a France with which Britain was at war. 'Citizens' who used it were easily depicted as treasonable supporters of the enemy. It was shaded out by the British oak, which was used by conservatives to identify opposition to political reform as the naturally British and patriotic view to take. Later radicals were to wrest the oak-symbol, and the songs in which it had become popular, to their cause rather than use a symbolic tree brought over from revolutionary France.

The oak was by 1798 once more the bulwark of the language of patriotism. The prospect of a French fleet crossing the channel made it pertinent as a symbol of the navy as well as the ancient constitution. Panic set in when 1,200 French soldiers were found to have landed almost unopposed on the Pembrokeshire coast in February 1797. A reprinted 'Hearts of Oak' from this period tried to rally Britons against larger French invasions:

> They swear they'll invade us, these terrible foes
> They frighten our women, our children and beaus
> But should their flat bottoms in darkness get o'er,
> Still Britons they'll find to receive them on shore.
> CHORUS
> Hearts of Oak are our ships, jolly Tars are our men
> We ever are ready,
> Steady boys, steady
> We'll fight and we'll conquer again and again.
>
> We'll still make them run and we'll still make them sweat,
> In spite of the Devil and Brussels gazette.
> Then cheer up my lads, with one heart let us sing,
> Our soldiers, our sailors our statesmen and king.
> Hearts of Oak, &c.[33]

Another version of the song, 'Hearts of Oak, Or, The British Empire', insisted on the Englishness of the oak that would defend king, country and religion:

> Our sailors are faithful, our soldiers are brave,
> Their King and their Country all anxious to save:
> And whilst life shall remain, to no traitors they'll yield,
> For virtue's their safeguard—Religion their shield.
> English oak are our ships, brave and loyal our men,

> All eager and ready,
> With hearts firm and steady,
> To thrash those invaders again and again.[34]

And 'The Patriot Briton; or England's Invasion' showed that the oak was a symbol of the nation as a whole: 'Never shall the Storms of France/ Rive, or blast, the British Oak!'[35]

By 1814 Napoleon had been defeated and exiled (although not for the last time), a defeat in which British oak, as commanded by Nelson, had played its part. But the patriotic oak did not die into neglect. It flourished in peacetime verse as a symbol of a Georgic Britain sheltered by a paternalist monarch. The author of 'August 1st 1814' owed a debt to Thomson's politics of landscape as he imagined a rural scene in which a generic 'rustic' looks to an oak to shelter his flock:

> A king more belov'd never honour'd a throne,
> Than he whom Britannia still calls her own ...
> ...
> The oak, our fam'd bulwark, seems nipt by the frost,
> And its limbs ev'ry sucker appear to have lost;
> While the rustic laments, as he leans on his spade,
> That his flock can no longer sport under its shade;
> Yet spring's genial heat shall its vigour restore,
> To bud bloom and shadow the valley once more;
> So Britain rejoice, that thy monarch remains,
> To protect thee, to bless thee, and cheer thy lov'd plains;
> And like the stout oak, may his virtues long bloom,
> Till the cold hand of death slope his path to the tomb![36]

The oak is 'nipt' because George III was, by 1814, not only old but mad. He had recovered from an earlier bout of madness: the oak image suggests that it would be natural for him to do so again. It also claims the Hanoverian king to be definitively British, making him the protector of a pastoral land of shepherds—appropriately enough since 'Farmer George' devoted much of his energy to a scheme to crossbreed native sheep. The poem is subtitled 'Printed in the Grand Jubilee Fair Held in Hyde Park Given in Commemoration of Peace. The Brunswick Family Ascending the British Throne, This Day One Hundred

Years and the Glorious Battle of the Nile'. Victory, peace, the monarchical tradition: these are symbolized by the oak that survives the frost and by the landscape it protects. And at the Jubilee Fair the oak itself was present in its naval form: mock sea battles re-creating Nelson's victories were staged.

By 1820 the political situation had changed again, and the traditionalist Georgic of 'August 1st, 1814' was challenged by a the radical use of the oak-symbol and of the patriotic songs in which that symbol had become popular. Economic depression had followed Napoleon's final defeat, and unrest had culminated in 1819 in the massacre of protesters at St Peter's Fields, Manchester. The ministry cracked down on the radical press, imprisoning many and forcing others into exile. But it could not prevent a deluge of songs, ballads and satires when, after George III's death, the new king attempted to have his wife Caroline deprived of a queen's rights and privileges on the grounds that she was an adulteress. Determined not to allow her access to his coronation or the title 'Queen', George IV had her name removed from the litany of the Church of England. He then caused a reluctant ministry to have Caroline 'tried', seeking both to deprive her of her rights as queen and to divorce her. A Bill of Pains and Penalties was put to the House of Lords because George, as a known adulterer himself, had no chance of obtaining his divorce in a jury trial. The country was outraged by the cruelty and hypocrisy of the attack, especially when the ministry's offer to bribe Caroline to stay abroad was published in the press by her supporters. Among those supporters was William Cobbett, the radical journalist whose *Political Register* carried nearly two thousand pages devoted to showing Caroline as the victim of the corrupt establishment. In Cobbett's press strategy, Caroline rather than the King became the proper embodiment of national virtues. She became the monarch to whom loyalty should be given. He argued that it would be un-patriotic and 'unmanly' not to take up Caroline's cause, quoting 'Rule Britannia' to imply that it would also be a violation of Britishness:

> if the people had remained passive; if their bosoms had not glowed with resentment; if they had not sworn to lose their

Fig. 1: Print of Queen Caroline. 'Britain's best hope!!
England's Sheet Anchor!!!'

lives to the last man rather than see her made a *martyr of*,
they themselves would have deserved the heaviest punish-
ments that God in his wrath can pour out upon a people.
Not to feel indignant; not to feel enraged at the publication
of a sentiment like this, would have argued the nation to be
the meanest, the most unmanly, the most cowardly, that
ever existed in the world.

'Blest Isle! with matchless beauties crown'd
And manly hearts to guard the fair'.

This boast, in a very celebrated English song, is by no means
an exaggeration.[37]

Radical prints also played on the patriotic images that Thomson
had helped to establish. In 'Queen Caroline. Britain's best
hope!! England's Sheet Anchor!!!' Caroline was depicted as
Britannia, holding the anchor of the ship firing its guns in her
honour. On the anchor is written 'Magna Carta. The People. Bill
of Rights. Constitution'. To her right a sailor shouts 'The Queen
and Old England for Ever!!' (Fig. 1). Thus the naval Muse of
Britain and her 'hearts of oak' were radicalized, used as a weapon
against the King and the ministry. In 'Queen Caroline Running
Down the Royal George' (Fig. 2) she was portrayed as a frigate
sinking a ship which resembles the King. His supporters
Wellington and Liverpool are left floundering in the water as the
Royal George sinks under the attack of Caroline's oaken vessel.
The caricature alludes to a real and notorious event: on 29
August 1782 the bottom fell out of the *Royal George* at Spithead
whilst she was being careened in preparation for repair. All hands
were drowned, and an admiralty enquiry subsequently found the
cause to have been the rotten state of her timbers. The British
oak of the navy's greatest ship had been used unseasoned, with
the consequence that, although apparently sound, it became
riddled with dry rot. The ship's name made its fate ironically
appropriate to the present King and the ship of state he
commanded.

The radicals' use of patriotic symbols against George was
effective: to the majority of the public his conduct showed 'Old
England' to be rotten within. The people believed they had a
better claim to the language of patriotism than did their King.

Fig. 2: Cartoon of 'Queen Caroline Running Down the
Royal George'

Opposition to monarch and ministry, so easily stigmatized as
disloyal in the 1790s, could now be expressed as a higher loyalty
to Britain and her Queen. And sailors and soldiers were inclined
to transfer their loyalty to Caroline: on 16 June a battalion of the
Guards had to be marched away from London when, on being
ordered to defend the House of Lords from the crowds, they
mutinied and drank the health of the Queen. Revolution was
widely predicted, though the Queen's supporters insisted on
their loyalty and made their protest by peaceful processions and
petitions.

Tory supporters of the King were few and hard pressed. They
reacted to George's unpopularity by trying to smear Caroline.
And they tried to wrest the traditional symbols of patriotism
from the hands of her radical supporters. Cobbett had used 'Rule
Britannia' against the King; he had also associated himself
with the oak tree.[38] Loyalists used this association against him,
jeering at his efforts to improve English silviculture by importing
foreign trees:[39]

He made the Farmers all believe he had a Tree to sell,
Which better than a British oak would stand, or quite as
    well;—
But when the fools had paid the price, they found, and not
    before,
This Locust-tree, like him who sold, was rotten at the core.[40]

In 1820 Cobbett had returned from exile in America with the bones of Tom Paine. To the author of this satire he was importing the hollow products of foreign climes, palming them off on the very men whose interests he claimed to represent. This was an astute point of attack on a man whose politics depended on his own and his public's belief that he embodied and would safeguard the rural traditions of England. That the attack failed is evidence of the social and political change which the trial of Caroline helped to accelerate. Cobbett could not successfully be branded, as Paine had been, as unBritish, as an importer of untrustworthy foreign ideas. Reform of parliament was precipitated as the people now regarded themselves and their champions as better guardians of British traditions and the national interest than were their aristocratic ministers and king. As Cobbett put it on 7 October: 'it required her case to be before us to convince a certain portion of the people of the lengths to which the system could go'.[41]

After the Caroline trial the belief that Britons were oaken in their native strength did not die, but it was no longer possible to argue, as Burke had done, that it was exclusively in the landowning classes that the oak-like constitution was conserved. For the landowning classes—or at least the monarch and the peers who were beholden to him—were not guarding 'the fair' Queen as the *Reflections on the Revolution in France* and as 'Rule Britannia' had stipulated. Cobbett challenged Burkean conservatism directly when he argued that the 'age of chivalry' was no longer preserved by the ruling classes: 'The spirit of that age is still left in England, but it appears to live only in the breasts of the people'.[42] The old oaks upon the great estates were still visible symbols of the landowners' power, but they were no longer proof of their exclusive right to govern. Georgic symbolism was now appropriated by the middle classes, who insisted that their own native strength and disinterested Britishness qualified them, as patriots, to defend, preserve but also reshape the historic form of government bequeathed to them.[43] Like Nelson's sailors, they had learnt the language of patriotism as defined by Thomson and Garrick. Unlike the sailors who died in battle, they were able to use that language to take power in the nation they loved. Secure in their belief in their 'manly' 'hearts of oak', they were able to secure reform without seeming to be disloyal and unBritish revolutionaries. The language of early eighteenth-century patriotism had triumphed in a manner unanticipated by those who wrote it—but that is a testament to its ability to shape an image of national character which formed the loyalties of the singers of halfpenny ballads as well as those of the readers of quarto poems. If Thomson's words did not actually rule Britannia, they did shape its people's understanding of its past and future. The myth of Britishness that he helped to create, if not Britain itself, would continue to grow like an oak.

NOTES

1.   'Hearts of Oak' was written during an invasion scare in the Seven Years' War. It was performed in *Harlequin's Invasion, or a Christmas Gambol* (London, 1759).

2.   Thomson's patriotic song first appeared in *Alfred. A Masque* (1740), co-authored by David Mallet with music by Thomas Arne. I take the text from James Thomson, *Poetical Works*, ed. J. Logie Robertson (London, 1908), pp. 422–23.

3.   John Charnock, *An History of Marine Architecture*, 3 vols (London, 1800–02), III, 171.

4.   Charnock, *Marine Architecture*, p. 172.

5.   'Nelson's Report of 1803', Appendix XVII of Cyril E. Hart, *Royal Forest. A History of Dean's Woods as Producers of Timber* (Oxford, 1966), pp. 312–14.

6.   The crooked 'compass' oak found in isolated trees was essential for the 'knee' timber used to join decks and stern posts to hull. For details of construction methods and discussion of the timber shortage see Robert Greenhalgh Albion, *Forests and Sea Power: The Timber Problem of the Royal Navy 1652–1862* (Harvard, 1926; repr. Hamden, CN, 1965).

7. Braham's popularity was matched by that of Charles Incledon, a former seaman who had fought in the West Indies and begun his career singing to officers on board his ship. A star at Covent Garden and Vauxhall Gardens, he was best remembered for his performances of 'Hearts of Oak', sometimes given in his sailor's clothes.

8. First performed at the Lyceum in Braham's operetta *The Americans*, 'The Death of Nelson' was revived the next year at Covent Garden and became a popular Victorian ballad. I quote it from G. J. Marcus, *Heart of Oak. A Survey of British Sea Power in the Georgian Era* (London, 1975), p. 258.

9. Gillian Russell, *The Theatres of War: Performance, Politics, and Society, 1793–1815* (Oxford, 1995), p. 13.

10. Edmund Burke, *Reflections on the Revolution in France*, ed. Conor Cruise O'Brien (London, 1982), p. 120.

11. Burke, *Reflections*, p. 181.

12. Roger Fisher, *Heart of Oak, The British Bulwark* (London, 1763), p. 7.

13. Robert Southey, *Essays, Moral and Political*, 2 vols (London, 1832), I, 11–12.

14. My text for *The Seasons* is James Thomson, *The Seasons*, ed. James Sambrook (Oxford, 1981).

15. The Oak Tree Society medal was distributed in 1750 at the time of Charles Edward's visit to London; it featured a withered oak with a sapling springing from its root and the legend REVERESCIT (It Flourishes). The oak also featured with the rose and thistle on glasses in which the Bonnie Prince's health could be drunk. See Noel Woolf, *The Medallic Record of the Jacobite Movement* (London, 1988), pp. 116–17, 127. I am grateful to H. H. Erskine-Hill for alerting me to this vein of symbolism.

16. My texts for *Liberty* and *Britannia* are taken from *Liberty, The Castle of Indolence And Other Poems*, ed. James Sambrook (Oxford, 1986).

17. The *Salopian Journal*, quoted in Russell, *The Theatres of War*, p. 63.

18. It was used, for instance, as the title of a book intended to engender patriotic feeling by praising the navy during World War Two: see C. King, *Rule Britannia* (London, 1941).

19. Thomson, *Poetical Works*, pp. 422–23.

20. Russell, *The Theatres of War*, p. 101.

21. Fisher, *Heart of Oak*, pp. ix, 36–37.

22. Madden Ballad Collection, vol. III, Cambridge University Library.

23. Quoted in B. Tunstall, *Admiral Byng and the Loss of Minorca* (London, 1928), p. 149.

24. The later date is favoured by R. N. Ringler, 'The Genesis of Cowper's "Yardley Oak"', *English Language Notes*, 5 (1967–68), 27–32.

25. The best modern edition of the poem is to be found in *The Poems of*

William Cowper, ed. John D. Baird and Charles Ryskamp, 3 vols (Oxford, 1980–95), III, 77–83. The poem was first published, without a number of passages cancelled by Cowper in MS, in *The Life and Posthumous Writings of William Cowper*, ed. William Hayley, 4 vols (London, 1803–06), IV, 405–16.

26. Details of the affair are given in Edward Hyams, *Capability Brown and Humphry Repton* (London, 1971), p. 44. See also the discussion in Tim Fulford, *Landscape, Liberty and Authority: Poetry, Criticism and Politics from Thomson to Wordsworth* (Cambridge, 1996), pp. 55–58.

27. Madden Ballad Collection, vol. XV, Cambridge University Library.

28. Madden Ballad Collection, vol. XV, Cambridge University Library.

29. See Simon Schama, *Citizens. A Chronicle of the French Revolution* (London, 1989), p. 492 and William Ruddick, 'Liberty trees and loyal oaks: emblematic presences in some English poems of the French Revolutionary period', in *Reflections of Revolution: Images of Romanticism*, ed. Alison Yarrington and Kelvin Everest (London and New York, 1993), pp. 59–67.

30. 'The Contrast. 1792. English Liberty. French Liberty. Which Is Best? A New Song. Liberty, Property—Old England For Ever', Madden Ballad Collection, vol. XV, Cambridge University Library.

31. Madden Ballad Collection, vol. XV, Cambridge University Library.

32. 'S. Gosnell Printer, Little Queen St. Holborn', Madden Ballad Collection, vol. XV, Cambridge University Library.

33. Madden Ballad Collection, vol. II, Cambridge University Library.

34. Madden Ballad Collection, vol. XV, Cambridge University Library.

35. Madden Ballad Collection, vol. XV, Cambridge University Library.

36. Madden Ballad Collection, vol. XV, Cambridge University Library.

37. *Political Register*, 15 July, XXXVI, 1259.

38. On Cobbett's appropriation of the oak symbol see Leonora Nattrass, *William Cobbett: The Politics of Style* (Cambridge, 1995), pp. 122ff.

39. On this and other of Cobbett's schemes for agrarian improvement see Daniel Green, *Great Cobbett: The Noblest Agitator* (London, 1983), pp. 312–13.

40. 'An Excellent New Song Called "Rascals Ripe!" In Which Some Account Is Given Of A Very Noted Character', Madden Ballad Collection, vol. XV, Cambridge University Library.

41. *Political Register*, XXXVII, 796.

42. *Political Register*, XXXVI, 1021.

43. On the use of Country-party symbolism by radicals in this period see Philip Harling, 'Leigh Hunt's *Examiner* and the Language of Patriotism', *English Historical Review*, 111 (1996), 1159–81 (p. 1178).

Thomson in the 1790s

JOHN BARRELL and
HARRIET GUEST

This essay is not an attempt to discuss, in general terms, the
reputation and reception of Thomson's poems in the 1790s.
Indeed, it ignores completely what was certainly, to readers of
that decade as of any other, the most important aspect of his
writing, his descriptions of natural scenery. Instead the essay tries
to exemplify, however selectively, how Thomson's poetry came
to be taken up in the controversies of the 1790s. It argues, to
begin with, that after 1789 the political passages and poems of
Thomson, and *Liberty* especially, became briefly 'readable' in a
way they had not been for decades: they were seen to offer an
account of political virtue, and of the consequences of the lack of
it, which could support a range of arguments, from liberal
Whiggism to popular radicalism, by which the French Revolution,
at least in its early stages, could be approved, and political reform,
in some degree or another, could be advocated at home. The
terms and conditions of this new readability, however, made it
short-lived; in the late 1790s, when the movement for parliamentary reform was largely repressed, and the nation became
arguably more unified under the threat of a French invasion, it
disappeared as quickly as it had appeared, and *Liberty* never again
achieved the importance it had briefly enjoyed. Throughout the
decade, however, Thomson's reputation had also continued to be
shaped by longer-term historical changes with an apparently
more oblique relation to discourses of public politics: in particular perhaps the privatization, the sentimentalization, the femin-
ization of literature, as opposed, in particular, to the discourses of
politics itself. The essay ends by glancing at the use made of a
particular passage of *The Seasons* by women novelists of the
1790s; and it suggests that here, too, where we might expect
Thomson's poetry to be removed from controversy, it was being

read in a new way, as a resource and reference point in an increasingly politicized discussion of sentimentality, femininity, and domestic life.

I

The history of the plan to place a monument to Thomson in Ednam, his native village, began with a chapter of accidents. Mainly through the efforts of Sir Walter Scott, an obelisk was eventually erected on Ferneyhill, south of the village, in 1820. Such a monument, though on a different site, had originally been proposed 30 years earlier by David Stewart Erskine, the 11th Earl of Buchan. On the anniversary of Thomson's birthday, 22 September 1790, Buchan assembled a select group of devotees at a Mrs Spinks' house in the village, to celebrate a 'Thomson Festival'. It was here that the plan was first conceived, and Sir Alexander Don and Samuel Robertson were invited to draw a plan of the intended monument. It was unfortunate that one of Thomson's sisters had chosen to die a few days earlier, and was being buried in Ednam churchyard while the drunken festivities were in progress. It was unfortunate that the next morning the carriage taking Buchan and his friends from Ednam to his nearby estate at Dryburgh was overturned. No one, however, was injured: the injury occurred the following year.

In the months following this first festival, Buchan secured the consent of the owner of Ednam Hill to the erection of the obelisk on his land; Ednam Hill, east of the village and nearer to it, is higher, more conspicuous and more shapely than Ferneyhill. He wrote letters to every influential Scotsman he could think of, soliciting subscriptions to pay for the monument. For whatever reason his appeals went unheard, and Buchan was obliged to opt for a more temporary monument to be unveiled at the 1791 festival. He arranged for Thomas Coutts, his London banker, to send up a plaster copy of the head and shoulders of Thomson as they appeared in Michael Spang's monument to the poet, after a design by James Adam, in Westminster Abbey; he planned to have this bust carried up Ednam Hill where he would crown it with a wreath of laurel. Six days before the festival it was race week at Dryburgh, the house was full of guests, and the bust 'was broken in a midnight frolic'. Undaunted, on 22 September Buchan and his friends climbed the hill and the Earl delivered a long eulogy to the poet, at the end of which he produced a copy of the 1730 quarto of *The Seasons*, given by Thomson to Buchan's father. 'And on it,' he concluded, 'since I have no bust of the poet to invest, I lay this garland of bays.'[1]

At this time, before the rise of Scott and the death of Burns, Thomson had a strong claim to be regarded as the national poet of Scotland.[2] Why then did Buchan's appeal fail? Some of those he approached may have been unwilling to entrust money to an impecunious aristocrat with a reputation for eccentricity, and a fondness for classical ceremonies in which he was at centre stage—most notoriously when, in the character of Apollo, he invited to tea 'nine young ladies of rank' whom he obliged dress as the Muses, and who ran 'giggling and screeching from the room' when the tea kettle was brought in by a little naked Cupid.[3] But according to one of Thomson's biographers, Robert Heron, who contributed a new life of the author to an edition of *The Seasons* published in 1793 in Perth, Buchan's scheme may have been 'defeated' by the 'eager and officious enthusiasm' with which he pursued it.[4]

This remark is certainly a coded reference to the political inflection Buchan had given to his scheme, and had intended to perpetuate in the obelisk. Buchan was an 'honest' Whig, alarmed at the degree to which the power of the Crown had increased and was increasing during the reign of George III. His main contribution to Scottish politics was his continued opposition to the system by which the 16 representative Scottish peers allowed to sit in the House of Lords, though in theory elected by the nobility of Scotland, were in effect nominated by the Prime Minister in London.[5] In 1792 he joined one of his younger brothers, the great liberal advocate Thomas Erskine, in the Friends of Liberty, the grouping of liberal Foxite Whigs (though Fox was not among them) united in opposing the corruption of the constitution and in proposing a moderate reform of the House of Commons. From 1789 until at least 1792 he was a fervent supporter of the revolution in France; and in 1792 he had written an essay on Thomson which, as well as describing his efforts to erect a monument to the poet, represented him as a prophet of that revolution, and as 'the bard of Liberty', one especially to be remembered at a time when 'the very sound and sight of the word LIBERTY has become disagreeable, if not terrible, to the fashionable world in Britain'.[6]

Buchan's life of Thomson appears in a volume alongside a life of Andrew Fletcher of Saltoun, who, like Thomson, is presented as a harbinger of a new age of 'philosophical politics', apparently now realized in America and France, and which 'Thomson, my favourite bard, and the bard of liberty, saw before his death, like another prophet from Pisgah, saw and rejoiced!' The reference here is to the final book, 'The Prospect', of *Liberty*, the poem which, though Thomson regarded it as his highest achievement, had always been, as the Tory Johnson had complacently remarked, the least regarded of his works. For Buchan, 'the highest encomium of Thomson is to be given him on account of his attachment to the cause of political and civil liberty'. *Liberty* was the greatest of Thomson's poems, the trumpet of a prophecy, either of an enlightened and democratic future for Britain or an irreversible decline into corruption and slavery. This prophecy had apparently been repeated by the elder Pitt, the Earl of Chatham, in a 'Pythonick' remark addressed to the young Buchan in the course of a conversation about Thomson's politics: 'either the parliament will reform itself from within, or be reformed with a vengeance from without'. By the early 1780s this prophecy had been taken up by 'honest', even republican Whig politicians, who now however saw no chance of the Commons reforming itself, and expected reform only from extra-parliamentary action. In this version Chatham's prophecy had become a founding doctrine of the Society for Constitutional Information (SCI), whose leaders, in 1794, would be charged with High Treason. At the end of his life of Thomson, Buchan reinforced Chatham's prophecy with another: 'I am the voice of one crying in the wilderness of politics—*Make straight your ways, for the empire of delusion is at an end.*'[7]

For Buchan, Johnson was among the greatest enemies both of

the political liberty of Britain and of Thomson's *Liberty*. According to Johnson, *Liberty* had arisen out of the clamour raised, by the opposition to Walpole, for a 'liberty, of which no man felt the want', and 'which was not in danger'. But if, as Johnson claimed, *Liberty* had 'called in vain upon her votaries to read her praises', this for Buchan was a part of that disregard for the 'free constitution' of Britain which had allowed 'a baneful aristocracy' to establish in Britain 'a system of corruption', and to defeat its essential principle, which was, claimed Buchan, 'the *autocracy* of the people'. Johnson, disingenuously, had refused 'to hazard either praise or censure' of the poem, for he had not read it through; he had *tried* to read it, 'and soon desisted'. With equal disingenuousness, Buchan in his eulogy replied: 'Of Johnson's criticism on the Poem of Thomson, entitled Liberty, I shall say nothing; but I will take the liberty to say that Britain knows nothing of the liberty that Thomson celebrates!'—and later added, in a sentence whose syntax Johnson would have marvelled at, 'No wonder that, when the brutal Johnson tried to read liberty when it first appeared, he soon desisted, when Johnson's countrymen try to read France's liberty, and desist!'[8]

Buchan's rhetoric is considerably more radical than his politics; he remains, in the life of Thomson, a supporter of the limited reform proposed by the London Friends of the People, which, like them, he advocates as the only means of silencing the call for universal manhood suffrage coming from political societies such as the SCI and the newly-formed London Corresponding Society (LCS). But if his appeal for subscriptions to the proposed monument at Ednam had been made in terms similar to those by which, in the life, the authority of Thomson was enlisted to justify the French Revolution and a measure of parliamentary reform, it is hardly surprising that it failed. For the appeal was made in the period when polite public opinion, following the publication of Burke's *Reflections on the Revolution in France*, was decisively abandoning support for the revolution; in the life, indeed, Thomson's poems were specifically prescribed as an antidote to the writings of 'raging Burke'.[9]

By the time of the second Thomson festival, still more by the publication of the life in 1792, the terms in which Buchan was

eulogizing Thomson, and still more, as we shall see, the iconography of his proposed monument, were coming to seem increasingly dangerous and disloyal. The old opposition version of
classical republicanism of the 1730s and 1740s, which Buchan
found in *Liberty*, depended for its constitutional legitimacy on a
careful observation of the distinction between the Crown—in the
shape, especially, of the Prime Minister, the Cabinet, the Privy
Council—and the king; indeed it emphasized this distinction, in
order to insist that only if the increasing power of the Crown was
curtailed could the king reign in the security that only a limited
monarchy had a right to enjoy. Opposition classical republicanism
was supposedly as friendly to a limited monarchy as it was hostile
to despotism. The revolution in France, however, and more especially events in Britain and France in 1791 and 1792—the attack
on the hereditary principle in the *Rights of Man*, the royal proclamation on May 1792 directed against Paine and (so they believed)
the Friends of the People; the widening split in the Whig party;
the triumph of Robespierre; the proclamation of the Republic;
the formation of the 'Loyal Associations' to defend 'Liberty and
Property against Republicans and Levellers'—all had the effect
of making the distinction, on which the rhetoric of opposition
classical republicanism depended, ever more blurred. Increasingly,
hostility to the growing power of the Crown was represented by
loyalists as hostility to the monarchy itself. By 1795 John Reeves,
the moving spirit behind the loyal associations, would represent
the ideology of the old Whigs as unqualified republicanism,
indeed as regicidal.[10]

The degree to which Buchan's representation of Thomson as
'the bard of liberty' must have been caught up in the increasing
hostility to the revolution and to the movement for parliamentary reform is dramatically suggested by the publication, in
Morison's 1793 edition of *The Seasons*, of the design for his
proposed obelisk.[11] Its iconography was based on that of Spang's
monument (Fig. 3), which had been erected in 1762, and which
depicted

> a figure of Mr Thomson sitting, who leans his left arm upon
> a pedestal, and holds a book with the cap of Liberty in his
> other hand. Upon the pedestal is carved a bas-relief of the

Fig. 3: James Caldwall, engraving of Michael Spang's monument to Thomson in Westminster Abbey, from *The Seasons, by James Thomson. A New Edition* (London, 1779).

Fig. 4: J. Fraser, after a design for an obelisk to Thomson by
Sir Alexander Don and Samuel Robertson, from *The Seasons,
by James Thomson. A New Edition* (Perth, 1793).

Seasons, to which a boy points, offering him a laurel crown
as the reward of his genius. At the feet of the figure, is the
tragic mask, and ancient harp.[12]

In Buchan's design (Fig. 4), against an obelisk of darker stone,
the four seasons support a sarcophagus on which Thomson
reclines; he is reading a book, again presumably *Liberty*, while
Nature kneels beside him, offering, in the words of the epitaph,
borrowed from *The Seasons*, to 'snatch' him to Heaven. But
where Adam had placed the tragic mask, Buchan's design has
something less stylized, more three-dimensional; it may also be
intended as a tragic mask, but the short Roman sword resting on
its neck, alongside a bundle of fasces, seems to invite us to read it
as the severed head of a despot, actual or imagined, whether
Pisistratus, or Tarquin, or Julius Caesar, or an allegory which
includes every tyrant or absolute monarch who attempts to stand
against 'the autocracy of the people'. If the republican rhetoric of
the monument—intended as tyrannicidal, of course, rather than
regicidal—was contentious enough in 1791 or 1792, when the
monument was presumably designed, it is difficult to imagine
how shocking it must have seemed when Morison published it—
after, that is, the execution of Louis XVI, and in the middle of the
loyalist alarm for the safety of George III that Louis's death
generated in Britain. By then the monument must have appeared
to associate Thomson not only with Jacobin republicans and
regicides in France, but with the supposedly regicidal ambitions
the Government was claiming to detect in the movement for
universal suffrage, a claim which led in the following year to the
indictment of the leaders of the LCS and SCI, for the treason of
'compassing and imagining the death of the king'.

II

'He treats the very word, LIBERTY, which, properly understood,
comprehends every thing that is dear to man, with an indecent,
and *contemptible contempt*.' Attacking Johnson in the course of
defending *Liberty*, Percival Stockdale describes the mixed, the

'well-proportioned' constitution of Britain as a compromise between aristocratic repression and popular licence; it is to be found, like liberty itself, 'half-way between the star-chamber of SAMUEL JOHNSON, and the tap-room of THOMAS PAINE'.[13] This was a description well calculated to please Buchan, to whom Stockdale's 1793 edition of *The Seasons* was dedicated, for it implies the distinction between the 'autocracy of the people', the notion that the Crown in Parliament rules with the consent of the people, and the 'sovereignty of the people', which presumes an unlimited power in the people to change the constitution at their own will. It was a wariness of supporting the doctrine of popular sovereignty that led the London Friends of the People to oppose universal manhood suffrage and to leave unchallenged the hereditary principle that Paine had so thoroughly ridiculed: for Buchan, an independent nobility was an essential safeguard of the liberty of Britain. And so of course it had been for Thomson himself.

We might expect, then, that *Liberty* would have had no appeal for the popular movement for parliamentary reform that emerged in the 1790s, first in Sheffield and then in London, and which adopted so much of the political programme set out in *Rights of Man*: universal manhood suffrage, economical reform, conventionism, and (or so the Government and its loyalist supporters insisted) abolition of the hereditary parts of the constitution. In fact, however, the rhetoric of the popular radical societies was almost as imbued with the aristocratic classical republicanism of writers like Thomson as it was with Paine's language of popular rights, and its ideology can partly be understood as an attempt to knot these two discourses together. For if Paine provided popular radicalism with arguments to establish the right of all men (and it is men we are speaking of) to be citizens, opposition classical republicanism offered a far more attractive and authoritative account of active, independent citizenship, of the disinterested public virtue essential to the citizen, and of the corruption of government which results when those in power pursue private ends in preference to the public good. If *Rights of Man* offered a vision of how a system of government might be originated on first principles, many in the radical movement found this prospect too vertiginous, or at least imagined that it might appear so to those it sought to win over. The radical societies preferred to insist that their aim was not to invent a new system, but to return the constitution to its former, its original purity; and to represent themselves as the heirs and adapters of the classical republican Whiggery of the early century, as well as of the honest Whiggery of the early 1780s that so many Whigs, the younger Pitt among them, had dishonestly abandoned. Thus Thomas Spence, for example, a member of the LCS, filled up most of his own periodical *Pig's Meat* with extracts from the Whig canon by writers such as Akenside, Churchill, Harington, Lyttelton, Sidney, Trenchard, as well from more modern writers like Barlow, Price and Volney. His aim was to provide the popular radical movement with a history, a canon, and in the process to demonstrate that the movement was as much part of the struggle to maintain the principles of the English revolution as were the polite and aristocratic writers whose works he anthologized.

Thomson's *Liberty* found among the members of the popular reform movement the enthusiastic readers that, according to Johnson, it had never earlier enjoyed. *Pig's Meat* included a lengthy extract from the first book of the poem, 'Antient and Modern Liberty Compared', a passage which Wordsworth, in the blissful dawn of his enthusiasm for the revolution, had also alluded to.[14] Charles Pigott, the old Etonian Jacobin and member of the LCS, in his pamphlet *Treachery no Crime*, quoted Buchan's discussion of *Liberty* with the elder Pitt.[15] Robert Thompson, an auctioneer, a founder member of the LCS, and author of the radical anthem 'God save the—RIGHTS OF MAN', published 'The Origin of Kings', a poem which, arguing that early monarchies were elective rather than hereditary, alludes at length to the opening lines of the second book, 'Greece'.[16] But it was these lines from the fifth book, 'The Prospect' (ll. 99–109), attacking the corruption of Walpole's ministry, that the popular reformers found most useful:

> Unblest by VIRTUE, *Government* a *League*
> Becomes, a *circling Junto of the Great*,
> To rob by Law: *Religion* mild, a *Yoke*
> To tame the stooping Soul, a *Trick of State*
> To mask their Rapine, and to share the Prey.
> What are without it *Senates*, save a Face

Of Consultation deep and Reason free,
While the determin'd Voice and Heart are sold?
What boasted *Freedom* save a sounding Name?
And what *Election* but a Market vile,
Of Slaves self-barter'd?

This attack on the corruption of the government, parliament and the electorate was at least as appropriate to the ministry of the younger Pitt as it had originally been to that of Walpole. The attention of the LCS was probably first directed to the passage by Thompson: in August 1792 it was used as the epigraph to the society's third address to the nation, *An Address from the London Corresponding Society to the Inhabitants of Great Britain on the Subject of a Parliamentary Reform*,[17] written by the then chairman, Maurice Margarot, who in 1794 would be transported to Australia following his conviction in Edinburgh for sedition. The address was reprinted in Sheffield by John Gales in the second volume of his periodical *The Patriot*, and was adopted by the Sheffield Society for Constitutional Information as the epigraph to its pamphlet of early 1794 *The People's Ancient and Just Liberties Asserted*.[18] The following year it was alluded to at length by James Sansom, in his poem *Oppression*, dedicated 'To all the Reforming Societies in Great Britain'.[19] But it was an animated discussion of the passage in the trial of Thomas Hardy, the secretary of the LCS, in November 1794, a discussion reprinted in every major London newspaper, that would have made the wider political public, the polite as well as the vulgar, aware that the radical societies had appropriated 'the bard of Liberty' to the cause of universal manhood suffrage.

Prosecuting Hardy, the Attorney General Sir John Scott led the jury at great length through the history of the society and its publications. When the address to the inhabitants of Great Britain was read to the court the epigraph was omitted, but Thomas Erskine, Hardy's counsel, insisted that the passage from Thomson be read also. In his reply to Scott for the defence, Erskine suggested to the jury that the court had responded to the delivery of this 'very bold motto' with an awed silence. And no wonder; for these, Erskine announced, 'are the words of Thomson'; 'it is under the banners of his proverbial benevolence, that these men are supposed to be engaging in plans of anarchy and murder'. Hardy, Erskine reminded the jury, was accused of intending to depose, to kill George III, and yet in this address, signed by Hardy himself, he was invoking a poem

> written under the auspices of his majesty's royal father, when heir apparent to the crown of Great Britain, nay, within the very walls of Carlton House ... it was under the roof of a PRINCE OF WALES that the poem of LIBERTY was written; and what better return could be given to a Prince for his protection, than to blazon, in immortal numbers, the only sure title to the crown he was to wear— THE FREEDOM OF THE PEOPLE OF GREAT BRITAIN?

It was, Erskine insisted, entirely absurd to assume

> that the unfortunate prisoner before you was plotting treason and rebellion, because, with a taste and feeling beyond his humble station, his first proceeding was ushered into view, under the sanction of this admirable person, the friend and the defender of the British constitution.[20]

Erskine ended this 'desultory digression', as he described it, by referring to the attempts of his brother to erect a monument to the 'immortal memory' of Thomson. He himself, Erskine reminded the jury, bore the same name as Buchan; and he rejoiced at the thought that if his brother's attempts were successful, his own name would 'descend to the latest posterity' by being forever coupled with Thomson's.[21] The digression of course was far from desultory: Thomson, Erskine was reminding the jury, was a patriot and a most loyal subject; Erskine's reverence for and desire to be associated with Thomson was an earnest of his own patriotism and loyalty; and if that was true of Erskine (and who would dare deny it?), how should it not be true of Hardy also?

For Erskine it was a mark of Hardy's humility, his desire to improve himself, his deference to the canon of the polite culture, that he should borrow the authority of Thomson to sanction his own political opinions. For the prosecution, however, the quotation was an act of appropriation, a theft; it was a mark of Hardy's insolence, indeed his perversity. 'Who will dispute any one

principle which it contains?' asked the Solicitor General, Sir John
Mitford, of the passage from *Liberty*: an odd question from him,
perhaps, in that he owed his seat in Parliament to the same corrupt
system of election that Thomson was attacking. 'And yet,' he
continued, 'if passages are to be taken from books, and applied to
such purposes, the best books may be perverted to the worst of
purposes.'[22] The worst of purposes meant, for the Solicitor
General, the attempt to establish a fully democratic constitution in
Britain; for though Hardy was tried for a conspiracy to kill the
king, the prosecution never pretended that he had any actual
design on the king's life; its argument was that the likely effect of
establishing universal manhood suffrage and the doctrine of
popular sovereignty would be the deposition and consequent
death of George III. The perversity, the act of theft that Hardy had
performed, was thus the appropriation of the words of a canonical
poet of the polite culture to the culture of popular radicalism.

And yet the canonical Thomson was not, by the 1790s,
Buchan's Thomson, nor Erskine's, nor Hardy's; it was the poet of
The Seasons, the poet of nature, and, increasingly, as we shall see,
of private and domestic, not of public virtue. If Mitford found
nothing to disagree with in this passage from *Liberty*, it may well
have been because the polite and cultivated loyalism he represented had found a way of reading Thomson's lines which was
perfectly compatible with the corrupt practices of Pitt's ministry.
This point is well suggested by a pamphlet which appeared in
January 1795, immediately after the acquittals of Hardy, Tooke
and Thelwall; it is one of a number of pamphlets which insisted
that, notwithstanding the acquittals, the charge of a conspiracy to
subvert the constitution had been fully proved at the trials. The
author of *Treason Triumphant over Law and Constitution!* had no
quarrel with Thomson's representation of 'the ruin of a state, from
a deprivation of virtue'; but, he managed to suggest, it was a failure
of *private* virtue that Thomson had in mind. The inappropriateness
of radical appropriations of Thomson was evident, he claimed,
from the fact that 'in all the reforming codes, we no where
descry an attempt at a reform of manners. On the contrary, the
generality of Reformers, are men of the most immoral characters,
and devoid of all true virtue'.[23] This manages to suggest, and to

suggest that Thomson believed, that 'true virtue' is nothing to do with 'INDEPENDENT LIFE', 'INTEGRITY IN OFFICE', 'A PASSION FOR THE COMMON-WEAL'—the public virtues listed by Thomson in the paragraph of 'The Prospect' immediately following the passage at issue. It is simply a matter of manners, of conduct, of the morality of private life. The convenience of this reading is not simply that it makes public life into a zone of amorality, in which a system of political corruption is supposed not to threaten the survival of the nation if it is conducted by men whose private morality is unimpeachable. The argument also implicitly invites a contrast between, on the one hand, George III and Pitt, both famous for the purity of their private lives, and, on the other, the sexual immorality imputed to Paine by loyalist propaganda, and the notorious private immorality of many of Erskine's political allies, notably Fox and Sheridan.

III

In September 1792 France was proclaimed a republic, and two months later, on 18 November at White's Hotel in Paris, the new republic was toasted by the members of the British Club. Other toasts were drunk to the National Convention, to 'the coming Convention of England and Ireland', to Thomas Paine, to 'the abolition of hereditary titles throughout the world', and to 'the Women of Great Britain, particularly those who have distinguished themselves by their writings in favour of the French revolution, Mrs Charlotte Smith and Miss H. M. Williams'.[24] It was Charlotte Smith's novel *Desmond*, published early in 1792, that the British Club must have had in mind in drinking her health, a novel in which Thomson is enlisted on the side of modernity by the hero, a supporter of French Revolution. The attack, in 'Winter', on the oppression and corruption of the legal system, is dismissed by the loyalist Mr Cranbourne as 'flowery declamation; fine sounding words about rights and liberties' which can impose only on 'superficial understandings'. As the argument continues, Thomson's vision of an uncorrupt, future Britain is implicitly but unmistakably linked by Cranbourne to the pernicious and impracticable Utopianism of Paine.[25] In the summer of 1793, Smith published her poem in blank verse, *The Emigrants*, perhaps the best English poem on the revolution to be published in the 1790s. The first of its two books is set in Brighton in November 1792, and it reveals that her support for the new France has barely survived the events of the previous autumn. The second book is set in April 1793, after the execution of Louis XVI, and when Britain and France are at war.

The Emigrants is a difficult poem for it has to articulate a difficult set of beliefs and attitudes, though one which was not unusual among British liberal intellectuals in the mid-1790s. Smith now wants to defend the revolution as it had been in the three years before the ascendancy of the Jacobins, and wishes to believe that the Jacobin terror, and the execution of Louis, were not its inevitable outcome. She deplores the war set in motion in 1792 by the Duke of Brunswick to restore Louis to the position he had enjoyed before 1789, and is still more horrified by Britain's entry into that war; but, while she still despises hereditary titles and the pageantry of courts, she believes that the best hope for France lies in the restoration of limited monarchy and of a king more loyal to that institution than Louis had been. She has no doubt that Britons enjoy more liberty than those now suffering under the 'lawless Anarchy' of France, yet sees the oppression exercised by the aristocracy and church in Britain in 1793 as only just preferable to the similar oppression in France before 1789 which had provoked the revolution, and she is appalled by the reactionary loyalism which, beginning as hostility to that revolution, is apparently bent also on undermining the remaining constitutional liberties of the British. As each of these positions is articulated, its qualifications have to be articulated also, in sentences which wind vigorously yet carefully down the page, unable to end until statement and counter-statement are precisely poised.

The 'emigrants' of the title are the French émigré clerics and aristocrats who have fled from France, who have sought and (to Britain's credit) have found refuge in the land of their traditional Protestant enemies. In her portrait of one of these refugees, an aristocrat longing to recover the power and privilege he had enjoyed before the revolution, Smith writes of his

high consciousness of noble blood,
Which he has learn'd from infancy to think
Exalts him o'er the race of common men:
Nurs'd in the velvet lap of luxury,
And fed by adulation—could *he* learn
That worth alone is true Nobility?
And that *the peasant* who, 'amid the sons
Of Reason, Valour, Liberty, and Virtue,
Displays distinguish'd merit, is a Noble
Of Nature's own creation!'—If even here,
If in this land of highly vaunted Freedom,
Even Britons controvert the unwelcome truth,
Can it be relish'd by the sons of France?[26]

The quotation these lines enclose is from Thomson's *Coriolanus*,[27] a tragedy which Smith may well have had in mind elsewhere in the writing of *The Emigrants*. The parallels between the two texts are obvious enough: a noble exile, driven by a popular rebellion from his native country, and planning, as did the French émigrés,[28] to invade it and reclaim his position; the eloquent opposition voiced by Galesus in Thomson's play and by Smith in her poem to aggressive war and to the ambition of one state to intervene in the internal affairs, however anarchic, of another; the concentration on how much of the cost of war and civil strife is borne by women; the commitment to public virtue, to 'Patriot Virtue', and to the classical republican vocabulary in which its value is proclaimed.

The immediate point of the quotation, however, appears to be similar to that made by Erskine in the trial of Hardy, and by Buchan in the opening sentence of the introduction to his *Essays*; that it is a measure of the ascendancy of reactionary loyalism in 1792 and after that such passages from Thomson should now appear subversive. As Smith puts it in her footnote that identifies the reference, 'These lines are Thomson's, and are among the sentiments which are now called (when used by living writers), not common-place declamation, but sentiments of dangerous tendency'.[29] Smith's immediate point is presumably that what, when the play was written, would have been received as an obvious truth, that commoners could aspire to the empty privileges of 'natural' nobility, will now be read, by those alarmed by the fate of nobility in France, and by the ridicule directed at the hereditary principle by Paine, as a call for the abolition of social distinction and the establishment of a constitution based on the equality of all men.

The footnote may be read as making a more indirect but more particular point. *The Emigrants* appeared a few months after the trial for seditious libel, in his absence, of Paine, in December 1792, for publishing Part II of *Rights of Man*. Those familiar with Thomson's play, or those encouraged by her footnote to seek it out, would have known that the lines Smith quotes are spoken by Cominius, one of the embassy sent to plead with Coriolanus to persuade the Volsci to make peace with Rome. The negotiations break down, and Cominius, disgusted at the intransigence of Coriolanus, addresses him thus:

> Yet I must tell thee, it would better suit
> A fierce despotic chief of barbarous slaves,
> Than the calm dignity of one who sits
> In the grave senate of a free republic,
> To talk so high, and as it were to thrust
> Plebeians from the native rights of man.

Two lines of angry expostulation from Coriolanus divide these lines from the sentence containing the lines Smith quotes. By indirection, then, Smith's footnote may remind her readers, that there was a time when it was not only acceptable but commendable to utter the words 'rights of man', as well as to suggest, as *Desmond* had done, a degree of consonance between Thomson's politics and Paine's.

Our sense of what might be going on here is reinforced by 'The Dead Beggar', one of two poems in *Elegiac Sonnets*, both dated to November 1792, both sited in Brighton, which evidently relate to the first book of *The Emigrants*. Here too we find an apparently radical sentiment in the text, this time a direct reference to the 'rights of man' and, in the footnote, a polemical disclaimer:

> Rejoice, that tho' an outcast spurn'd by Fate,
>   Thro' penury's rugged path his race he ran;

In earth's cold bosom, equalled by the great,
    Death vindicates the insulted rights of Man.

The note remarks that the poem has

> incurred blame for having used in this short composition,
> terms that have become obnoxious to certain persons. Such
> remarks are hardly worth notice; and it is very little my
> ambition to obtain the suffrage of those who suffer party
> prejudice to influence their taste; or those who desire that
> because they have themselves done it, every one else should
> be willing to sell their best birth-rights, the liberty of
> thought, and of expressing thought, for the *promise* of a
> mess of pottage.[30]

This note describes very well the political atmosphere of the mid-
1790s in Britain, the inducements of patronage, of preferment, of
profit, in parliament, in the professions, in trade, offered in
exchange for expressions of loyalty to the crown and of enmity
to revolution or reform. Like the footnote to *The Emigrants*,
however, it raises a question which, when the poems were
written, Smith may well have been finding too difficult to answer.
After the events of 1792, is she still defending, is she still advo-
cating, equality and the rights of man as these had been established in France and advocated, in England, by Paine? Or is she
defending the phrase, 'rights of man', on the grounds that to
believe in such rights is not necessarily to endorse a French, or a
Paineite definition of them?—objecting to the tendency of
loyalism to identify certain words and phrases as the infallible
marks of disloyalty, and to conflate the language of true liberty
with the language of republican 'anarchy'. It is not entirely clear,
and for this essay, at least, the point matters less than the fact that
Smith, like Buchan and like Erskine, found it appropriate to reach
for the political poetry of Thomson to demonstrate how much
more restrictive the limits of acceptable political discourse had
become in the mid-1790s than when Thomson was writing.

IV

Elsewhere in *The Emigrants* Charlotte Smith seems, like many of her contemporaries, to read Thomson as it were through the medium, the filter of William Cowper. In the prefatory letter which dedicates the poem to Cowper, she represents herself as having 'read THE TASK almost incessantly from its first publication to the present time', and as composing her own poem while the cadences of Cowper's still resonate in her mind. Cowper is initially invoked, as we might expect, as the poet of private life, the celebrator of rural retirement and the domestic fireside. But Cowper's example has also, Smith suggests, taught her to consider her personal sufferings as extending into a sympathetic involvement in the fate of victims of political oppression: it is the forceful impression of Cowper's poetry which has led her to write from 'an heart, that has learned, perhaps from its own sufferings, to feel with acute, though unavailing compassion, the calamity of others'. In conclusion, she represents Cowper as the champion of a set of political beliefs inseparable from the vocabulary of liberty and public virtue which 'it was once the glory of Englishmen to avow and defend'.[31] Her Cowper has a doubled role as the hero of Foxite Whiggery, as well as the defender of domesticity, and it is in imitation of him that Smith represents herself as a heroine of private and maternal sensibility whose capacity for sympathy impels her to champion the political cause of liberty.

Smith's more explicit and direct expression of allegiance to Cowper rather than Thomson may suggest that she, like other women writers of the late eighteenth and early nineteenth centuries, values Thomson's work particularly for the (more or less indirect) relation it could seem to describe between the political values of classical republicanism and a sentimental idea of domesticity. For in the later 1790s, the passage from *The Seasons* that is most frequently cited or referred to is the praise of domestic happiness that concludes 'Spring'. The passage, so often selected for illustration in editions of *The Seasons* in the three decades after 1790 (see Figs. 5 and 6),[32] celebrates the delights of marriage which has its basis in 'Perfect Esteem enliven'd by Desire/ Ineffable, and Sympathy of Soul', the shared

T. Stothard del.   *P. Audinet sculp.*

Fig. 5: Philippe Audinet after Thomas Stothard,
Paternal Instruction: illustration to Thomson's 'Spring', from
The Seasons, by James Thomson (London, 1794).

Fig. 6: Francesco Bartolozzi after William Hamilton, illustration
to Thomson's 'Spring', from *The Seasons, by James Thomson*
(London, 1797).

joy of parents who 'teach the young Idea how to shoot'. In
perhaps the most frequently cited lines from the passage,
Thomson writes:

> O speak the Joy! ye, whom the sudden Tear
> Surprizes often, while you look around,
> And nothing strikes your Eye but Sights of Bliss,
> All various Nature pressing on the Heart:
> An elegant Sufficiency, Content,
> Retirement, rural Quiet, Friendship, Books,
> Ease and alternate Labour, useful Life,
> Progressive Virtue, and approving HEAVEN.
> These are the matchless Joys of virtuous Love;
> And thus their Moments fly.

In conclusion the poet claims that all seasons are sweet to the happy pair, until finally 'Together down they sink in social Sleep' and ascend to a heaven which makes permanent the bliss they have enjoyed on earth.[33] In novels as diverse as Regina Roche's Gothic-erotic *The Children of the Abbey* (1796) and Hannah More's *Coelebs in Search of a Wife* (1808), this passage is alluded to with a familiarity that suggests it has become a necessary part of the cultural equipage of sentimental femininity.[34] Indeed, in *Northanger Abbey* (written 1798–99?), it appears as one of the three quotations from eighteenth-century verse the knowledge of which Catherine Morland regards as essential to a properly sentimental heroine.[35]

Mary Wollstonecraft seems to express a common perception of Thomson's work when she writes, alluding explicitly to *Liberty*, that:

> Liberty, though reckoned the grand source of the sublime, has seldom, we believe, acted as a muse to warm the breast with true poetic fire, that presumed to sing her praise; lost in contemplating the noble deeds she inspired, like Caesar, she forgets to speak of herself, and dwells on the praises of the heroes whom she guides up the steps of glory.[36]

Anna Seward, for example, in her detailed commentary on *The Seasons*, seems primarily interested in close verbal criticism, but she pauses to note that she, perhaps like Wollstonecraft, finds lists of heroes unpoetic: 'I do not like the frequency of complimentary addresses to the actual persons of the author's day ... they ruefully encumber the poetry.' She prefers the landscapes and 'episodes', or the 'charming eulogium on virtuous love, and connubial bliss'. She singles out for particular praise the account of 'the virtuous man in retirement', and notes that this provides the basis for Cowper's account of the pleasures of peeping 'through the loop-holes of retreat', concluding that the later poet 'has risen above his original in this passage'. Neither Wollstone-craft nor Seward objects to the nature of Thomson's political views; Seward indeed makes the pantheon of Whig heroes in 'Summer' an exception to her dislike of complimentary addresses, commenting that 'the list of British heroes, sages, and patriots, must be welcome to every mind attached to its country, and admiring virtue'.[37] But they seem to prefer Thomson as the poet of sentiment, the source perhaps of something like that 'infinite consolation' that Smith finds in Cowper's poetry.[38]

The image of Thomson as the exponent of what has come to be seen as a distinctively middle-class and sentimental domesticity is put to striking use in Mary Hays's *Memoirs of Emma Courtney* (1796). The first part of Hays's novel offers a detailed account of the early circumstances and education which the heroine believes are largely responsible for her subsequent career; her passionate pursuit of the man she loves and equally impassioned political idealism. As a result of her education, the novel claims, Emma Courtney becomes the personification of feminine sensibility, though the narrative remains extraordinarily ambivalent about whether that sensibility is virtuous or corrupt. The heroine spends her early years in the house of her uncle, a successful merchant involved in trade with the West Indies, whose love for his wife and children is strengthened by the 'frequent absences and meetings' his business entails. She writes of him that:

> A walk or a ride in the country, with his wife and little ones, he accounted his highest relaxation:—on these occasions he gave himself up to a sweet and lively pleasure; would clasp them alternately to his breast, and, with eyes overflowing with tears of delight, repeat Thomson's charming description of the joys of virtuous love—
> 'Where nothing strikes the eye but sights of bliss,
>   All various nature pressing on the heart!'
> This was the first picture that struck my young imagination, for I was in all respects, considered as the adopted child of the family.[39]

The information that the heroine's uncle, 'though with few advantages of education', takes pleasure in hearing his niece at the age of six read aloud his 'favourite authors, Pope's Homer and Thomson's Seasons', and is apparently in the habit of repeating Thomson's praise of domestic life, seems to indicate that the early years she spends in his household are passed in a secure haven of seclusion and stability.[40] It would seem to be the pleasure of reading oriental romances with her aunt, and later devouring Plutarch and Rousseau in the house of her profligate and politically radical father, that cause Emma Courtney to depart from this Thomsonian model into her later career of sensibility.

There may be some suggestion, in Hays's novel, that Thomsonian domesticity is a little too blissful, and may possibly provide the hotbed for germinating the seeds of excessive sensibility. The heroine notes that 'Caressed by my aunt, flattered by her husband, I grew vain and self-willed', though she adds that her desires were always overridden by her sense of justice. In Frances Burney's *Camilla*, first published in the same year as *Emma Courtney*, the passage from 'Spring' seems to be used as an ambivalent marker of both excessive sentimentality and ideal domesticity. The heroine and her party come across 'a well dressed elegant young man' in a bookshop, where he is absorbed in reading the passage, and the account of his behaviour, and of their responses to it, is intriguingly indeterminate. Melmond, the young man, is first presented as 'wrapt in what he was reading with a pleasure amounting to ecstasy': he writhes, gestures and grimaces, exclaims aloud, and 'almost devoured with kisses the passages that charmed him'. When he recognizes the company, he insists on reading aloud 'the truly elegant and feeling description that concludes Thomson's Spring ... too much delighted with the pathos of his own voice in expressing the sentiments of the poet, to deny himself a regale so soothing to his ears'. The narrative clearly indicates suspicion of the extent to which Melmond is pleased with his own capacity to respond to the sentiment of the passage, of the self-congratulation involved in his 'exaltation of delight in literary yet domestic felicity', but suspicion of the young man's sentimental enthusiasm is carefully dissociated from criticism of the passage itself. The virtuous and dependable hero, for example, 'stood pleased and attentive to hear him' because the hero is 'caught up by the rehearsal of his favourite scheme of human happiness, which no time, no repetition can make vapid to a feeling heart'. The capacity to respond to the reading with pleasure clearly indicates virtuous sentiment, even though that cannot be demarcated unambiguously from the enthusiasm that later develops into the alarmingly pathological symptoms of excessive sensibility.[41]

In *Emma Courtney* reference to the passage seems more obviously to indicate the opposition between the uncle's house and the licentious morals and political views of the heroine's father; perhaps to indicate a sort of feminine safe haven from a world of politics dominated by the lists of great men that seemed so unappealing to Wollstonecraft and Seward. But it is interesting that in Elizabeth Hamilton's satirical parody of Hays's novel, in her *Memoirs of Modern Philosophers* (1800), the detailed account of the childhood of Bridgetina Botherim, the figure who caricatures Emma Courtney and Mary Hays herself, omits the reference to Thomson as a formative influence on its heroine, for it has another use for the passage. Emma Courtney notes, as we have mentioned, that she is caressed and flattered by her aunt and uncle, and she also recalls that 'I hated the needle:—my aunt was indulgent, and not an hour passed unamused:—my resources were various, fantastic, and endless'.[42] It is this aspect of her childhood which Hamilton identifies as the source of her later folly. Hamilton's satirical heroine is brought up by her mother, an over-industrious notable housewife (Emma Courtney's aunt is 'careful and oeconomical').[43] In Hamilton's novel, the leisure afforded Bridgetina by her mother's industry lies at the root of her excessive sensibility. Bridgetina explains:

> As I never at any time debased myself by houshold cares, never attended to any sort of work, I always enjoyed the inestimable privilege of leisure. Always idle, always unemployed, the fermentation of my ideas received no interruption. They expanded, generated, increased. The society of the philosophers gave a fresh supply to the fuel of my mind. I became languid, restless, impatient, miserable. But a mind of *great powers* cannot long remain in a state of inactivity; its sensations are ever ready to be called forth. *The romantic, frenzied feelings of sensibility will soon generate an opportunity for their exertion.*[44]

Bridgetina's frenzied sensibility is the fruit of the indolence she enjoyed as a child.

In contrast to this account of Bridgetina's upbringing, Hamilton offers an account of domestic life which insists on the recognition of women's domestic work as a form of productive labour. The 'Conclusion' to the novel opens with an epigraph from Cowper on domestic happiness as the nurse of virtue, and closes with a lengthy quotation from Thomson's lines on the domestic happiness of virtuous lovers. Finally the narrator reflects that these lovers are:

> Happy even in *'this corrupt wilderness of human society,'* where any degree of happiness is, in the dark and gloomy dogmas of modern philosophy, represented as impossible. Impossible, however, it never will be found by those who seek for it in the right path of regulated desires, social affections, active benevolence, humility, sincerity, and a lively dependance on the Divine favour and protection.[45]

Hamilton argues that domesticity is the basis of feminine self-esteem because it is the source of social affections and active benevolence. Her account of the domestic role of women is neatly summarized here in the notion of 'lively dependance'. Dependence here is not represented as servile, as Emma Courtney repeatedly insists, but is active, social, productive. In Hamilton's reading of Thomson's lines, women as well as men might 'speak the Joy' they feel in 'Ease and alternate Labour, useful Life'.

In the later 1790s, and the early decades of the nineteenth century, the nature of domesticity, as Davidoff and Hall have so thoroughly demonstrated, is endlessly celebrated and discussed as the key to the English national and imperial character.[46] In that discussion, Thomson's lines are explicitly or implicitly taken to portray an ideal of family life that is subject to continual reinterpretation and negotiation. Thomson the poet of sentimental domesticity became a key point of reference in a different kind of contention, about the politics of gender and of private life. Meanwhile the poet of *Liberty* was forgotten. When in 1814 Buchan finally managed to raise a monument to liberty in the Borders, it was the colossal statue of Wallace overlooking

Dryburgh, cheaply and cheerfully carved in red sandstone by John Smith, a local mason. When Scott raised his obelisk to Thomson on Ferneyhill—another cheap effort, with none of the elaborate sculpture, in the style of a funerary monument, envisaged by Buchan—it commemorated Thomson as the author of the *Seasons* alone.[47]

NOTES

1. See David Stewart Erskine, Earl of Buchan, *Essays on the Lives and Writings of Fletcher of Saltoun and the Poet Thomson* (London, 1792), pp. 239–42; *The Lady's Magazine*, 21 (October 1790), 526; and *Gentleman's Magazine*, 61, Part II (November 1791), 1019–21 and 1083–85. The bust was later repaired and presented by Buchan to the architect James Craig; see *The Seasons, by James Thomson. A New Edition* (Perth, 1793), p. xlix.

2. The most recent attempt to represent Thomson as a distinctively Scottish poet is Mary Jane W. Scott's *James Thomson, Anglo-Scot* (Athens and London, 1988).

3. Alexander Fergusson, *The Honourable Henry Erskine, Lord Advocate for Scotland* (Edinburgh, 1882), pp. 485–86.

4. *Seasons* (Perth, 1793), l.

5. Fergusson, *Henry Erskine*, esp. pp. 489–91; Henry W. Meikle, *Scotland and the French Revolution* (Glasgow, 1912), pp. 12–13.

6. Buchan, *Essays*, p. i.

7. Buchan, *Essays*, pp. xxvi–xxvii, 214–17.

8. Johnson, *Lives of the English Poets*, 2 vols (London, 1952), II, 352, 359; Buchan, *Essays*, pp. xxxiii–iv, 259, 217. In the *Gentleman's Magazine* (see above, n. 1), the remark about British liberty appears thus: 'I am sorry to be obliged to own, that Britain, especially Scotland, knows but too little of the liberty that Thomson celebrates!' It is not clear whether the later version, in *Essays*, is a deliberate strengthening of Buchan's original speech as reported in the magazine, or whether the magazine chose to tone down Buchan's words, and to point them away from England, more towards the specific problems of parliamentary representation in Scotland.

9. Buchan, *Essays*, pp. xxxvii–viii, 250.

10. See [John Reeves], *Thoughts on the English Government Addressed to the Quiet Good Sense of the People of England. In a Series of Letters. Letter the First* (London, 1795).

11. Thomson, *Seasons*, opposite p. l.

12. *The Works of James Thomson*, 4 vols (Edinburgh, 1774), I, xxvii–xxviii.

13. *The Seasons, by James Thomson; with ... Notes to the Seasons, by Percival Stockdale* (London, 1793). The remark appears on the penultimate page of the unpaginated 'Notes'. Stockdale's prefatory 'life' of Thomson is a lazy abridgement of Johnson's, which oddly preserves some of Johnson's contemptuous remarks on *Liberty*; see p. xiv.

14. *Pig's Meat; or, Lessons for the People* (London, 1795), III, 117–19. For Wordsworth, see *Descriptive Sketches*, ed. Eric Birdsall (Ithaca and London, 1984), p. 108 and especially l. 706.

15. Charles Pigott, *Treachery no Crime, or the System of Courts* (London, 1793), pp. 140–41.

16. [Robert Thompson], *To the Public, alias 'The Swinish Multitude'* (London, 1794), pp. 4–6.

17. London: [London Corresponding Society] 1792.

18. *The Patriot: or, Political, Moral, and Philosophical Repository* (London, 1793), II, 73; *The People's Ancient and Just Liberties Asserted, in the Trial of William Penn, & William Mead* (Sheffield, 1794), title page.

19. James Sansom, *Oppression; or, the Abuse of Power. With the Recovery and Establishment of Freedom in America and France, a Poem ... addressed to the Reforming Societies in Great Britain* (London, 1795), IV, 6 and 8.

20. *A Complete Collection of State Trials*, 30 vols, ed. William Cobbett and T. B. Howells (London, 1816–22), XXIV, 387 and 928.

21. Cobbett and Howells, *State Trials*, XXIV, 929.

22. Cobbett and Howells, *State Trials*, XXIV, 1238.

23. *Treason Triumphant over Law and Constitution! Addressed to both Houses of Parliament* (London, 1795), p. 30.

24. David V. Erdman, *Commerce des Lumières: John Oswald and the British in Paris, 1790–1793* (Columbia, 1986), p. 230.

25. Charlotte Smith, *Desmond. A Novel*, 3 vols (London, 1792), I, 185–86.

26. *The Emigrants*, Book I, ll. 235–47, in *The Poems of Charlotte Smith*, ed. Stuart Curran (New York and Oxford, 1993), pp. 143–44. Smith uses the lines from Thomson again in her sonnet 'To the shade of Burns'; see Curran, p. 71.

27. Thomson, *Coriolanus. A Tragedy*, Act III, Scene iii.

28. See *The Emigrants*, Book II, where the émigré invasion is described.

29. Curran, *Poems of Charlotte Smith*, p. 144n.

30. Curran, *Poems of Charlotte Smith*, pp. 96n and 97.

31. Smith, Dedication to *The Emigrants*, in Curran, *Poems of Charlotte Smith*, pp. 132 and 134.

32. For some other illustrations of this passage, see Thomas Rothwell after Woolley, *Seasons* (London, 1802); James Fittler after William

Hamilton, in *Seasons* (London, 1802); Thomas Bewick after John Thurston, *Seasons* (London, 1805); Charles Warren after Thomas Uwins, *The Seasons and Castle of Indolence* (London, 1820). Some of these show a family with children; some a young married couple; and a longer treatment of this passage than we have room for would demonstrate how in novels, too, it is used in reference both to happy and virtuous parenthood and to conjugal love in anticipation of the arrival of children.

33. Thomson, *The Seasons*, ed. James Sambrook (Oxford, 1981), 'Spring', ll. 1121–22, 1153, 1157–67, 1174.

34. Roche, *The Children of the Abbey*, various edns, ch. 57; More, *Coelebs in Search of a Wife*, various edns, ch. 27.

35. Jane Austen, *Northanger Abbey*, various edns, vol. 1, ch. 1.

36. [Mary Wollstonecraft], review of *Poems*, by D. Deacon, Article xviii, *Analytical Review*, vol. VII, 1790, in *The Works of Mary Wollstonecraft*, ed. Janet Todd and Marilyn Butler, 7 vols (London, 1989), VII, 266.

37. *The Letters of Anna Seward: Written between the years 1784 and 1807*, ed. A. Constable, 6 vols (Edinburgh, 1811), letter xiii, to Thomas Park, Lichfield, 10 May 1798, V, 89, 88; letter xiv, to Thomas Park, Lichfield, 19 May 1798, V, 97, 98; letter xiii, V, 91.

38. Smith, Dedication to *The Emigrants*, in Curran, *Poems of Charlotte Smith*, p. 132.

39. Mary Hays, *Memoirs of Emma Courtney*, ed. Eleanor Ty (Oxford, 1996), p. 12.

40. Hays, *Emma Courtney*, pp. 11, 14.

41. Fanny Burney, *Camilla: or a Picture of Youth*, ed. Edward A. Bloom and Lillian D. Bloom (Oxford, 1983), pp. 99, 100–01.

42. Hays, *Emma Courtney*, p. 15.

43. Hays, *Emma Courtney*, p. 11.

44. Elizabeth Hamilton, *Memoirs of Modern Philosophers*, 2nd edn, 2 vols (London, 1800), II, 93–94.

45. Hamilton, *Modern Philosophers*, III, 365–66.

46. Leonore Davidoff and Catherine Hall, *Family Fortunes: Men and Women of the English middle class 1780–1850* (London, 1987), ch. 3.

47. The obelisk is unfortunate in its position. Ferneyhill, as we have noted, is south of Ednam; and no doubt in order to preserve the lettering from the effects of permanent shadow and the weather from the north, the slate plaque bearing the 'epitaph' was placed on the south side of the monument. This has the unpatriotic though not wholly inappropriate effect of turning the obelisk away from Ednam, so that it faces across Kelso to the border with England.

'That is true fame':
A Few Words about Thomson's Romantic Period Popularity

JOHN STRACHAN

I

In the period which we now label 'Romantic', the universality of the appeal of Thomson's *The Seasons* was axiomatic. Ralph Cohen has ably demonstrated 'its development as a popular poem'[1] in the late eighteenth and early nineteenth centuries and lists some 274 editions published between 1789 and 1830. Thomson's 'writings are everywhere, and in all hands' declares the *Penny Magazine* in 1842: 'If to be popular, in the best meaning of the word, that is, to be universally read and understood long after all temporary tastes and influences have ceased to act, be the best test of a poet's genius, then we must place the author of the "Seasons" high indeed in the intellectual scale'.[2] In the first section of this essay, I intend drawing out the implications of critical debate about Thomson's popularity, a popularity which as Cohen states creates 'a serious issue in the domain of literary history'.[3] Beginning with a neglected essay by John Wilson (a piece ignored even by Cohen), I will discuss how the consideration of Thomson's popularity (defined by Thomas Campbell as the poet's appeal 'to the universal poetry of the human breast'),[4] plays an important role in several of the most notable critical debates of the Romantic period. In the later portion of the essay, and using the work of the now neglected but once best-selling poet Robert Bloomfield, I move on to examine how Thomson's influence is evident in the 'popular' (defined here in terms of the material facts of sales and editions) descriptive nature poetry of the Romantic period.

II

In 1842, the poet, satirist and critic John Wilson published 'An Hour's Talk about Poetry' in *The Recreations of Christopher North*. The piece, a revised and enlarged version of an essay originally published in *Blackwood's Edinburgh Magazine* in October 1831[5] offers an important meditation on the significance of Thomson in the late Georgian period. Though one hesitates to apply the label 'magisterial' to any piece of writing from the pen of the mercurial Wilson, whose best work is characterized by an unsettling mixture of vivacity and savagery, the essay offers a wide-ranging examination of the state of contemporary poetry and is, perhaps, more the work of Professor Wilson, holder of the chair of Moral Philosophy in the University of Edinburgh, than the 'Kit North' of the *Noctes Ambrosianæ*. Wilson's self-appointed task is to look for a 'Great Poem' and he surveys a broad and representative range of the verse of the time in search of this somewhat elusive phenomenon. Though his is a 'poetical age', Wilson cannot locate one modern example of the great poem. Those of us used to regarding the period under survey, roughly speaking 1790–1830, as one best characterized by the achievements of canonical Romanticism might find Wilson's opening gambit a little surprising: 'Ours is a poetical age; but has it produced one "Great Poem"? Not One'.[6] And perhaps just as surprising is the poetic terrain over which he ranges in search of the quintessential poem of the age, which is notably different from the twentieth century's Romantic landscape, dominated, as it has been until very recently, by the so-called 'Big Six' of Wordsworth, Coleridge, Blake, Byron, Shelley and Keats. *Seriatim*, Wilson discusses Rogers, Crabbe, Bowles, Campbell, Montgomery, Moore, Burns, Wordsworth, Coleridge, Southey, Scott and Byron. After individual examinations of these figures, he moves on to discuss women poets ('the Glory of Female Genius'): Tighe, Hemans, Landon and Norton amongst others; the school of 'uneducated poets' in the tradition of Burns: Hogg, Cunningham, Bloomfield and Clare; and the 'national' poetry of Scotland: Beattie, Grahame, Moir and Pollok. Whatever the merits of these writers, and Wilson affords praise to them all separately, none of them has produced a 'Great Poem'. Writing without knowledge of *The Prelude*, Wilson feels that even Wordsworth has not reached the highest plateau of excellence: 'But has he—even he—ever written a Great Poem? If he has—it is not the Excursion'.[7]

Abandoning his search for a contemporary example of poetic greatness, Wilson is forced to move his focus further back into the eighteenth century. He eventually finds examples of the 'Great Poem' in Cowper, and, most particularly, in Thomson: 'Are then the Seasons and the Task Great Poems? Yes'.[8] *The Seasons* possesses a kind of neo-pantheistic grandeur: 'that Poem must be great, which was the first to paint the rolling mystery of the year, and to show that all its Seasons are but the varied God? The idea was original and sublime'.[9] In a judgment which exemplifies Romantic period attitudes to the poet, Wilson argues that it is *The Seasons* rather than *The Castle of Indolence* or *Liberty* which is the poet's quintessential work:

> The Castle of Indolence is distinguished by purer taste and finer fancy; but with all its exquisite beauties, that poem is but the vision of a dream. The Seasons are glorious realities; and the charm of the strain that sings the 'rolling year' is its truth.[10]

Wordsworth himself had drawn a contrast between *The Seasons* and *The Castle of Indolence* in his 1815 'Essay, Supplementary to the Preface'. The former has become omnipresent whilst the latter languishes in disregard: 'that fine poem was neglected on its appearance, and is at this day the delight of only a few'.[11] *Liberty* is even more neglected in this period. Josiah Conder, writing in the *Eclectic Review* for June 1827, argues that were it not for *The Seasons*, Thomson would no longer be read: 'the Author of Liberty and Britannia would have been forgotten'.[12] The relative inattention to *Liberty* in the 1790s is perhaps particularly remarkable, given that 'liberty' is a word of such central cultural power and resonance in England during the decade after the French Revolution. Though George Canning begins *The Poetry of the Anti-Jacobin* (1799) by ironically quoting 'Rule Britannia' ('The Muses still with freedom found') against 'liberty's friends' in the 'coy muse of Jacobinism', Thomson's political verse is generally not used as a model in this period. From the left, the friend of liberty Mary Wollstonecraft's description of *Liberty* as 'uninteresting and coldly diverse'[13] is fairly typical. From the right, the powerful satirical voices of Canning, William Gifford and T. J. Mathias take their lead from Pope and the patriotism of *Liberty*'s 'fearless eye' is ignored. William Boscawen's *The Progress of Satire: An Essay in Verse* (1798), which tracks the history of satire from Juvenal to Pope, sums up the opinion of this body of politically charged verse. For Boscawen, Thomson is to be placed firmly in the tradition of nature poetry rather than the politically engaged line of Pope, the 'skilful maker of the moral lay':[14]

> Such genuine numbers flowed from Thomson's tongue,
> When, at the Muse's call, to genius true,
> All nature rose majestic to his view.[15]

Boscawen's attitude is that commonly found in more orthodox literary criticism. Wilson's account of Thomson, for instance, simply ignores the poet's political verse. It is *The Seasons* which is established, to borrow a phrase from the August 1811 number of the *Christian Observer*, as 'a poem fertile in the most astonishing displays of genius'.[16]

'An Hour's Talk about Poetry' is an important document in the history of Romantic period criticism of Thomson. However, the essay's significance has not been registered before. Even Cohen's compendious critical survey *The Art of Discrimination: Thomson's The Seasons and the Language of Criticism* (1964) nowhere mentions Wilson's essay. For Wilson, Thomson's genius emerges fully formed and without poetic ancestry: 'to what era, pray, did Thomson belong? To none. Thomson had no precursor—and till Cowper no follower. He effulged all at once sunlike—like Scotland's storm-loving, mist-enamoured sun, which till you have seen on a day of thunder, you cannot be said ever to have seen the sun'.[17] Wilson goes on to make the grandiloquent claim that thousands of years will elapse before such another poem as *The Seasons* is written: 'some six thousand years having elapsed between the creation of the world and of that

poem, some sixty thousand will elapse between the appearance of
that poem and the publication of another equally great'.[18]

I would argue that Wilson's notion of the 'Great Poem' rebuts
an equivocal estimation of Thomson enshrined in a famous anecdote about *The Seasons*. This can be traced to Hazlitt's 'My First
Acquaintance with Poets', first published in *The Liberal* in April
1823, where Hazlitt describes his trip with Coleridge to Linton:

> we found a little worn-out copy of the *Seasons*, lying in a
> window-seat, on which Coleridge exclaimed, '*That* is true
> fame!' He said Thomson was a great poet, rather than a
> good one; his style was as meretricious as his thoughts were
> natural.[19]

As a critic, Wilson vacillated between fearsome abuse[20] and
enthusiastic praise of Coleridge and he had an intimate, if antipa-
thetic, knowledge of Hazlitt's work, having spent much of his
youth baiting 'pimpled Hazlitt' in the pages of *Blackwood's*. To
my mind, 'An Hour's Talk about Poetry' repudiates Coleridge's
mixed testimonial on Thomson ('a great poet, rather than a good
one') by elevating the poet of *The Seasons* above the whole range
of contemporary verse. Wilson meets Coleridge on his own
ground, inverting his critical lexicon; here Thomson's 'greatness'
is celebrated rather than being qualified. However, this is more
than clever critical footwork on Wilson's part. He is contributing
to an ongoing Romantic period discussion of Thomson's popularity and significance, evident in the critical writings of the likes
of Campbell, Coleridge, Hazlitt, Jeffrey and Wordsworth, a
controversy which is itself part of some of the most important
literary debates of the period.

The terms on which Coleridge's compliment of Thomson is
backhanded are reinforced by another of Hazlitt's well-rehearsed
yarns, where he makes the poet's ambivalence about popular
taste and distrust of popularity clear:

> He had been to see the *Castle Spectre* by Monk Lewis, while
> at Bristol, and described it very well. He said 'it fitted the
> taste of the audience like a glove'. This *ad captandum* merit
> was however by no means a recommendation of it,

according to the severe principles of the new school, which reject rather than court popular effect.[21]

A similar distrust of 'popular effect' underpins Coleridge's comment on Thomson, which has often been cited, but little analysed (even Cohen is uncharacteristically unforthcoming about the anecdote). 'Meretricious' is not a hastily chosen word. As in his description of Lewis courting popularity, the poet's language mixes eroticism with the mercantile. As so often in Coleridge's *obiter dicta*, what appears to be a casual remark is, whether or not we agree with it, both subtle and critically suggestive. The *Oxford English Dictionary* defines 'meretricious' in two ways: 'Of, pertaining to, characteristic of, or befitting a harlot; having the character of a harlot' and 'Alluring by false show of beauty or richness; showily attractive. Now often applied to the style of a painter or a writer'. For Coleridge, however pure and 'natural' Thomson's 'thoughts' might be, he markets them in a catchpenny style, courting popular effect 'I' the manner of a whore'. To Coleridge, labouring in his self-appointed mission to create the taste by which he was to be appreciated, the popularity of the unlikely harlot Thomson, his 'true fame', is a leaden influence on the contemporary reading public. Time and again in Romantic period criticism, the name of Thomson is linked to debates about taste and popularity. Hazlitt's 1818 lecture 'On Thomson and Cowper', which contains the first published version of the Coleridge anecdote, where the poet appears as an anonymous 'man of genius', explicitly links Thomson's 'true fame' with his popularity. Hazlitt labels Thomson 'the most popular of all our poets, treating of a subject that all can understand, and in a way that is interesting to all alike, to the ignorant or the refined, because he gives back the impression which the things themselves make upon us in nature. "That," said a man of genius, seeing a little shabby copy of Thomson's Seasons lying on the window-seat of an obscure county alehouse—"That is true fame!".'[22]

Hazlitt's stress on the poet's popularity and the universality of his appeal is something of a critical commonplace in this period. For example, Percival Stockdale writes in 1793 that 'Perhaps no Poems have been read more generally, or with more pleasure than the Seasons of THOMSON'.[23] In his essay on Thomson in the *Specimens of the British Poets; with Biographical and Critical Notices, and an Essay on English Poetry* (1819), Thomas Campbell is almost embarrassed to criticize poetry so widespread in its appeal:

> It is almost stale to remark the beauties of a poem so universally felt—the truth and general interest with which he carries on through the life of the year; the harmony of succession which he gives to the casual phenomena of nature; his pleasing transition from native to foreign scenery; and the soul of exalted and unfeigned benevolence which accompanies his prospects of the creation.[24]

Though Campbell faults the declamatory style of portions of *The Seasons*, for him the poem ultimately offers 'the pure contemplation of nature, and appeals to the universal poetry of the human breast'.[25] For both Campbell and Wilson, Thomson's 'universality' informs the poet's success. Like his countryman before him, Wilson argues that Thomson's popularity is rooted in its universality: 'There is no mystery in the matter. Thomson—a great poet—poured his genius over a subject of universal interest; and "The Seasons" from that hour to this—then, now, and for ever—have been, are, and will be loved, and admired by all the world'.[26] Wordsworth's 1815 essay puts a similar argument less charitably: 'Thomson was fortunate in the very title of his poem, which seemed to bring it home to the prepared sympathies of every one'.[27] The poet goes on to echo Coleridge's Linton sentiments, again linking the unanimity of response to Thomson to his stylistic inadequacies: 'in the next place, notwithstanding his high powers, he writes a vicious style; and his false ornaments are exactly of that kind which would be most likely to strike the undiscerning'.[28] Here again Thomson's poetry and its true fame participates in central hermeneutical debates between the lakers and other critical camps. Thomson's popularity is of significance to more than the poet's various publishers; what Wilson calls Thomson's 'national popularity'[29] involves issues of great significance in the early nineteenth century.

Moving from Wilson to the other great Scottish literary critic of the period, Francis Jeffrey of the *Edinburgh Review*, we see an even stronger link made between literary quality and popularity. In his March 1819 review of Campbell's *Specimens*, Jeffrey declares that 'The character of our poetry depends not a little on the taste of our poetical readers ... Present popularity, whatever disappointed writers may say, is, after all, the only safe presage of future glory'.[30] Jeffrey clearly has Wordsworth in mind here; his argument castigates the discussion of popularity to be found in the 'Essay, Supplementary to the Preface' (discussed below) where Thomson plays such a pivotal role. Whatever their differences, Jeffrey, Wilson, Wordsworth and Coleridge all acknowledge that 'popular effect' is a key determinant of cultural power. Much of Jeffrey's famous venom against the lake poets derives from their supposed endorsement of a 'false taste' and repudiation of the predilections of 'ordinary readers of poetry'.[31] Time and again, Jeffrey lambastes Wordsworth—as Byron does later in the 'Dedication' to Canto I of *Don Juan*—with the charge of literary solipsism. Wordsworth has deliberately cut himself off from the popular taste of 'the public'. And, significantly, Jeffrey's criticism of Thomson specifically refers to the poet's popularity. In his August 1811 review of Weber's edition of Ford's *Dramatic Works*, Jeffrey sees Thomson as a poet who is instrumental in returning English poetry to its original state, after the depredations of the corrupting 'French taste' of the Restoration and the early eighteenth century:

> Thomson was the first writer of any eminence who seceded from it, and made some steps back to the force and animation of our original poetry. Thomson, accordingly, has always been popular with a much wider circle of readers, than either Pope or Addison; and ... has drawn, even from the fastidious, a much deeper and more constant admiration.[32]

The *Edinburgh*'s editor's preoccupation with popularity as a central criterion in determining poetic value is also evident in the work of another of his distinguished roster of contributors, Thomas Campbell, himself an enormously successful poet in the first 20 years of the nineteenth century. Campbell's April 1808

Edinburgh review of *Lectures on Eminent English Poets*, a book by that indefatigable Thomsonian Percival Stockdale, is a central text in Romantic period criticism of Thomson. Campbell argues that Thomson's 'popularity exceed[s] that of all other poets, even those who are not his inferiors in genius'.[33] *The Seasons* has a readership to be measured in some seven figures and Thomson's poetry 'yields more intense delight in the present perusal, than others of high merit'.[34] Ploughing an intellectual furrow close to that of Stockdale himself, who had argued in his 1793 edition of *The Seasons* that the poem addresses 'the common knowledge, and the common sentiments of mankind',[35] Campbell takes an explicitly associationist line in his examination of the prominence of *The Seasons*:

> But the Seasons present to us imitations of nature, which the eye delights not merely to revisit, but to rest and to muse upon. In the placid and still nature of the objects, we have time to gather a multitude of associations. There is scarce a reader of Thomson, whose own mind will not furnish recollections in proof of this. The features of nature, in Thomson's description, are without vagueness or indistinctness, but still general and applicable, by association, to the particular scenery which is freshest and pleasantest in the actual remembrance of every individual among the million who read him.[36]

Or as Stockdale puts it: 'particularly in *this* Poet, a little natural object, apparently insignificant of itself, takes consequence, from its association to others, and very much heightens and enforces the awful or beautiful assemblage'.[37] The psychological principle of associationism, declares Campbell, enables one to explain the extraordinary popularity of *The Seasons*: 'it accounts for our recurring to it so often'.[38]

For Campbell, Thomson's popularity lies in a mixture of the universality of his themes and a more material expression of taste, his million readers. Wide readership and universal acceptance of eminence, however unlikely it might seem to us today, are virtues often attributed to Campbell in his day. However, they are attributes which are notoriously lacking in this period by a poet who was by then, after the eclipse of Southey, the *Edinburgh*'s *bête noire*, William Wordsworth. Small wonder that a discussion of Thomson becomes part of the quarrel between Wordsworth and the Scotch reviewers. The 'Essay, Supplementary to the Preface', with its famous dictum, borrowed from Coleridge, that 'Every author, as far as he is great and at the same time *original*, has had the task of *creating* the taste by which he is to be enjoyed',[39] is a sustained meditation on poetic popularity ('Away, then, with the senseless iteration of the word, *popular*')[40] which directly engages with Jeffrey's preference for the 'most popular poetry of the world'[41] exemplified by Thomson. Wordsworth is similarly preoccupied with audience (or, rather, his comparative lack of one) and his distinction between the 'PUBLIC' (Jeffrey's favoured model) and his own rather metaphysical notion of the 'PEOPLE' is part of his attempt to repudiate Jeffreyian criticism. Whether or not 'popular' is a senseless word, it is a word which is inextricably linked to Thomson in this period. Sadly for Wordsworth, the 'PUBLIC' are not listening to him, preferring instead the supposedly 'vicious style' of Thomson.

Perhaps unsurprisingly in the face of public apathy and the critical hostility which had greeted the publication of *Poems in Two Volumes* (1807), Wordsworth attempts to demonstrate how poetry of permanent value is neglected by contemporary audiences. The case of Thomson consequently raises particular problems for the poet. Not only is *The Seasons* the supreme example of the popular; Thomson also seems to have been a poet whose success, if we are to believe Patrick Murdoch, was immediate. Wilson, remember, sees Thomson 'effulg[ing] all at once sunlike'. *Ergo*, Wordsworth must have a Thomson whose true genius is only appreciated after his death. The poet has to work hard in the face of the generally acknowledged early success of 'Winter': 'How was it received? "It was no sooner read," says one of his contemporary biographers, "than universally admired"'.[42] As Wordsworth admits, 'This case appears to bear strongly against us'.[43] Consequently, an appreciation of the true value of Thomson must be divided from his early success. Hence Wordsworth's distinction, borrowed from the unlikely figure of

Samuel Johnson, 'between wonder and legitimate admiration'. Paradoxically, Wordsworth's argument that Thomson was responsible for bringing nature back to poetry is very close to Jeffrey's assertion that the poet was instrumental in a revival of the traditions of English poetry. Due to the supposed dearth of 'image[s] of external nature' between the publication of *Paradise Lost* and *The Seasons*, the public have lost the 'art of seeing':

> Wonder is the natural product of Ignorance; and as the soil was *in such good condition* at the time of the publication of the Seasons, the crop was doubtless abundant. Neither individuals nor nations become corrupt all at once, nor are they enlightened in a moment. Thomson was an inspired poet, but he could not work miracles ... much of what his biographer deemed genuine admiration must in fact have been blind wonderment.[44]

Forcing Thomson to fit his central argument, Wordsworth maintains that it was only in the mid-1750s, i.e. after the poet's death, that Thomson's true genius was first acknowledged: 'nor are we able to collect any unquestionable proofs that the true characteristics of Thomson's genius as an imaginative poet were perceived, till the elder Warton, almost forty years after the publication of the Seasons, pointed them out by a note in his Essay on the Life and Writings of Pope'.[45] Even now, Wordsworth tartly suggests, the despised public do not truly appreciate their hero; the poet dismissively argues that the popular taste is simply for the episodes:

> [Thomson's] false ornaments are exactly of that kind which would be most likely to strike the undiscerning. He likewise abounds with sentimental common-places ... In any well-used copy of the Seasons the book generally opens of itself with the rhapsody on love, or with one of the stories (perhaps Damon and Musidora).[46]

To Wilson, Wordsworth's posturing is tendentious, if not dishonest, as Thomson has been read and understood from the first publication of 'Winter': 'Thomson ... leapt at once into a glorious life, and a still more glorious immortality'.[47] In his 'A

Few Words about Thomson', also published in the *Recreations*,
Wilson attempts systematically to demolish Wordsworth's line
on Thomson. Point by point, Wilson repudiates the 'Essay,
Supplementary to the Preface'. On the supposedly fortuitous
choice of *The Seasons* as the title for a poem, Wilson declares
'Thomson, in one sense, was fortunate in the title of his poem
[but] Genius made that choice not fortune'.[48] The 'Essay'
reflects badly upon Wordsworth rather than Thomson ('Having
shown!!! Why, he has shown nothing but his own arrogance'):[49]

> Wordsworth labours to prove, in one his 'postliminious
> prefaces,' that the true spirit of the 'Seasons,' till long after
> their publication, was neither felt nor understood. In the
> conduct of his argument he does not shine. That the poem
> was at once admired he is forced to admit; but then,
> according to him, the admiration was false and hollow—it
> was regarded but with that wonder which is the 'natural
> product of ignorance'.[50]

The fundamental argument of the 'Essay' is lamentably miscon-
ceived: 'Never did the weakest mind ever fall into grosser contradictions than does here one of the strongest, in vainly labouring
to bolster up a silly assertion, which he has desperately ventured
on from a most mistaken conceit that it was necessary to account
for the kind of reception which his own poetry had met with
from the present age'.[51] Crucial to Wilson's argument is an
assault upon Wordsworth's account of the initial reception of
The Seasons:

> though the descriptive poets during the period between
> Milton and Thomson were few and indifferent, no reason is
> there in this world for imagining, with Mr Wordsworth, that
> men had forgotten both the heavens and the earth. They had
> not—nor was the wonder with which they must have
> regarded the great shows of nature the 'natural product of
> ignorance,' then, any more than it is now, or ever was during
> a civilised age. If we be right in saying so—then neither could
> the admiration which the 'Seasons', on the first appearance of
> that glorious poem, excited, be said with any truth, to have
> been a 'wonder, the natural product of ignorance'.[52]

Wilson concludes that Wordsworth is employed in an arrogant and élitist attack upon the popular taste of the public: 'Such is the reasoning (!) of one of the first of our English poets, against not only the people of Britain, but mankind';[53] 'What a nest of ninnies must people in general be in Mr Wordsworth's eyes'.[54] In a flash of the old acerbity, Wilson sarcastically asks 'And is the "Excursion" not to be placed by the side of "Paradise Lost", till the Millennium?'[55]

III

In a critical manoeuvre which looks uncontroversial to our understanding of the poetry of the early nineteenth century, Wilson's 'An Hour's Talk about Poetry' sees Thomson and Cowper directly inspiring modern verse: 'These two were "Heralds of a mighty train ensuing"'.[56] On the face of it, this appears to anticipate the lineage of literary history as we understand it today, the line from Milton, Thomson and Cowper through to Wordsworth. However, Wilson's mighty train has some unlikely participants. Though he includes the familiar figures of Byron, Coleridge and Wordsworth, Wilson's emphasis is upon the now-neglected likes of Rogers, Campbell, Scott and Bloomfield. Burns excepted, Wilson's inventory might seem like an ill-assorted, even motley collection of minor poets. Nonetheless, Wilson's inventory is but the commonplace consensus catalogue of the poets favoured by the middle-class reading audience of the time. And what Wilson is doing is setting out a canonical taxonomy of authors who have rather fewer reservations about Thomson than Wordsworth and Coleridge. In 'An Hour's Talk about Poetry', Thomson, like Cowper, is a contemporary poet who belongs to the modern age: 'add them, then, to the worthies of our own age, and they belong to it'.[57] If our critical focus is exclusively upon Wordsworth, Coleridge and what Jeffrey calls the poetical 'revolutionists', then we get a somewhat distorted picture of Thomson's importance in the earlier nineteenth century. Instead of being an occasionally inspired but often misguided grandfather, Thomson becomes an avuncular and animate presence. Because of the canonical peripeteia which has overtaken the poetry of the early nineteenth century and our consequential preoccupation with addressing Romanticism as the period's central literary formation, Thomson's influence in the early nineteenth century has tended to be forgotten. In particular, Thomson has a great influence on much of the nature poetry of the time, on the likes of Robert Bloomfield, the Suffolk peasant poet who enjoyed great success in the first decades of the nineteenth century. Some of the best-selling poetry of the period between 1789 and 1830 is influenced by *The Seasons*, in varying degrees of indebtedness, and is certainly more closely related to Thomson than is the tradition of mainstream Romanticism. Wordsworth's literary theory is generally seen as assailing the malign nature of eighteenth-century paradigms. However, in the poet's various polemical prefaces the *avant garde* is repudiating *contemporary* taste and *contemporary* models as much as historical ones. For both the readers and many of the poets of the day see Thomson as a living figure in the late Georgian period. Moving from popular taste to popular models, the rest of this essay will examine Thomson's status as a living influence in that period.

For many writers of the early nineteenth century, *The Seasons* possesses great contemporary potency as a literary model. Anna Laetitia Barbauld's 'Eighteen Hundred and Eleven' (1812) characterizes the poem in terms of its contemporary and educative power: 'In Thomson's glass the ingenuous youth shall learn/ A fairer face of Nature to discern'.[58] Thomas Dermody's 'Hymn to the Memory of Thomson', published in *The Harp of Erin* (1807), makes the same point:

> Then oft let Genius young peruse
> That page divine, with studious care;
> Meanwhile the much-astonish'd muse
> Finds her own soul reflected there.[59]

The Seasons survives into the nineteenth century, to revisit the *Christian Observer*'s term, as a 'fertile' poem which is employed as a model by a significant number of contemporary poets. James Beattie, whose *The Minstrel* (1771–74), formally indebted to

Thomson, was still highly popular in this period, offers a practical demonstration of Barbauld's dictum: 'Thomson was an
honour to his country and to mankind, and a man to whose
writings I am under very particular obligations: for if I have any
true relish for the beauties of nature, I may say it with truth, that
it was from from Virgil and Thomson that I caught it'.[60] The
poet's legacy is best found and his influence best felt in alternative late eighteenth- and early nineteenth-century literary traditions; to some extent in the likes of Beattie and Campbell,
certainly in the work of their fellow Scot D. M. Moir,[61] but in
particular in the enormously popular figure of that enthusiastic
devotee of Thomson, Robert Burns, and in the nature poetry of
the time for which the term 'Romantic' fails to account, in such
works as Robert Bloomfield's *The Farmer's Boy* (1800) and the
Thomsonian epigone James Grahame's *British Georgics* (1809).
The latter is the most Thomsonian of all Romantic period poems,
indebted to *The Seasons* to the point of resembling a formal
imitation. Bloomfield and Burns, of course, are the foremost
'peasant poets' of the age, examples of what Wilson calls the
'unlettered muse', and both enjoyed the status of best-sellers. In
terms of total numbers of editions, Burns is the most popular
poet living in the Romantic period, bar none. There is a vibrant
strand of well-received nature poetry, peasant or otherwise,
which was popular in the period—Burns, Bloomfield, even Clare
and Grahame—to which the term 'Romantic' does not apply or
where great critical ingenuity (perhaps tendentiousness is a
better term) must be used to make it apply. And Thomson
informs this tradition. As well as focusing upon the often highly-
qualified attitudes of Wordsworth and Coleridge, scholars of
Thomson's influence in the Romantic period should address this
tradition, for it is there where the poet's influence is perhaps best
felt. Detailed accounts of Thomson's influence are not the
province of this essay and indeed, the poet's influence on Burns
and Fergusson is treated elsewhere in this book by Gerard
Carruthers. Instead, I have chosen to examine how Thomson's
presence loomed large in the popular descriptive nature poetry of
the Romantic period by using the now forgotten work of Robert
Bloomfield as a key example.

IV

To the poetry-reading public of the first decade of the nineteenth century, the year 1798 was notable for the emergence of a highly significant new nature poet, a provincial writer who was preoccupied with the experience of the rural poor, a poet notable for endorsing the notion of 'simplicity' and for his powerful descriptions of natural scenery. For 1798 saw the composition of Robert Bloomfield's *The Farmer's Boy; A Rural Poem*. Bloomfield (1766–1823) was born in Honington, Suffolk, of peasant stock. Though he presents himself as a bucolic soul in his poetry, Bloomfield's physical infirmities meant that he was of little practical use as a farmer's boy. Consequently, he was sent to London to work as a cobbler. As a boy, Bloomfield's first introduction to poetry came from *The Seasons*. His brother George's biographical sketch, included in the prefatory material to *The Farmer's Boy*, declares that 'ROBERT ... spent all his leisure hours in reading the *Seasons* ... I never heard him give so much praise to any Book as to that'.[62] Borrowing from George Bloomfield's account, the *Monthly Mirror* declares that Thomson's poem directly prompted *The Farmer's Boy*: 'with his mind glowing with the fine Descriptions of rural scenery which he found in Thomson's *Seasons* ... he collected the materials which gave rise to the poem now before us'.[63] The poem's early sequences capture its flavour:

> 'Twas thus with GILES: meek, fatherless, and poor;
> Labour his portion, but he felt no more;
> No stripes, no tyranny his steps pursu'd;
> His life was constant, cheerful, servitude:
> Strange to the world, he wore a bashful look,
> The Fields his study, Nature was his book;
> And, as revolving SEASONS chang'd the scene
> From heat to cold, tempestuous to serene,
> Though every change still varied his employ,
> Yet each new duty brought its share of joy.[64]

The Farmer's Boy, completed in April 1798, was published in 1800. The volume was an immediate success. As the *Dictionary of*

National Biography notes, 'The success of the "Farmer's Boy"
was remarkable; 26,000 copies, it is estimated, were sold in less
than three years'. Compare this with the *Lyrical Ballads*' print
run of 2,250 in four editions over seven years (and there is
evidence of the existence of remainders as late as 1808). Vernor
and Hood paid the enormous sum of £4,000 for the copyright of
The Farmer's Boy in 1800. Compare this with the £2,000 paid to
Scott for *Rokeby* in 1812, the £1,000 per poem paid to Byron for
The Bride of Abydos and *The Giaour* in 1813 and, indeed, the £80
paid by Longman for the second edition of the *Lyrical Ballads* in
the same year as Bloomfield received his £4,000. W. H. Ireland
writes in 1815 that 'If the rapid sale of a work can speak for
its merits, the *Farmer's Boy* must claim the most unbounded
commendation: beauties it certainly does possess, what will ever
rank it a favourite with the British public'.[65] In the second edition
of *The Farmer's Boy*, also published in 1800, in sentiments
directly opposed to the argument which Wordsworth was to
make some 15 years later, Bloomfield's patron Capel Lofft
praises the judicious taste of the 'British public'. Instead of
relying upon posterity, the contemporary audience has instantly
granted Bloomfield his due reward: 'I rejoice in that Fame which
is just to living Merit, and wants not for the Tomb to present the
tardy and then unvalued wreath'.[66]

Wordsworth is faced with a public which preferred the trans-
mutation of *The Seasons* into heroic couplets in *The Farmer's Boy*
to the poetical innovations of the *Lyrical Ballads*. The *New
London Review*'s April 1800 review of the poem sees the poem as
epoch making, in terms which the modern reader would reserve
for Wordsworth. Bloomfield is notable for his emphasis upon
'primitive simplicity'[67]: 'In short ... THE FARMER'S BOY may
be looked upon as a new model of genuine pastoral'.[68] Wilson's
argument in 'An Hour's Talk about Poetry' that 'The Farmer's
Boy is a wonderful poem—and will live in the poetry of
England'[69] might seem perverse to us today, but it is unremark-
able in its period. And Thomson is an ineluctable presence in
both the shaping and the reception of Bloomfield's poetry. *The
Farmer's Boy* was introduced, read and reviewed with constant
reference to *The Seasons*. Indeed, it was not considered odd for

nineteenth-century publishers to print *The Seasons* and *The Farmer's Boy* in the same volume, as in Scott, Webster and Geary's popular edition of 1842.[70] Much of the *Mirror*'s review dwells on the correlations between the two poets:

> THOMSON has described the various operations of the four seasons, and their influence on mankind in general. His subject was vast and unlimited; the living volume of nature was before him, in all its comprehensive grandeur, and minute varieties, and he had to select, without restriction, whatever pleased his imagination, or interested his heart. Mr Bloomfield, with poetical powers that seem not to stand in need of 'circumscription or confine,' has contented himself with tracing the occupation of the *Farmer's Boy*, through the vicissitudes of the year, and with describing the more homely, but not less picturesque ... scenery which falls within the survey of the humble rustic. ... he was thus enabled to derive intellectual improvement from his daily labours, and to look *through nature, up to nature's* GOD ... hence the vein of genuine piety, the feeling, truth, and engaging simplicity, which are every where discoverable in this delightful poem.[71]

Nathan Drake declares in the second edition (1800) of his *Literary Hours* that 'in true *pastoral* imagery and simplicity, I do not think any production can be put in competition with it, since the days of Theocritus'.[72] Drake argues that Bloomfield is influenced, inevitably, by Thomson and Cowper: 'Thomson and Cowper were enabled to unfold their scenery with such distinctness and truth, and on this plan, whilst wandering through his native fields, attentive to "each rural sight, each rural sound" has Mr Bloomfield built his charming poem'.[73] He maintains that *The Farmer's Boy* displays 'the individuality, fidelity, and boldness of description, which render Thomson so interesting to lovers of nature'.[74] At times, Bloomfield even outstrips his model; Drake cites similar passages on 'Lambs at play' in *The Seasons* and *The Farmer's Boy* and concludes that here 'the Farmer's Boy is in every respect superior'.[75]

Lofft, who wrote the preface to *The Farmer's Boy*, does his best to distinguish Bloomfield from his poetic mentor in the description of his first reading of the poet's manuscript:

> At first I confess, seeing it divided into the four Seasons, I had to encounter a prepossession not very advantageous to my writer, that the Author was treading in a path already so admirably trod by THOMSON; and might be adding one more to an attempt already so often, but so injudiciously and unhappily made, of transmuting that noble Poem from Blank Verse into Rhime.[76]

Lofft continues: 'although the delineation of RURAL SCENERY naturally branches itself into these divisions, there was little else except the General Qualities of musical ear; flowing numbers, Feeling, Piety, poetic Imagery and Animation, a taste for the picturesque, a true sense of the natural and pathetic, force of thought, and liveliness of imagination, which were in common between Thomson and this Author'.[77] Thus apart from his theme, subject, tone and imagery, Bloomfield owes little to Thomson. This is a curiously self-defeating argument. Stripping away the Thomsonian elements from Bloomfield leaves the poet resembling a swimmer who returns to the river bank to discover that his clothes have been stolen. Certainly the *Monthly Mirror* stressed the close link between the two poets, venturing the opinion that Thomson now had a rival:

> This favoured child of Genius and the Muse, who, with no adscititious advantages of birth, fortune, education or connexion, has produced a poem which may be read with delight, even after Thomson, and, in some respects, may challenge a competition with the *Seasons* of that author.[78]

In its notice of *The Farmer's Boy*, the *New London Review* makes a similar point:

> we question much, with all the stores of classic erudition, with all the fascinating luxury of selected language, polished to a voluptuous correctness for future admiration, whether THOMSON himself, all-charming as he was to 'exalt his voice to ages,' and countenanced by LYTTELTON and the

most distinguished wits of his time, could, on the same
foundation, and with the same materials, produce a chaster
or more fanciful piece than this of ROBERT BLOOM-
FIELD, a *journeyman shoemaker*.[79]

The *New London* 'earnestly recommend[s]' *The Farmer's Boy* 'to
every taste',[80] setting out 'to give the PUBLIC an idea of the very
numerous beauties which this poem possesses'.[81] In the face of
these constantly articulated comparisons between Bloomfield
and Thomson, the satirist W. H. Ireland dismissed the connection:

> I love native worth, and will ever enthrone it:
> Ne'ertheless, in their plaudits some friends over warm,
> The dictates of reason wou'd fain take by storm;
> Such critics as boldly advanc'd potent reasons,
> To prove *Farmer's Boy* vied with *Thomson*'s fam'd *Seasons*:
> Productions that never can parallel chime,
> The one pure simplicity;—th' other sublime.[82]

The *New London*'s reviewer goes to great lengths to demonstrate that there is nothing patronizing about his eulogistic
recommendation of Bloomfield: 'This may be deemed the
extravagant panegyric of a mind influenced by the first emotions
of astonishment, and impelled by one motive, that of the
author's "book-learned" ignorance, to concede all other objec-
tions: but such is not the case'.[83] To the *New London*, though
Bloomfield is a peasant, his work bears comparison with its
great inspiration, *The Seasons*. The narrative of Bloomfield's
Damascene conversion at the hands of Thomson will send out
resonances to students of another peasant poet, John Clare,
whose purchase of *The Seasons* in his adolescence was a shaping
force in his development. Though the reception of Clare in terms
of volume of sales did not equal that of *The Farmer's Boy*, the
poet was received and reviewed as a contributor to the clearly
established Thomsonian line of Burns and Bloomfield. The
prevalence of Thomson as a poetic model for pastoral poetry in
the early nineteenth century, evident in the reception of *The
Farmer's Boy*, implicit in the literary theory of the 'Essay,
Supplementary to the Preface', exasperated the *British Critic*

which, in its usual uncharitable but mordantly amusing manner, lamented in its June 1821 review of Clare's *The Village Minstrel, and Other Poems* and the soldier poet Robert Millhouse's *Vicissitude; a Poem, in four Books* that 'Nothing is more easy for any person, of moderate talents [who] is in possession of Thomson's Seasons and Beattie's Minstrel, and one or two other poems of that class, to cultivate a talent for making verses; to learn to cut out watch-papers with his toes would be far more difficult'.[84] The ranks of 'uneducated poets', it implies, are populated entirely by slavish devotees of *The Seasons*, who, in imitation of Burns, insolently present themselves in the tradition of Thomson.

As well as associating Bloomfield with Thomson, the *New London's* review of *The Farmer's Boy* explicitly associates his 'beautiful poem' with Burns, turning from the Scottish poet 'with a softer, and scarcely an inferior admiration, to the placid attractions and pastoral philosophy of THE FARMER'S BOY'.[85] That enthusiastic Thomsonian the Earl of Buchan certainly saw Bloomfield in the line of Burns and Thomson, penning an address 'To the Readers of Bloomfield's "Wild Flowers"', which includes a moment where Buchan seems to pass on Thomson's laurels to the farmer's boy: 'I invited him down into Scotland that I might have him at Dryburgh Abbey, and show him the pastoral scenes that adjoin to it, the pure parent stream of Eden, and of Tweed, where Thomson first tuned his pastoral pipe'.[86] Capel Lofft excitedly wrote to Bloomfield urging him to take up Buchan's offer of the address, which would firmly link Bloomfield to the great Scottish poets: Buchan is 'A friend of poetry [and] a friend of liberty' who is notable for 'his attachment to the memory of Thomson, of Burns'.[87] Bloomfield is joining what is seen as a clearly established poetic tradition. In the case of Bloomfield, Thomson directly informs the popular poetry of the early nineteenth century. An exclusive preoccupation with high Romantic judgments on Thomson does insufficient justice to the true importance of the poet in the 'Romantic period', a period which is perhaps more Thomsonian than Wordsworth and Coleridge's self-representations and critical judgments would imply.

NOTES

1. Ralph Cohen, *The Art of Discrimination: Thomson's The Seasons and the Language of Criticism* (London, 1964), p. 412.

2. *Penny Magazine*, 11 (1842), 113.

3. Cohen, *Art of Discrimination*, p. 396.

4. Thomas Campbell, *Specimens of the British Poets; with Biographical and Critical Notices, and an Essay on English Poetry*, 7 vols (London, 1819), V, 218.

5. [John Wilson] 'An Hour's Talk about Poetry', *Blackwood's Edinburgh Magazine*, XXX (September 1831), 475–90.

6. [John Wilson] *The Recreations of Christopher North*, 3 vols (Edinburgh & London, 1842), I, 267.

7. Wilson, *Recreations*, I, 275. In his 'A Few Words about Thomson', Wilson compares *The Excursion* and *The Seasons* more particularly: 'And is there not a charm in the free, flowing, chartered libertinism of the diction and versification of the "Seasons"—above all, in the closing strains of the "Winter" and in the whole of the "Hymn", which inspires a delight and wonder seldom breathed upon us—glorious poem, on the whole, as it is— from the measured march of the "Excursion"' (Wilson, *Recreations*, III, 234).

8. Wilson, *Recreations*, I, 328.

9. Wilson, *Recreations*, I, 328.

10. Wilson, *Recreations*, I, 328.

11. *The Prose Works of William Wordsworth*, ed. W. J. B. Owen and Jane Worthington Smyser, 3 vols (Oxford, 1974), III, 75.

12. *Eclectic Review*, N.S., XXVII (June 1827), 511.

13. *The Works of Mary Wollstonecraft*, ed. Janet Todd and Marilyn Butler, 7 vols (London, 1989), VII, 266.

14 [William Boscawen], *The Progress of Satire: An Essay in Verse* (London, 1798), p.10.

15. Boscawen, *Progress of Satire*, p. 2.

16. *The Christian Observer*, X (August 1811), 509.

17. Wilson, *Recreations*, I, 327.

18. Wilson, *Recreations*, I, 328.

19. *The Complete Works of William Hazlitt*, ed. P. P. Howe, 21 vols (London and Toronto, 1932), XVII, 120.

20. The fearsome assault on the *Biographia* in the October 1817 number of *Blackwood's*, which led the poet to consider a libel suit, is probably Wilson's.

21. Hazlitt, *Works*, XVII, 118.

22. Hazlitt, *Works*, V, 87–88.

23. *The Seasons, by James Thomson; With his Life, an Index, and Glossary, A Dedication to the Earl of Buchan, and Notes to the Seasons, by Percival Stockdale* (London, 1793). The comment introduces Stockdale's 'Notes' (though not paginated, these follow p. 221).

24. Campbell, *Specimens*, V, 217.

25. Campbell, *Specimens*, V, 218.

26. Wilson, *Recreations*, III, 256–57.

27. Wordsworth, *Prose Works*, III, 74. Conder agrees: 'Thomson deserves great credit for the choice of his subject, and though his theme and his genius were not very well suited to each other, it was a fortunate match for the fame of the Poet' (*Eclectic Review*, N.S. XXVII (June 1827), 511).

28. Wordsworth, *Prose Works*, III, 74.

29. Wilson, *Recreations*, III, 234.

30. *Edinburgh Review*, XXXI (March 1819), 466.

31. *Edinburgh Review*, XXXI (March 1819), 466.

32. *Edinburgh Review*, XVIII (August 1811), 282.

33. *Edinburgh Review*, XII (April 1808), 80.

34. *Edinburgh Review*, XII (April 1808), 81.

35. In Stockdale's 'Notes' to *The Seasons, by James Thomson*.

36. *Edinburgh Review*, XII (April 1808), 80.

37. In Stockdale's 'Notes' to *The Seasons, by James Thomson*.

38. *Edinburgh Review*, XII (April 1808), 81.

39. Wordsworth, *Prose Works*, III, 80.

40. Wordsworth, *Prose Works*, III, 83.

41. *Edinburgh Review*, XI (October 1807), p. 217.

42. Wordsworth, *Prose Works*, III, 72.

43. Wordsworth, *Prose Works*, III, 73.

44. Wordsworth, *Prose Works*, III, 74.

45. Wordsworth, *Prose Works*, III, 74–75.

46. Wordsworth, *Prose Works*, III, 74.

47. Wilson, *Recreations*, III, 256.

48. Wilson, *Recreations*, III, 251.

49. Wilson, *Recreations*, III, 250.

50. Wilson, *Recreations*, III, 248.

51. Wilson, *Recreations*, III, 252.

52. Wilson, *Recreations*, III, 250–51.

53. Wilson, *Recreations*, III, 256.

54. Wilson, *Recreations*, III, 255–56.

55. Not even then. Wilson, *Recreations*, III, 256.

56. Wilson, *Recreations*, I, 327.

57. Wilson, *Recreations*, I, 327.

58. *The Works of Anna Laetitia Barbauld. With a Memoir by Lucy Aikin*, 2 vols (London, 1825), I, 237.

59. Thomas Dermody, *The Harp of Erin, Containing the Poetical Works of the Late Thomas Dermody*, 2 vols (London, 1807), I, 255.

60. Cited in Thomas Campbell, *An Essay on English Poetry; with Notices of the British Poets* (London, 1846), p. 265.

61. Moir's attitude is encapsulated in 'Thomson's Birth-Place' by

'Delta', published in *Blackwood's Edinburgh Magazine*, XXIX (January 1831), 127–28.

62. Robert Bloomfield, *The Farmer's Boy; A Rural Poem* (London, 1800), p. x.

63. *The Monthly Mirror*, IX (March 1800), 159.

64. Bloomfield, *Farmer's Boy*, p. 5.

65. [W. H. Ireland] *Scribbleomania; or, The Printers Devil's Polichronicon. A Sublime Poem* (London, 1815), p. 44.

66. Robert Bloomfield, *The Farmer's Boy*, 2nd ed. (London, 1800), p. vii.

67. *New London Review*, III (April 1800), 324.

68. *New London Review*, III (April 1800), 324–25.

69. Wilson, *Recreations*, I, 325.

70. *The Seasons and Castle of Indolence, by Thomson. The Farmer's Boy, Rural Tales, Banks of the Wye, &co. &co, by Bloomfield* (London, 1842).

71. *Monthly Mirror*, IX (April 1800), 227. The *Mirror*'s notion of the 'living volume of nature' is an unacknowledged borrowing from Stockdale's argument, in the 'Notes' to *The Seasons*, that the poem offers 'transcripts made immediately from the living volume of NATURE'.

72. Nathan Drake, *Literary Hours or Sketches Critical and Narrative*, 2 vols (Sudbury, 1800), II, p. 443.

73. Drake, *Literary Hours*, II, 453.

74. Drake, *Literary Hours*, II, 445.

75. Drake, *Literary Hours*, II, 457.

76. Bloomfield, *The Farmer's Boy*, p. ii.

77. Bloomfield, *The Farmer's Boy*, p. ii.

78. *The Monthly Mirror*, IX (March 1800), 163.

79. *New London Review*, III (April 1800), 323.

80. *New London Review*, III (April 1800), 324.

81. *New London Review*, III (April 1800), 326.

82. Ireland, *Scribbleomania*, pp. 45–46. Bloomfield himself explicitly distinguishes his work from the preoccupations of sublime poetry in the address to the muse at the beginning of *The Farmer's Boy*: 'No *Alpine* wonders thunder through my verse,/ The roaring cataract, the snow-topt hill,/ Inspiring awe, till breath itself stands still:/ Nature's sublimer scenes ne'er charm'd mine eyes' (pp. 3–4).

83. *New London Review*, III (April 1800), 323.

84. *British Critic*, N.S. XV (June 1821), 660. This jibe may well have been influenced by Jeffrey's January 1809 *Edinburgh* review of the *Reliques of Robert Burns*: 'we can see no reason for regarding the work of Burns chiefly as the wonderful work of a peasant, and thus admiring it in much the same way as if it had been written with his toes'.

85. *New London Review* , III (April 1800), 323.

86. *Selections from the Correspondence of Robert Bloomfield The Suffolk Poet*, ed. W. H. Hart (London, 1870), p. 39.

87. Bloomfield, *Selections*, p. 42.

Notes on Contributors

JOHN BARRELL is Professor of English at the University of York, and the author of various books on British culture of the eighteenth and early-nineteenth centuries, most recently *Imagining the King's Death*, to be published by Oxford University Press in March 2000.

GERARD CARRUTHERS is a graduate of the Universities of Strathclyde and Glasgow. He has held posts at Glasgow and Aberdeen Universities, and is now a lecturer in English Studies at the University of Strathclyde where he teaches American, English and Scottish literatures. He has published on Burns, the Scottish Enlightenment, Alexander Geddes, Walter Scott and a variety of twentieth-century topics.

ROBIN DIX is a Lecturer in English at Durham University. His publications include a facsimile edition of the collection of Akenside manuscripts at Amherst College (1988), an edition of Akenside's *Poetical Works* (1996), and various articles on eighteenth-century poetry, aesthetics, and bibliography. He is currently working on a critical study of Akenside and eighteenth-century philosophical poetry.

TIM FULFORD is Professor of English at Nottingham Trent University. Among his books are *Romanticism and Colonialism* (Cambridge, 1998), *Romanticism and Masculinity* (Basingstoke, 1998), *Landscape, Liberty and Authority: Poetry, Criticism and Politics from Thomson to Wordsworth* (Cambridge, 1996), and *Coleridge's Figurative Language* (London, 1991).

HARRIET GUEST is co-Director of the interdisciplinary Centre for Eighteenth-Century Studies at the University of York, and the author of *A Form of Sound Words: The Religious Poetry of Christopher Smart* (Oxford, 1989) and of various essays on Pacific exploration, on femininity, and on other eighteenth-century topics. Her latest book, *Small Change: Women, Learning, Patriotism, 1760–1810*, will be published by the University of Chicago Press in 2000.

BREAN S. HAMMOND is Professor of English at the University of Nottingham. He is the author of several books and articles on eighteenth-century topics, the most recent being *Professional Imaginative Writing in England, 1660–1740* published by OUP. He is a recent President of the British Society for Eighteenth-Century Studies.

W. B. HUTCHINGS is Senior Lecturer in English Literature at the University of Manchester. He is the author of *The Poetry of William Cowper* (1983) and co-editor of *Thomas Gray: Contemporary Essays* (1993) in the Liverpool University Press 'English Texts and Studies' series. He is presently editing the poems of William Collins, Oliver Goldsmith and Thomas Gray, and Jane Austen's *Emma*, for the British Heritage Database.

ROBERT INGLESFIELD is a Lecturer at Birkbeck College, University of London, and is currently working on volume 6 of the Oxford English Texts edition of Robert Browning's *Poetical Works*.

GLYNIS RIDLEY is a Lecturer in Eighteenth-Century Studies in the School of English at The Queen's University of Belfast and a member of the Executive Committee of the British Society for Eighteenth-Century Studies. She has published on a diverse range of eighteenth-century topics, from cookbooks to gardens and prose fiction to the rhetorical tradition. She is currently working on *Divided by a Common Language*—a study of English and American national stereotypes developed around the War of Independence—for the University of Delaware Press, which was begun in 1998–99 during a Visiting Fellowship at the Institute for Advanced Studies in the Humanities at the University of Edinburgh.

JOHN STRACHAN is is Reader in Romantic Literature at the University of Sunderland. His publications include *Parodies of the Romantic Age* (5 vols, 1999), co-edited with Graeme Stones, and *Poetry* (2000), co-authored with Richard Terry. He is currently working on several books and editions, including *A Cultural History of Romanticism* (for Blackwell), *The Poetry of Leigh Hunt* (Pickering and Chatto) and *Romanticism: A Glossary* (Edward Arnold).

RICHARD TERRY is Reader in Eighteenth-Century English Literature at the University of Sunderland. He has published numerous articles on aspects of eighteenth-century literature, especially to do with parody and burlesque. A long-term project on literary historiography between 1660–1781 will be published soon.

Index

Addison, Joseph, 7, 20–21; *Cato*, 20–22, 23–24, 26, 27, 31; *Spectator*, 73, 74, 79

Akenside, Mark, 3, 130, 138 n. 22, 156, 161 n. 16, 227

Alfred, King, 106–07

Arne, Thomas, 197

Arnold, Matthew, 166

Athens, ancient, 120–21, 128

Augustus, 121, 128, 131

Austen, Jane, 239

Barbauld, Anna Laetitia, 260, 261

Barrow, Isaac, 75, 102–03

Baumgarten, A. G., 50

Barrell, John, 4–5, 11

Beattie, James, 260–61, 267

Berkeley, George, 71

Bickham, George, 110

Blair, Rev. Robert, 176

Bloomfield, Robert, 12, 259, 262–67

Bolingbroke, Henry St John, Viscount, 17, 22, 32, 96, 124, 125, 134, 136 n. 9, 143

Boscawen, William, 250

Braham, John, 193

Brown, John, 71, 150

Buchan, David Stewart Erskine, 11th earl of, 11, 165, 218–25, 229, 233, 235, 243–44, 267

Buchanan, Dugald, 167

Burke, Edmund, 193–94, 202, 203, 212, 221

Burney, Frances, 241–42

Burns, Robert, 10, 12, 165–66, 167, 174, 179, 180, 181–87, 219, 261, 267

Byng, John, Admiral, 202

Byron, George Gordon, Lord, 254, 259, 263

Camden, William, 147–48

Campbell, Thomas, 251, 253–55, 259, 261

Canning, George, 249–50

Carew, Thomas, 146

Carey, Henry, 17

Caroline, Queen, 11, 208–12

Carruthers, Gerard, 10

Celtic culture, 143–44, 152, 166–68

Charles II, King, 123, 192

Charnock, John, 191–92, 196

Chaucer, Geoffrey, 147, 150

Chesterfield, Philip Dormer Stanhope, 4th earl of, 109–10, 112

Cicero, 79, 128

Clare, John, 261, 266–67

Clerk, Sir John, 169–70, 175

Cobbett, William, 208, 211–12

Cobham, Richard Temple, Viscount, 101–12 *passim*

Cohen, Ralph, 4, 247, 250

Coleridge, Samuel Taylor, 1, 11, 44, 251–52, 254, 256, 259, 260

Collins, William, 9, 118, 127, 130–31, 141–42, 160, 165

Condor, Josiah, 249

Cooper, Anthony Ashley, *see* Shaftesbury, earl of

Corneille, Pierre, 20, 129

275